Y0-ACA-309

SYMBOLS FOR THEME CORRECTION

A   THE COMMA

A1   Compounds
A2   Compound and compound-complex sentences
A3   Non-restrictive modifiers
A4   Non-restrictive appositives
A5   Introductory expressions with appositives
A6   Independent sentence elements
A7   Sentence modifiers
A8   Elements not in normal sentence position
A9   Direct quotations
A10 Dates and addresses
A11 To prevent misreading
A12 Degrees and titles
A13 Echo questions
A14 Contrasted items

B   PARENTHESES

B1   Appositives
B2   Interpolated elements

C   THE DASH

C1   Shifting or interruption of thought
C2   Appositives
C3   Interpolated elements
C4   Explanatory elements

D   BRACKETS

Explanatory notes or additions

E   THE SEMICOLON

E1   Compound and compound-complex sentences
E2   Compounds with internal comma punctuation

F   THE COLON

F1   Direct quotations
F2   Appositives
F3   Explanatory elements

G   THE PERIOD

G1   Declarative sentences
G2   Imperative sentences
G3   Abbreviations

H   THE QUESTION MARK

H1   Interrogative sentences
H2   Interrogative non-sentences

I   THE EXCLAMATION POINT

I1   Exclamatory sentences
I2   Exclamatory elements

J   QUOTATION MARKS

J1   Titles
J2   Direct quotations
J3   Position of other marks of punctuation
J4   Single quotation marks

PUNCTUATION AND MECHANICS

K THE APOSTROPHE

K1 Possessives
K2 Contractions
K3 Plurals of letters, figures, and words

L THE HYPHEN

L1 Compound words
L2 Divided words

M ITALICS

M1 Titles
M2 Names of ships, trains, and airplanes
M3 Letters and words used as such
M4 Foreign words
M5 Emphasized words

N CAPITAL LETTERS

N1 Beginning of sentence
N2 Beginning of quoted sentence
N3 Beginning of line of poetry
N4 Proper nouns and adjectives
N5 Important words in titles
N6 Pronoun *I*
N7 Words referring to Deity

OTHER SYMBOLS FOR CORRECTING THEMES

adj   Adjective
adv   Adverb
agr   Subject-verb agreement
awk   Awkward phrasing or construction
cap   Capital letter (See N in Appendix)
case   Wrong case
coh   Coherence
cs   Comma splice (See A2, E1, and G1 in Appendix)
cst   Construction; faulty sentence structure
dng   Dangling modifier
frag   Fragmentary sentence
id   Faulty idiom
inc comp   Incomplete comparison
inf   Too informal
ital   Italics (See M in Appendix)
lc   Lower case; do not capitalize
mean   Meaning not clear
mm   Misplaced modifier
no abb   Do not abbreviate
no ¶   No new paragraph
om   Omission of word or words
¶   New paragraph
‖ cst   Parallel construction
ref   Faulty pronoun reference
rep   Undesirable repetition
seq tn   Sequence of tenses
shift   Shift in tense, person, or number
sp   Spelling
sub   Subordinate this idea
tn   Wrong tense
tr   Trite
vb fm   Verb form
voice   Wrong voice of verb
wd ord   Word order
wdy   Wordy
ww   Wrong word

WRITING GOOD PROSE

WRITING GOOD PROSE

A Simple Structural Approach

FOURTH EDITION, COMPLETELY REVISED

Alexander E. Jones
Butler University

Claude W. Faulkner
University of Arkansas

PE
1408
J763
1977

WITHDRAWN FROM
CALARTS LIBRARY

Charles Scribner's Sons   New York

CALIFORNIA INSTITUTE
OF THE ARTS LIBRARY

Copyright © 1977, 1971, 1968, 1961 Charles Scribner's Sons

Library of Congress Cataloging in Publication Data
Jones, Alexander E.
    Writing good prose.

    1. English language—Rhetoric. I. Faulkner, Claude Winston,
1916-   joint author. II. Title.
PE1408.J763 1977   808'.042   76-57149
ISBN 0-684-14865-X

This book published simultaneously in the United States of America
and in Canada—Copyright under the Berne Convention

All rights reserved. No part of this book may be reproduced in any
form without the permission of Charles Scribner's Sons.

11 13 15 17 19 Q/P 20 18 16 14 12 10

Printed in the United States of America

Acknowledgments

We wish to express our appreciation to all of the people who have helped us during the preparation of this completely revised, simplified edition of *Writing Good Prose*. We are especially grateful for the encouragement and helpful suggestions which we have received from students and teachers who have used the three previous editions.

A.E.J.
C.W.F.

Preface

After reading Emerson's *Essays, First Series*, Thomas Carlyle was moved to comment on Emerson's prose style. The individual sentences, he felt, were strong and simple, clear and beautiful. Nevertheless, they did not always "entirely cohere"; they "did not, sometimes, rightly stick to their foregoers and their followers: the paragraph not as a beaten *ingot*, but as a beautiful square *bag of duck-shot* held together by canvas."

By deleting the adjective *beautiful* from Carlyle's phrase, one arrives at a description of much student writing: a number of separate statements which have not been fused into a clear and unified treatment of the topic, but which have instead been poured loosely into a container known as an "essay." The result is a piece of prose which lacks coherence and therefore does not "stick together."

Such lack of coherence should be of great concern to both the student and his instructor. For the basis of all effective communication is a clear and coherent arrangement of related ideas. If a composition presents a tightly knit, well-organized discussion of its subject, it is potentially a good piece of writing. Errors in mechanics and blunders in word choice are, of course, blemishes; but the composition is at least a diamond in the rough, which can be improved through further polishing. On the other hand, flawless grammar, punctuation, spelling, capitalization, and diction are of little value if the student has been unable to arrange his ideas effectively. In fact, a perfect command of the mechanics of writing will only render more obvious a student's inability to organize his ideas, for the reader will have the feeling that the whole composition is much less than the sum of its parts.

As its title indicates, *Writing Good Prose* is designed to train the student in the writing of well-organized compositions. It neither seeks to present a complete analysis of prose style nor strives to make the student a professional author. Instead, it attempts to train him in writing skills which will be sufficient for all the ordinary purposes of life.

By introducing the student to materials of gradually increasing complexity, this book acquaints him with the basic structure of expository prose. He first writes pairs of related main clauses, then composes longer passages and complete paragraphs. Only after he has developed some skill in handling these smaller units of prose is he allowed to attempt full-length essays.

While studying *Writing Good Prose,* the student will learn to express himself clearly and effectively. Once he has mastered the five basic structural patterns of expository prose, he can adapt them to the ideas which he wishes to present. And he can be confident that his writing will be a unified and coherent discussion of his subject.

ALEXANDER E. JONES   CLAUDE W. FAULKNER

Table of Contents

Preface vii

Chapter 1. Meaning Relationships and Linking Devices 1

  A. What Meaning Relationships Are 2

  B. What Linking Devices Are 3

      1. Automatic Linking Devices 4

        a. Repetition 4

        b. Pronoun Reference 6

      2. Deliberate Linking Devices 7

        a. Parallelism 8

        b. Nouns Summarizing Previous Assertions 9

        c. Meaning Links 9

          (1) Meaning Links Pointing Backward 9

          (2) Meaning Links Pointing Forward 11

          (3) A Special Note Concerning Meaning Links 13

  C. Meaning Relationships and Associated Linking Devices 13

Chapter 2. Pairs of Independent Clauses 15

  A. Enumerative Meaning Relationships 16

      1. Related Action 16

      2. Parallel Idea 17

  B. Equal Meaning Relationships 19

      1. Contrast 19

      2. Alternative 20

      3. Balanced Comparison 21

      4. Result 22

      5. Cause 23

      6. Question 24

      7. Answer 25

  C. Unequal Meaning Relationships 26

      1. Definition 27

      2. Amplification 29

      3. Sample Item 31

      4. Sample Fact 32

    5. Supporting Data... 35
    6. Generalization 36
    7. Inference 37
  D. Coordination Versus Subordination... 39

Chapter 3. The Five Patterns of Prose 44
  A. The Five Basic Patterns 44
    1. Enumeration.. 44
    2. Equal Pair... 46
    3. Unequal Pair 47
    4. Chain... 48
    5. Leapfrog 49
  B. Review of the Five Basic Patterns... 51
    1. Enumeration... 51
    2. Equal Pair.. 51
    3. Unequal Pair 51
    4. Chain... 52
    5. Leapfrog 52

Chapter 4. The Cluster.. 53
  A. Varieties of Clusters 54
    1. The Enumerative Cluster 54
    2. The Equal-Pair Cluster.. 55
    3. The Unequal-Pair Cluster.. 56
    4. The Chain Cluster 57
    5. The Leapfrog Cluster 58
  B. A Special Note on the Enumerative Cluster 58
  C. Clusters Within Clusters.. 59
  D. Clusters Relating to Clusters 60
  E. Grouping and Punctuation of Clauses in Patterns Containing Clusters 62

Chapter 5. The Paragraph.. 68
  A. Basic Patterns of Paragraph Development 69
    1. The Enumerative Paragraph 69
    2. The Equal-Pair Paragraph 70
    3. The Unequal-Pair Paragraph.. 71
    4. The Chain Paragraph 72
    5. The Leapfrog Paragraph 72
  B. The Topic Statement... 72
    1. Topic Statement at Beginning 73
    2. Topic Statement at End 75
    3. Topic Statement in Middle 76
    4. No Topic Statement.. 76
  C. The "Laws" of the Paragraph 77
    1. Unity... 78
    2. Coherence... 78
    3. Completeness 79
    4. Emphasis.. 80
    5. Variety... 81

Chapter 6. The Essay: Preliminary Considerations 84
  A. The Parts of an Essay 84
    1. The Introduction 84
    2. The Body 85
    3. The Conclusion 87
  B. Outlining 88
    1. The Steps in Outlining 88
    2. The Formal Outline 89
    3. Diagramming Essay Structure 91
  C. Varieties of Introductions 93
    1. Introductions Presenting a General Explanation of the Subject 93
    2. Introductions Presenting an Example 94
    3. Introductions Presenting a Definition 94
    4. Introductions Presenting Cause and Result 94
    5. Introductions Presenting Comparison and Contrast 95
    6. Introductions Presenting a Question 95
    7. Introductions Presenting Narrative Materials 95
  D. Varieties of Conclusions 96
    1. Conclusions Presenting a Summary 96
    2. Conclusions Presenting a Final Generalization 97
    3. Conclusions Presenting a Final Inference 97
    4. Conclusions Presenting a Striking Example 97
    5. Conclusions Presenting an Analogy 98
    6. Conclusions Presenting a Parting Question 98
    7. Conclusions Presenting a Call to Action 98
    8. Conclusions Presenting a Forecast 99
    9. Conclusions Presenting a Denouement 99
    10. Conclusions Presenting Narrative Materials 99
  E. Transitional Elements 100
    1. Automatic Linking Devices 100
    2. Deliberate Linking Devices 100
    3. Special Transitional Devices 101

Chapter 7. The Essay: Types of Enumeration 103
  A. Narration 103
  B. Process Explanation 106
  C. Description 109

Chapter 8. The Essay: Types of Enumeration (Continued) 113
  A. Listing of Points 113
  B. Point-by-Point Contrast 119
  C. Special Two-Point Patterns 123

Chapter 9. The Essay: Equal-Pair and Unequal-Pair Patterns 126
  A. The Equal-Pair Pattern 126
  B. The Unequal-Pair Pattern 131

Chapter 10. The Essay: Chain and Leapfrog Patterns 136
A.   The Chain Pattern... 136
B.   The Leapfrog Pattern 138

Chapter 11. The Essay: Expanded Patterns 141
A.   Varieties of Paragraph Clusters 141
B.   Topic Statements and Subtopic Statements....................... 145
1. The Absorbed Topic Statement............................. 147
2. The Detached Topic Statement 148
C.   Progressing from Accurate Outline to Successful Essay 148

Exercises 157

Appendix: Punctuation and Mechanics............................... 259

WRITING GOOD PROSE

1

Meaning Relationships
and Linking Devices

Prose is made up of sentences. And writing effectively is, in essence, a matter of composing clear individual sentences and joining these sentences together to form larger prose units whose meaning can be readily grasped by the reader.

The writer must make it easy for the reader to follow his ideas from one sentence to the next. Furthermore, he must make sure that his larger prose units—paragraphs and complete essays—have structural patterns which will help the reader to see how the major ideas fit together. We will first study the smaller units of prose.

Actually, the smallest prose unit that expresses a complete idea is not the sentence as such but the *independent clause*—a group of words containing a *subject* (a word or word-group which indicates a person or thing about which something is said) and a *verb* (a word or word-group which says something about the subject, indicating action, possession, or state of being). As its name suggests, the independent clause is capable of standing alone and thus may, by itself, constitute a simple, basic sentence.

Here are some examples of such basic sentences with the subjects in boldface type and the verbs in italics:

Dogs *bark*.
The **log** *burned* rapidly.
We *like* music.
When *did* the **train** *leave*?
Bill *is* a reporter.
She *seemed* graceful.
What wonderful pies your **mother** *makes*!
Tighten the bolt with a socket wrench.

Note that in the last sentence the subject *you* is "understood" rather than expressed.

Two or more independent clauses may join together to form a sentence:

My friend needs a car; however, he can't afford to buy one.
    (There are two independent clauses.)

The sky became dark, lightning began to play along the horizon, and the first large drops of rain splattered on the sidewalk.
    (There are three independent clauses.)

But notice that the independent clauses in these last two sentences could stand by themselves:

> My friend needs a car. However, he can't afford to buy one.

> The sky became dark. Lightning began to play along the horizon. And the first large drops of rain splattered on the sidewalk.

Obviously, it is the independent clause—rather than the sentence—which is the basic unit of prose.

The first step in improving your ability to write good prose is to develop greater skill in linking one independent clause to another independent clause. There are two ways in which pairs of clauses may be connected: by *Meaning Relationships* and by *Linking Devices*. This chapter will help you to understand how pairs of independent clauses are joined by these two types of linkage. Later, you will study in more detail the most important varieties of Meaning Relationships and the specific Linking Devices associated with each one.

A. WHAT MEANING RELATIONSHIPS ARE

Meaning Relationships are "thought links" between independent clauses. If two independent clauses are to form a coherent unit, there *must* be a clear Meaning Relationship between them. Note the following examples:

> My brother drifted through high school, studying as little as possible. Consequently, he is having a lot of difficulty with his college courses.
>> (The second clause presents a result of the fact stated in the first clause. Thus, the two clauses are connected by the Meaning Relationship of Result.)

> I know that I should get more exercise than I do. However, I don't feel that I can spare the time from my work.
>> (The second clause presents an idea which is in contrast with the idea expressed in the first clause. Thus, the two clauses are connected by the Meaning Relationship of Contrast.)

Since Meaning Relationships are as complex as the human mind itself, we cannot consider every possible variety. We shall, however, examine those which we use most often. If you learn to employ these common Meaning Relationships effectively in the various prose patterns which we shall study, you should also be able to handle without difficulty the less common Meaning Relationships which are not specifically treated in this book.

All Meaning Relationships fall into three classes: *Enumerative Meaning Relationships, Equal Meaning Relationships,* and *Unequal Meaning Relationships.* Let us see what each involves.

Enumerative Meaning Relationships. The first class of Meaning Relationships includes *Related Action* and *Parallel Idea.* In each of these, there is an *enumeration,* or listing, of clauses which present thoughts of the *same type.* Note the following:

> The student collected as much information as he could about surface conditions on Mars. Then he began to organize the material he had gathered.

> A good diamond cutter must have a keen eye; he must also have a steady hand.

In both passages, the second clause duplicates the type of thought contained in the first clause. The first passage deals with related *actions*, the second with parallel *ideas*.

Equal Meaning Relationships. The second class of Meaning Relationships includes *Contrast, Alternative, Balanced Comparison, Result, Cause, Question,* and *Answer.* In each of these, the idea expressed by the second clause is *equal* in importance to that expressed by the first clause, and each clause is balanced against the other. Note the following:

> The hinny is the hybrid offspring of a stallion and a female donkey. The mule, on the other hand, is the hybrid offspring of a mare and a male donkey.

In this passage, the second clause presents a new idea which *contrasts* with that in the first clause. The two ideas are equal in significance, and each of the clauses balances the other.

Unequal Meaning Relationships. The third class of Meaning Relationships includes *Definition, Amplification, Sample Item, Sample Fact, Supporting Data, Generalization,* and *Inference.* In each of these, the idea expressed by one of the clauses is more important than the idea expressed by the other clause.

In Definition, Amplification, Sample Item, Sample Fact, and Supporting Data, the idea expressed by the second clause is *less significant* than that expressed by the first clause. The second clause is restricted to increasing our understanding of the first clause. It does this by giving additional details or facts. Note the following:

> Very few people in the United States have ever seen a hinny. This rare animal is the hybrid offspring of a stallion and a female donkey.

This passage illustrates the Meaning Relationship of *Definition*. The second clause offers a definition of the term *hinny* used in the first clause; hence, it increases our understanding of the first clause.

In Generalization and Inference, the idea expressed by the second clause is *more significant* than the idea expressed by the first clause. Note the following:

> In the mouth and stomach of the frozen mammoth, scientists found unwilted, undigested leaves and flowers. Some incredible catastrophe must have frozen the huge beast solid in a matter of seconds.

This passage illustrates the Meaning Relationship of *Inference*. The second clause sets forth a logical inference, or conclusion, based upon the data presented in the first clause, and that inference is more significant than the evidence from which it was derived.

DO EXERCISE 1

B. WHAT LINKING DEVICES ARE

As we have seen, each pair of independent clauses must be linked through a Meaning Relationship. In addition, the clauses are ordinarily connected by one or more *Linking Devices*—"word links" which tie the two clauses together and may also reinforce the "thought link" of the Meaning Relationship. Note the following examples:

> My cousin is working part-time after school. *He* wants to earn enough money to buy a car.
> (The word *he* refers to *cousin* in the first clause and thus ties the clauses together.)

> The rain is still pouring down. *Therefore*, the parade will have to be postponed.
> (The word *therefore* points back to the preceding clause and thus ties the two clauses together. At the same time, it emphasizes that the Meaning Relationship between the clauses is Result.)

Linking Devices fall into two classes—*Automatic* and *Deliberate*. As their name suggests, we ordinarily use Automatic Linking Devices instinctively, without being aware that we are doing so. They occur naturally as the result of the subject which we are discussing. On the other hand, we usually employ Deliberate Linking Devices consciously, when we feel the need for a stronger connection between the two clauses. Let us examine each class briefly.

1. AUTOMATIC LINKING DEVICES

The Automatic Linking Devices are *Repetition* and *Pronoun Reference*. Although these linking devices do occur automatically, they may not always occur in such a way that they tie the two clauses together smoothly and clearly. Therefore, you must be aware of the nature of these "word links" so that you can revise your work effectively. In particular, you may need to decide whether to repeat a word used in the preceding clause or to substitute a synonym or a pronoun. And you may need to clarify a passage in which there is a confusing use of a pronoun.

a. *REPETITION*

Perhaps the most common variety of Automatic Linking Device is *Repetition*. There may be repetition of *word-form*, repetition based upon *synonyms*, repetition involving *class-member concepts*, and repetition involving *whole-part concepts*.

Word-Form. In repetition of *word-form*, a prominent word or word-group occurring in the first clause reappears in the second clause, producing a sort of "echo effect." The repetition may be exact—that is, both elements may have precisely the same form and meaning and be used as the same part of speech:

> The people do not want *war*. Yet *war* seems inevitable.
> (The word *war* in the second clause is identical in form and meaning with the word *war* in the first clause. Moreover, in both clauses the word *war* is a noun—that is, a word which is the name of a person or thing.)

Of course, repetition is not always as exact as in the example just given. The two elements may differ in form, function, or both:

> Ordinarily my *teeth* give me little trouble, but this front *tooth* aches whenever I eat ice cream or drink hot coffee.
> (The noun *tooth* in the second clause has the same general meaning as the noun *teeth* in the first clause, but the two words differ in form, *tooth* being singular and *teeth* plural.)

> I have always liked baked *squash*, but I do not enjoy my grandmother's *squash* biscuits.
> (The word *squash* in the second clause is identical in form and meaning with the word *squash* in the first clause, but the word functions in the first clause as a noun and in the second clause as an adjective—that is, as a word modifying a noun or a pronoun.)

As the above examples demonstrate, repetition of word-form helps to link clauses. In addition, the repeated element is often made more emphatic. Note, for example, the stress upon *we shall fight* in the following passage:

> We shall defend our island, whatever the cost may be. *We shall fight* on the beaches, *we shall fight* on the landing grounds, *we shall fight* in the fields and in the streets, *we shall fight* in the hills; we shall never surrender.

This sort of repetition must not be used carelessly. Examine the following pair of clauses:

> Last summer I took a *trip to Mexico*. During my *trip to Mexico* I had a chance to try out the Spanish I had learned in high school.

Instead of helping to link the clauses, such repetition merely results in an awkward waste of words.

Every instance of word-form repetition must be examined carefully. Is it effective in helping to link the clauses, or is it merely clumsy? After producing a rough draft of his composition, the writer should go over the material carefully, eliminating any awkward or monotonous repetition which he discovers:

Last summer I took a trip to Mexico. While there, I had a chance to try out the Spanish I had learned in high school.

Synonyms. If repeating the form of a word seems awkward, you may use repetition based on *synonyms*—words or word-groups which repeat the meaning, but not the form, of an element in the preceding clause. Here are examples of this kind of repetition:

Today a teenager is apt to feel that he must have his own *automobile*. Sharing the family *car* does not satisfy him.
    (The word *car* is a synonym for the word *automobile*; both words function as singular nouns.)

A hungry *baby* is apt to be fretful. Well-fed *infants* are generally happy and placid.
    (The word *infant* is a synonym for the word *baby*, but *infants* is plural, *baby* singular.)

Although synonyms lack the strong emphasis which may sometimes be achieved through word-form repetition, they have the advantage of not growing monotonous.

To find a synonym for a word, you can use a dictionary or a thesaurus—a special collection of synonyms. But a word of caution is necessary. You must be sure that the synonym you select is truly appropriate. For instance, suppose you have written the following:

According to some music critics, Mischa Solomon is the most gifted concert violinist of our day. However, this great violinist has never been popular with the general public.

The repetition of *violinist* is clumsy. Perhaps, though, the only synonym you can find is *fiddler*:

According to some music critics, Mischa Solomon is the most gifted concert violinist of our day. However, this great fiddler has never been popular with the general public.

It is obvious that *fiddler*, which suggests a square-dance musician rather than a concert artist, is not a suitable synonym. Therefore, if you can find no better synonym for *violinist*, you should use some other form of repetition, such as *this great artist* or simply *he*.

Class-Member Concepts. Another variety of repetition involves the use of *class-member concepts*. The class is, of course, the group to which the members belong. For instance, if we use *evergreen* as the name of a class, then *cedar, pine, fir, spruce, balsam,* and *hemlock* are members of that class. Notice, however, that a *member* of a *larger class* may in turn be subdivided and thus serve as a *class* in relation to its *members*. The class *animal* has *bird* as a member; the smaller class *bird* has *waterfowl* as a member; the still smaller class *waterfowl* has *duck* as a member; and the even more limited class *duck* has *mallard* as a member. In other words, the terms *class* and *member* are relative terms, and an item can be identified as constituting a *class* or a *member* only in relation to some other item.

In class-member repetition, usually one clause contains an element naming a general class, and the other an element naming a member of that class. Sometimes, however, the class is merely implied, each clause containing an element naming a different member of that class. Here are some examples:

I am very fond of *Italian food*. Last night I stopped at a drive-in and ate a triple order of *spaghetti*.
    (The word *spaghetti* in the second clause names a member of the class *Italian food* in the first clause.)

A full-grown *Chihuahua* may weigh as little as one pound; an adult *Saint Bernard* may weigh nearly three hundred pounds.
    (*Chihuahua* and *Saint Bernard* are members of the unnamed class *dog*.)

Ordinarily the use of class-member concepts is truly automatic and occurs naturally as a result of the subject which the writer is discussing.

One special variety of class-member repetition deserves consideration. Sometimes a class noun in one clause and a member noun in another clause refer to the *same thing*. Note the following:

> For several minutes the *shark* swam in large circles around the terrified skin-diver; then the great *fish* turned and glided swiftly toward him.

It is obvious that the class noun *fish* in the second clause refers to the same creature as the member noun *shark* in the first clause. The writer has used *fish* merely to avoid an awkward repetition of *shark*.

Compare the passage just given with the following example of ordinary class-member usage:

> A great white *shark* fatally wounded a skin-diver near Sydney, Australia, last month; however, most species of *fish* in the ocean are not dangerous to swimmers.

Note that in this pair of clauses the noun *fish* does *not* refer to the same thing as the noun *shark*. Rather, the word *fish* names a broad class to which this particular shark belongs.

Here is another example of the use of a class noun to avoid awkward repetition of a member noun:

> *Lou Gehrig* obviously deserved his nickname of "Iron Man." This amazing *athlete* played in 2,130 consecutive baseball games.

Note the demonstrative adjective *this* before *athlete*. When the member noun and the class noun refer to the same thing, the class noun is often preceded by *this, that, these,* or *those*.

Whole-Part Concepts. Closely related to class-member linkage is repetition involving *whole-part concepts*. One clause contains an element naming the whole of something, the other an element naming a specific part of that whole. Sometimes, however, the whole is merely implied, each clause containing an element naming a different part. Here are some examples:

> The *rocket* exploded soon after lift-off. Later investigation disclosed that a small *valve* had failed to close properly.
> > (The word *valve* in the second clause names a part of the whole *rocket* in the first clause.)

> The *fuel pump* may be acting up, or there may be dirt and water in the *carburetor*.
> > (The *fuel pump* and the *carburetor* are parts of the unnamed whole *automobile engine*.)

As is the case with class-member concepts, the use of whole-part concepts is ordinarily automatic and occurs naturally as a result of the subject which the author is discussing.

b. *PRONOUN REFERENCE*

Pronoun Reference is the second variety of Automatic Linking Device.

As we have already noted, a noun is the name of a person or thing—for example, *teacher, chair, cat, Abraham Lincoln, South America, loyalty, happiness, wetness*. A pronoun is a word which stands for (that is, which is used in place of) a noun—for example, *I, you, he, it, this, that, who, which*. Any word or word-group to which a pronoun refers is called its *antecedent*.

A pronoun in the second of a pair of independent clauses may refer to a word or word-group in the first clause. Moreover, in informal writing the demonstrative pronouns *this* and *that* may refer to the entire preceding independent clause. In either instance, by referring to its antecedent the pronoun forms an obvious link between the two clauses. Here are some examples of Pronoun Reference:

Queen Victoria had great faith in *Disraeli,* her Prime Minister. Indeed, *she* seemed to consider *him* the source of all wisdom.

(The pronoun *she* refers to its antecedent *Queen Victoria*; the pronoun *him* refers to its antecedent *Disraeli*.)

Fred made an A on his last chemistry test. That really surprised me.
(The pronoun *that* refers to the entire preceding statement.)

Although we ordinarily use pronouns automatically, we sometimes employ them deliberately to avoid awkward repetition of their antecedents. Notice how clumsy the following passage is without the use of pronouns:

Queen Victoria had great faith in Disraeli, her Prime Minister. Indeed, Queen Victoria seemed to consider Disraeli the source of all wisdom.

A judicious use of pronouns enables the skillful writer to avoid such awkwardness.

Whenever you use a pronoun, you must make sure that its antecedent is immediately and unmistakably clear. Otherwise, the reader may be confused, and the pronoun will thus be ineffective as a Linking Device. Note the following example of faulty pronoun reference:

The tiger's tail lashed angrily. Then *it* sprang at the hunter.
(The pronoun *it* seems—incorrectly—to refer to *tail*.)

The writer can revise the passage so that the correct antecedent of *it* is immediately clear to the reader:

The *tiger* lashed its tail angrily. Then *it* sprang at the hunter.
(The pronoun *it* refers to its antecedent *tiger*.)

Or he can revise the passage in such a way as to get rid of the pronoun entirely:

The tiger's tail lashed angrily. Then the huge beast sprang at the hunter.
(The pronoun *it* has been eliminated by substituting *the huge beast*.)

DO EXERCISE 2

2. DELIBERATE LINKING DEVICES

So far we have been examining Automatic Linking Devices. Although we use them frequently, we ordinarily devote little thought or effort to doing so. Just the opposite is true of *Deliberate Linking Devices*. When we use them, we almost always do it consciously. Let us suppose that you have written the following:

Emily continued to smile sweetly. I knew that she was very angry.

It is obvious that the connection between these two statements is not clear. Indeed, the reader is likely to be confused: Is a sweet smile Emily's usual indication of anger? Note the difference when we insert a Deliberate Linking Device:

Emily continued to smile sweetly. I knew, *however*, that she was very angry.

Now the two clauses are tightly linked, and the Meaning Relationship is clearly *Contrast*. The simple addition of *however* has greatly improved the passage. In most cases, just as in this example, a writer uses Deliberate Linking

Devices in his prose to make the progression of ideas clear by eliminating any possible ambiguity (or uncertainty) of meaning.

Three types of Deliberate Linking Devices deserve our consideration. They are *Parallelism, Nouns Summarizing Previous Assertions,* and *Meaning Links.*

a. *PARALLELISM*

Two independent clauses may contain equivalent grammatical units which are strikingly similar in their structure and word order. In such instances, all or part of the second clause repeats—either exactly or approximately—the structure of the first clause and hence points back to it:

> In the fall he coaches football. In the spring he coaches baseball.
> (The second clause repeats the structure of the first clause. Note that repetition of structure may involve repetition of key words as well.)

> Jefferson Botts—a tall, lean, awkward boy—shambled into the room. His mother—a short, stout, determined woman—bustled after him.
> (The second clause repeats the structure of the first clause and hence points back to it.)

Of course, such use of parallel structure is effective only when the linked clauses are *noticeably* similar. A reader would not be aware of any Parallelism in the following clauses:

> I brought my umbrella, for it looks like rain.

Actually, there is some repetition of structure: each clause does contain a subject followed by a verb. But a reader would not sense any "echo effect" since almost every clause has this same general structure.

Before we leave Parallelism, a word of caution is necessary. In your writing you should avoid two kinds of errors involving Parallelism: *Lack of Parallelism* and *False Parallelism.*

Lack of Parallelism. Sometimes a writer carelessly uses dissimilar constructions to express similar ideas. Such pointless inconsistency of structure is *Lack of Parallelism.* Here is an example:

> At Thanksgiving my cousin Harold always sends our family a dressed turkey; a big box of candy and nuts is always sent by him at Christmas.

Parallel phrasing greatly improves the passage:

> At Thanksgiving my cousin Harold always sends our family a dressed turkey; at Christmas he always sends a big box of candy and nuts.

In your own writing, you should use similar constructions to express such similar ideas.

False Parallelism. Just the opposite of Lack of Parallelism is *False Parallelism,* which involves the use of parallel constructions to express ideas that are *not* truly similar or equivalent. Here is an example:

> Laura Hunt is a psychology major, and she is the newly-elected president of the student council.

The Parallelism of structure here is false because it implies, incorrectly, that the two clauses present ideas of comparable importance. Actually, either idea could be considered more important than the other, but the two ideas cannot be considered to be of equivalent significance. Thus, the writer can better express his true meaning by subordinating whichever idea he considers to be of lesser importance. Perhaps the writer's true meaning is as follows:

> Laura Hunt, a psychology major, is the newly-elected president of the student council.

Or perhaps it is this:

Laura Hunt, the newly-elected president of the student council, is a psychology major.

In either case, subordinating one of the two ideas makes clear the writer's feeling about their relative importance. Of course, the resulting sentence no longer contains two linked independent clauses. But that is as it should be, since the writer actually has only one main idea to express.

DO EXERCISE 3

b. *NOUNS SUMMARIZING PREVIOUS ASSERTIONS*

A second variety of Deliberate Linking Device involves the use of a *Noun Summarizing a Previous Assertion.* You can form a link between two independent clauses by using in the second clause a noun which summarizes an assertion appearing in the first clause. Nouns most frequently used in this fashion include *accomplishment, achievement, action, belief, custom, fact, idea, point, possibility, problem, promise, statement,* and *theory*. Here are two examples of clauses linked through the use of a Noun Summarizing a Previous Assertion:

> *The seal across the flap of the envelope has been broken*. That *fact* suggests that someone has read the document.
> (The noun *fact* summarizes the entire preceding independent clause.)

> He claimed *that the bus had swerved in front of the truck*, but the bus driver emphatically denied that this *statement* was true.
> (The noun *statement* summarizes *that the bus had swerved in front of the truck* in the preceding clause.)

Note that, in addition to linking the two independent clauses, the summarizing noun enables the writer to avoid awkward repetition of the original assertion.

c. *MEANING LINKS*

The final variety of Deliberate Linking Device is by far the most important: it is the *Meaning Link*. We can define a Meaning Link as *a word or word-group in one clause which points to another clause and at the same time helps to indicate the Meaning Relationship between the two clauses.*

A majority of Meaning Links *point backward* to an earlier clause; some, however, *point forward* to a later clause. Let us examine each kind briefly.

(1) Meaning Links Pointing Backward

A Meaning Link which *points backward* may be any of the following parts of speech: coordinating conjunction, conjunctive adverb, adverb, adjective, noun, or verb.

Coordinating Conjunction. A *coordinating conjunction* is a word which connects two equal grammatical units—for example, *sink* or *swim, cats* and *dogs*.

A coordinating conjunction can be used to introduce an independent clause—even a clause functioning as a separate sentence. When used in this way, it points back to the preceding clause and helps to indicate the Meaning Relationship between the two clauses:

> An ozone layer high above us in the stratosphere is necessary to guard us from the sun's ultraviolet rays, *but* ozone down here in the air we breathe is definitely poisonous.
> (The coordinating conjunction *but* points back to the first clause and shows that the Meaning Relationship between the two clauses is Contrast.)

The coordinating conjunctions used as Meaning Links Pointing Backward are *and, but, or, for,* and *nor.*

Conjunctive Adverb. Two clauses may be linked by a *conjunctive adverb,* a word or word-group which has an unusual dual function. It loosely modifies the whole independent clause of which it is a part and at the same time connects that clause with another independent clause.

A conjunctive adverb can point backward to a preceding clause and emphasize the Meaning Relationship between the clauses. Thus it greatly assists the reader in moving from one idea to the next:

> The hunter thought he had shot a fine deer. *However,* he soon discovered that his victim was actually a Jersey cow.
>> (The conjunctive adverb *however* points back to the preceding clause and shows that the Meaning Relationship between the clauses is Contrast. Notice that the reader is prepared for a contrasting idea before he reaches the subject of the second clause.)

A very large number of conjunctive adverbs may be used as Meaning Links Pointing Backward. Of these, the most important are *accordingly, actually, again, also, apparently, as a matter of fact, as a result, at any rate, besides, but also, certainly, consequently, for example, for instance, furthermore, hence, however, in addition, in any case, indeed, in fact, in other words, instead, in the second place, likewise, meanwhile, moreover, nevertheless, next, obviously, of course, on the other hand, probably, second, similarly, so, that is, then, therefore, though, thus, to be sure, too,* and *yet.*

Adverb. An *adverb* is a word or word-group which modifies another word or word-group other than a noun or pronoun—usually a verb, an adjective, or another adverb (for example, *swam* **slowly, very** *tall,* **quite** *easily*).

Two clauses may be linked by an adverb in the second clause which, in addition to functioning as a modifier in its own clause, points back to the preceding clause and helps to indicate the Meaning Relationship between the two clauses. This type of adverb differs from the conjunctive adverb in that, although it also points back to the idea in another clause, it does not connect the two clauses *grammatically.* Here is an example:

> The station wagon had been going more than sixty miles per hour. The motorcycle had been traveling even *faster.*
>> (The adverb *faster,* which modifies the verb *had been traveling,* points back to the preceding clause and helps to indicate that the Meaning Relationship between the clauses is Contrast.)

In the example just given, *faster* is the comparative degree of the adverb *fast;* the superlative degree would be *fastest.* The comparative degree of an adverb indicates a greater (or a lesser) amount of a quality as compared with the amount displayed by some other thing. The superlative degree of an adverb indicates the greatest (or the least) amount of a quality as compared with the amounts displayed by at least two other things. For instance, we can say that the station wagon is going *fast* (displaying the quality of speed), the motorcycle is going *faster* (displaying greater speed than that of the station wagon), and the patrol car is going *fastest* (displaying the greatest speed of the three vehicles). Here are some other examples:

POSITIVE DEGREE	COMPARATIVE DEGREE	SUPERLATIVE DEGREE
hard	*harder*	*hardest*
near	*nearer*	*nearest*
soon	*sooner*	*soonest*
well	*better*	*best*
badly	*worse*	*worst*
rapidly	*less rapidly*	*least rapidly*
boldly	*more boldly*	*most boldly*

Any comparative or superlative adverb may function as a Meaning Link Pointing Backward.

In addition, the following adverbs are frequently used as Meaning Links of this kind: *accordingly, also, comparably, differently, finally, next, previously, similarly,* and *then.*

Adjective. As we have already seen, an *adjective* is a word which modifies a noun or a pronoun—for example, *green, tall, costly, smooth, wet, stupid,* and *important*.

Two clauses may be linked by an adjective in the second clause which, in addition to modifying a noun in its own clause, points back to a preceding clause and helps to indicate the Meaning Relationship between the two clauses:

> The pep club may go to the basketball tournament in private cars. An *alternate* plan would be to charter a bus for the entire group.
>> (The adjective *alternate*, which modifies the noun *plan*, points back to the preceding clause and helps to indicate that the Meaning Relationship between the clauses is Alternative.)

Like adverbs, most adjectives have the property of expressing degrees of comparison. Here are some examples:

POSITIVE DEGREE	COMPARATIVE DEGREE	SUPERLATIVE DEGREE
cool	*cooler*	*coolest*
sweet	*sweeter*	*sweetest*
happy	*happier*	*happiest*
respectable	*less respectable*	*least respectable*
beautiful	*more beautiful*	*most beautiful*
good	*better*	*best*

Any comparative or superlative adjective may function as a Meaning Link Pointing Backward.

In addition, the following adjectives are frequently used as Meaning Links of this kind: *added, additional, alternate, alternative, another, comparable, contrasting, different, final, last, next, opposite, related, resulting, second, similar,* and *such*.

Noun. Two clauses may be linked by a *noun* in the second clause which points back to the first clause and helps to indicate the Meaning Relationship between the two clauses:

> The last six issues of the student newspaper have stressed the need for more school spirit. The *reason* for the editor's interest in this topic is the extremely poor attendance at every basketball game this year.
>> (The noun *reason* points back to the preceding clause and shows that the Meaning Relationship between the clauses is Cause.)

The nouns which most frequently function as Meaning Links Pointing Backward are *alternative, answer, cause, conclusion, consequence, contrast, effect, evidence, example, explanation, illustration, inference, instance, interpretation, meaning, proof, reason, result, reverse,* and *truth*.

Verb. Occasionally two clauses may be linked by a *verb* in the second clause which points back to the preceding clause and helps to indicate the Meaning Relationship between the two clauses:

> According to data sent back by space probes, the surface temperature of Venus is higher than the melting point of lead. We *must conclude* that no life as we know it exists on that planet.
>> (The verb *must conclude* points back to the preceding clause and helps to indicate that the Meaning Relationship between the clauses is Inference.)

Only a few verbs can function as Meaning Links Pointing Backward. The most common are *conclude, deduce,* and *infer*.

(2) Meaning Links Pointing Forward

Less common than Meaning Links which point backward are those which *point forward*. The Meaning Link in the first clause points forward to the second clause and causes the reader to expect it. The primary function of a Meaning Link Pointing Forward is to indicate the *relative order* or *importance* of each clause in a listing of related actions or parallel ideas or to indicate that a statement is a *hypothesis* or *theory* which will be reinforced by supporting data. It may be any of the following parts of speech: conjunctive adverb, adverb, adjective, noun, or verb.

Conjunctive Adverb. Two clauses may be linked by a *conjunctive adverb* in the first clause which loosely modifies the entire first clause and points forward to the second clause:

> *In the first place*, the job will give me valuable sales experience. In the second place, the money I earn will help to pay my college expenses.
>> (The conjunctive adverb *in the first place* points forward to the second clause by implying that a second fact will follow.)

The following conjunctive adverbs frequently function as Meaning Links Pointing Forward: *above all, apparently, at first, at the beginning, at the outset, beyond doubt, beyond question, first, in all probability, initially, in the beginning, in the first place, not only, obviously, on the one hand, originally, primarily, probably, to begin with, undoubtedly, unquestionably, without doubt.*

Adverb. Two clauses may be linked by an *adverb* in the first clause which (unlike a conjunctive adverb) modifies the verb in that clause and which also points forward to the second clause:

> Human beings *first* landed on the moon on July 20, 1969. And, in little more than three years they reached the lunar surface safely five more times, thereby proving that the success of the original mission had not been merely a lucky accident.
>> (The adverb *first*, which modifies the verb *landed*, suggests that at least one more item will be mentioned; it thus points forward to the second clause.)

Many comparative and superlative adverbs can function as Meaning Links Pointing Forward. In addition, the following adverbs are occasionally used not only to modify verbs in the clauses in which they appear but also simultaneously to function as Meaning Links which point forward: *chiefly, first, initially, mainly, originally, primarily.*

Adjective. Two clauses may be linked by an *adjective* in the first clause which points forward to the second clause:

> The *chief* concern of any school is to educate the students who attend it. An additional concern must be to give some attention to the general welfare of those students.
>> (The adjective *chief*, which modifies the noun *concern*, suggests that at least one less important item will follow and thus points forward to the second clause. Note, however, that there would be no such suggestion if one or more items of lesser importance had preceded the use of the word *chief*.)

The following adjectives frequently function as Meaning Links Pointing Forward: *chief, essential, first, foremost, initial, introductory, main, major, minor, original, paramount, preliminary, preparatory,* and *primary*. In addition, a superlative adjective may be used in such a way that it points forward to a following statement. If one clause refers to "our *gravest* danger," the next clause may then deal with one or more lesser dangers.

Noun. Two clauses may be linked by a *noun* in the first clause which points forward to the second clause:

> A good *beginning* would be to pass stricter laws concerning stream pollution. The next step would be to stock the rivers with large-mouth bass, which thrive in water that would kill trout.
>> (The noun *beginning* suggests that at least one subsequent step will be mentioned. It thus points forward to the second clause.)

The following nouns frequently function as Meaning Links Pointing Forward: *beginning, commencement, introduction, outset, precedence, priority,* and *start*.

Verb. Two clauses may be linked by a *verb* in the first clause which points forward to the second clause:

A forest fire often *starts* as a tiny wisp of smoke from a carelessly discarded cigarette. It may end as a raging inferno that destroys forest, wildlife, and even man himself.
> (The verb *starts* suggests that something will follow. It thus points forward to the second clause.)

The following verbs often function as Meaning Links Pointing Forward: *begin, commence, initiate, introduce, precede,* and *start.*

(3) A Special Note Concerning Meaning Links

As we have seen, Meaning Links are often helpful in indicating the Meaning Relationship between two independent clauses. If each of the clauses contains an equivalent Meaning Link, the two Meaning Links should be parallel in form.

For example, if the Meaning Link Pointing Forward in the first clause is *in the first place*, the Meaning Link Pointing Backward in the second clause should be *in the second place*—not *furthermore, moreover, second,* or *secondly*. Similarly, if the Meaning Link Pointing Forward is *first*, the Meaning Link Pointing Backward should be *second*—not *in the second place* or *secondly*. And, if the Meaning Link Pointing Forward is *on the one hand*, the Meaning Link Pointing Backward should be *on the other hand*—not *however, in contrast,* or *on the contrary*.

If two clauses are connected by a pair of coordinating conjunctions, the first conjunction points forward, the second backward. Here are two examples:

Either do your job, *or* take the consequences.

Not only did he lose the book, *but* he *also* forgot who had loaned it to him.

Here, again, the two Meaning Links must match each other. Such a sentence as the following will confuse the reader:

Not only did he lose the book; *in addition*, he forgot who had loaned it to him.

C. MEANING RELATIONSHIPS AND ASSOCIATED LINKING DEVICES

As we have already seen, there are three classes of Meaning Relationships: *Enumerative Meaning Relationships, Equal Meaning Relationships,* and *Unequal Meaning Relationships.*

As we study each variety, we shall diagram Meaning Relationships by using the following devices: (a) a box to indicate each independent clause, (b) an arrow to show that a clause is related to a previous clause, (c) the label "Statement" (or, if appropriate, "Question") in the first box to show that the first clause is the beginning of the passage, (d) a label in each additional box to specify the Meaning Relationship of its clause to the clause indicated by the arrow. Here is an example:

The customs officials suspected him of smuggling diamonds into the United States. Consequently, they searched him and his luggage thoroughly.

In our study of each Meaning Relationship, we shall examine the various Linking Devices associated with it.

Using broken-line boxes and arrows, we may also add Deliberate Linking Devices to our diagrams of Meaning Relationship patterns. Note the following diagram:

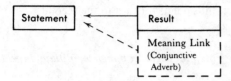

The customs officials suspected him of smuggling diamonds into the United States. *Consequently,* they searched him and his luggage thoroughly.

DO EXERCISES 4 AND 5

2

Pairs of Independent Clauses

In Chapter 1 we learned that two related independent clauses are connected by a Meaning Relationship. In this chapter we will examine the most common Meaning Relationships in detail. First, however, we need to consider the different ways in which a writer can group a pair of independent clauses to get the particular effect that he desires.

Perhaps he wishes to emphasize the importance of the idea in each clause by making the clauses stand alone as separate sentences. If so, he will begin each clause with a capital letter and end it with a period (or question mark, or exclamation point). We can represent this grouping as follows:

CAP _____ . **CAP** _____ .

The rocket exploded soon after lift-off. Later investigation disclosed that a small valve had failed to close properly.

Often, though, a writer feels that two ideas fit together so closely that they should be grouped in a single sentence. If he does not employ a coordinating conjunction to link the clauses, he must use a semicolon to separate them:

CAP _____ ; _____ .

A full-grown Chihuahua may weigh as little as one pound; an adult Saint Bernard may weigh nearly three hundred pounds.

If a writer does employ a coordinating conjunction to link the clauses, he will ordinarily use a comma to separate them:

CAP _____ , $\left\{ \begin{array}{l} \text{and} \\ \text{but} \\ \text{for} \\ \text{nor} \\ \text{or} \end{array} \right\}$ _____ .

My friend needs a car, but he can't afford to buy one.

However, even if a writer does link the clauses with a coordinating conjunction, he will normally use a semi-colon—rather than a comma—to separate them if there are any commas *inside* the clauses near the break between them:

$$\textbf{CAP} \underline{\hspace{4cm}}, \underline{\hspace{2cm}}; \left\{ \begin{array}{l} \text{and} \\ \text{but} \\ \text{for} \\ \text{nor} \\ \text{or} \end{array} \right\} \underline{\hspace{4cm}}, \underline{\hspace{2cm}}.$$

I interviewed Mr. Simpkins, the principal; and my brother interviewed Mr. Smith, the superintendent.
(The semicolon is used because of the comma after *Simpkins,* which is near the break between the independent clauses.)

As we study the various kinds of Meaning Relationships, we will examine sample clause-pairs grouped in all of these ways.

In Chapter 1 we saw that all Meaning Relationships fall into three classes: *Enumerative Meaning Relationships, Equal Meaning Relationships,* and *Unequal Meaning Relationships.* In examining each variety of Meaning Relationship, we shall first consider the Meaning Relationship alone and then see what Deliberate Linking Devices may accompany it.

A. ENUMERATIVE MEANING RELATIONSHIPS

Sometimes the second of two linked independent clauses duplicates the type of thought expressed by the first clause, and the two clauses therefore constitute an *enumeration* or *listing* of thoughts of the same kind. There are two Meaning Relationships which involve Enumeration. They are *Related Action* and *Parallel Idea.*

1. RELATED ACTION

When two independent clauses are linked through *Related Action,* each clause presents a separate happening or action, and these happenings are arranged in chronological order (that is, in the order of their occurrence) to form a single series of connected events.

Suppose you have written the following sentence: "The quarterback faked a handoff to the fullback." You might continue: "Then, holding the ball against his hip, he circled right end for the touchdown." It is obvious that your two clauses are linked through Related Action. On the other hand, it is equally obvious that the following clauses are *not* linked through Related Action since the second clause does not present an action: "The quarterback faked a handoff to the fullback. However, the opposing team was not fooled."

The Meaning Relationship of Related Action, then, requires three things: (1) each clause must present an action, (2) each action must be a part of the same series of connected events, and (3) all of the actions in the series must be presented in chronological order. In the following example, note that all three requirements are met:

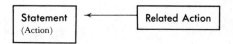

Joyce read the letter silently. When she had finished, she tossed it into the wastebasket.
(The two clauses form a single chronological series of connected events.)

Of course, Related Action is not the only Meaning Relationship that can join two clauses which present actions. Several other Meaning Relationships—especially Contrast, Result, and Cause, and occasionally Balanced Comparison—can also connect action clauses.

Examine the following sentence: "Outside the cabin, the cold winter wind howled savagely; but inside, a fire roared in the fireplace, filling the room with warmth." Although each of these clauses presents an action, they are *not* parts of a single series of connected events, and the Meaning Relationship between them is *not* Related Action. Rather, as the Meaning Link *but* indicates, the Meaning Relationship is Contrast.

Before we can say that two action clauses are connected through Related Action, we must make sure that the second clause does not contain any Meaning Links which show it to be a *contrasting* action, a *resulting* action, a *causing* action, or a *comparable* action. Instead, the second clause must present an *equivalent* action—one of several happenings in a single chronological series of connected events.

Two clauses which are joined through Related Action may contain certain Meaning Links which show time relationships between the clauses. Among the most important are the following conjunctive adverbs: *after, afterwards, finally, first, initially, last, later, next, now, second, then.* Here is an example:

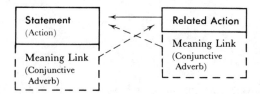

First, the scuba diver cleared the water from his breathing hose. *Next,* he emptied his flooded face mask.

> (The conjunctive adverb *first* points forward to the second clause, and the conjunctive adverb *next* points backward to the first clause; together, they indicate the order in which the actions occur.)

If you wish to determine whether the Meaning Relationship between two action clauses is Related Action when there is no Meaning Link, try inserting *then* or *next* between the two clauses. If the Meaning Relationship is Related Action, the revised passage will have the same sense as the original.

2. PARALLEL IDEA

When two independent clauses are linked through *Parallel Idea,* the second clause expresses the *same type of idea* as that presented in the first clause. In other words, the two clauses constitute an *enumeration of equivalent ideas.*

Suppose you have written the following sentence: "W. C. Fields was one of the most talented comedians America has produced." You might then continue: "He was also a fantastically skilled juggler." These two statements present parallel ideas—the first, the idea that Fields was a great comedian; the second, the idea that he was a great juggler.

To emphasize the parallelism of idea involved in this Meaning Relationship, the clauses usually employ Parallelism of structure. Here is an example:

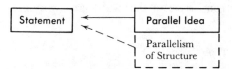

This book presents an obviously biased analysis of Kennedy's foreign policy, and it contains many serious errors of fact.

(The two clauses are linked by Parallelism of structure.)

Linking Devices are almost always present when two clauses are joined through Parallel Idea. In addition to Parallelism, the most important Linking Devices used are the following Meaning Links: the coordinating conjunctions *and, nor, not only . . . but (also)*; the conjunctive adverbs *above all, again, also, at first, besides, finally, first, further, furthermore, in addition, initially, in the first place, in the second place, last, moreover, next, primarily, second, secondarily, secondly, too*; the adverbs *first, last, next, primarily, secondarily*; the adjectives *added, additional, another, final, first, foremost, former, fourth, further, last, latter, main, major, minor, next, other, preceding, previous, primary, second, secondary, third*. We have already seen examples using the conjunctive adverb *also* and the coordinating conjunction *and*; here are two additional examples using Meaning Links to indicate the Meaning Relationship of Parallel Idea:

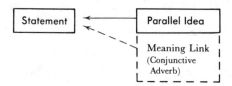

Professor E. R. Smith is probably the world's leading expert on quicksand; he is *also* an ardent spelunker and an authority on the caves of Indiana.

(The conjunctive adverb *also* links the two clauses and indicates that the Meaning Relationship between them is Parallel Idea.)

Mrs. Hawthorne has one of the finest collections of nineteenth-century valentines in existence. *In addition,* she owns some rare examples of British Christmas cards from the Victorian era.

(The conjunctive adverb *in addition* links the two clauses and indicates that the Meaning Relationship between them is Parallel Idea.)

If the Meaning Relationship between two clauses is Parallel Idea, you can reverse the order in which the clauses appear, and the revised passage will still make sense. For instance, the last example could have been written as follows:

Mrs. Hawthorne owns some rare examples of British Christmas cards from the Victorian era. In addition, she has one of the finest collections of nineteenth-century valentines in existence.

Of course, the original order of the clauses is probably preferable; nevertheless, the revised order does make perfectly good sense.

As another test to see whether two clauses are linked by Parallel Idea, you can insert the Meaning Links *first* and *second* or substitute them for any Meaning Links already present. If the Meaning Relationship is Parallel Idea, the basic meaning of the passage will remain the same. For instance, the example given above could be written as follows:

First, Mrs. Hawthorne has one of the finest collections of nineteenth-century valentines in existence. *Second,* she owns some rare examples of British Christmas cards from the Victorian era.

If you can apply *both* of these tests without changing the original sense of the two clauses, you can be sure that the Meaning Relationship is Parallel Idea.

DO EXERCISES 6 AND 7

B. EQUAL MEANING RELATIONSHIPS

Sometimes the second of two linked independent clauses presents an idea which is *unlike* that expressed by the first clause but *equal* to it in importance. In other words, the two ideas are of different types but possess equal significance, and we may therefore say that the two clauses have an *Equal Meaning Relationship.*

There are seven important varieties of Equal Meaning Relationship. They are *Contrast, Alternative, Balanced Comparison, Result, Cause, Question,* and *Answer.*

1. CONTRAST

When two independent clauses are linked through *Contrast,* the clauses present *important points of difference.*

Suppose you have written the following sentence: "The nurse shark is a relatively timid fish which almost never molests human beings." You might then wish to offer a contrast: "The tiger shark is a viciously aggressive fish which thoroughly deserves its reputation as a man-eater."

In this sample passage, the two linked clauses deal with different things—the nurse shark and the tiger shark. However, it is not merely the sharks themselves which are contrasted. Rather, it is two *ideas* about the sharks— namely, that one is timid and harmless, the other aggressive and dangerous. Thus, the Meaning Relationship of Contrast involves a contrast of entire clauses.

In employing Contrast, you must obey the following principles:

1. Your contrasting clauses must deal with *things* which display *significant points of similarity.* You can profitably contrast the flavor of a blackberry with that of a raspberry. But it would be a waste of time to contrast the flavor of a blackberry with that of a tiger shark (though both are edible), for the things being contrasted would lack significant points of similarity.

2. Your contrasting clauses must present *ideas* which display *significant points of similarity* as well as *significant points of difference.* You can profitably contrast the size of a black bear with that of a grizzly bear. But it would be a waste of time to contrast the size of a black bear with the color of a grizzly bear, for the two ideas would involve characteristics which lack significant points of similarity. On the other hand, it would also be a waste of time to contrast the appearance of one brand-new dime with that of another brand-new dime, for the two ideas involve characteristics which lack significant points of difference—and hence do not actually involve a contrast.

In the following example, note that the entire second clause is contrasted with the entire first clause:

When threatened by danger, the hog-nosed snake will often play dead, lying limply on its back. The green water snake, on the other hand, will attack fearlessly if disturbed, striking repeatedly in utter fury.

(The idea expressed by the second clause contrasts with that expressed by the first clause.)

In the Meaning Relationship of Contrast, the two clauses are often parallel in structure. Such parallelism is apparent in this passage: "This year I am taking nothing but required courses—English literature, advanced algebra, chemistry, and American history. Next year I shall be free to take nothing but electives—psychology, sociology, descriptive astronomy, and art appreciation." It is also present in the following example:

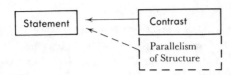

The average person can barely lift his own weight; a tiny ant can lift fifty times its own weight.
(The two contrasting clauses are linked by Parallelism of structure.)

In addition to Parallelism of structure, the most important Linking Devices associated with Contrast are certain Meaning Links which point backward: the coordinating conjunction *but*; the conjunctive adverbs *however, in contrast, nevertheless, on the contrary, on the other hand, yet*; comparative and superlative adverbs and adjectives; the adverb *differently*; the adjectives *conflicting, contrary, contrasting, different, differing, dissimilar, opposing, opposite, unlike, varying*; the nouns *contrast, exception, opposite, reverse*; and the verbs *contrast, differ.*   Here is an example:

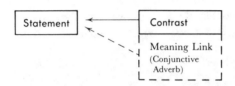

The average person can barely lift his own weight; a tiny ant, *however*, can lift fifty times its own weight.
(The conjunctive adverb *however* points back to the preceding clause and indicates the Meaning Relationship of Contrast between the clauses.)

2. ALTERNATIVE

Another common Equal Meaning Relationship is *Alternative,* in which the first clause makes a statement and the second presents an alternate possibility.

Suppose you have written this sentence: "The President may sign the bill reluctantly as the best he can get from Congress at the present time."   You might then continue as follows: "Or he may veto it, intending to call a special session of Congress later this year."   In this way you acquaint the reader with the various alternatives open to the President.

When clauses are linked through Alternative, the second clause usually is parallel with the first clause in structure:

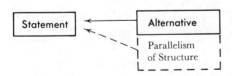

I can leave the car for you in front of the gymnasium, or I can pick you up at the library a few minutes before twelve.
(The second clause presents an alternative to the idea expressed by the first clause. The two clauses are linked by Parallelism of structure.)

In addition to Parallelism of structure, the most important Linking Devices associated with Alternative are certain Meaning Links: the coordinating conjunctions *or, either . . . or*; the conjunctive adverbs *again, alternatively*; the adjectives *alternate, alternative*; the noun *alternative*. We have already examined two examples using the coordinating conjunction *or*; here is another example using a Meaning Link to indicate the Meaning Relationship of Alternative:

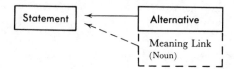

The Legislature may find it necessary to increase the state sales tax. One *alternative* would be to add a surcharge to the state income tax.

   (The noun *alternative* points back to the preceding clause and indicates the Meaning Relationship of Alternative between the clauses.)

In pairs of clauses linked by Alternative, there is always an element of Contrast. Consequently, it is sometimes only the Meaning Link that determines whether a Meaning Relationship is Alternative or Contrast. Note the following examples:

   I may go to school next fall, *or* I may decide to work full-time. (Alternative)

   I may go to school next fall; *however,* I may decide to work full-time. (Contrast)

Remember that the Meaning Link *on the other hand* does *not* indicate Alternative. When it appears, it shows that the Meaning Relationship between the clauses is Contrast:

   I may go to school next fall; *on the other hand,* I may decide to work full-time. (Contrast)

3. BALANCED COMPARISON

When two independent clauses are linked through *Balanced Comparison,* the clauses present *significant points of similarity.*

Suppose you have written the following sentence: "The female English sparrow courts the male by fluttering her wings like a fledgling and begging him to feed her." You might then wish to offer a comparison: "In similar fashion, the female wolf often woos the male by romping like a playful puppy and soliciting gifts of food."

In this sample passage, it is not merely the two female creatures which are being compared. Rather, it is two *ideas* about them—namely, their similar behavior during courtship. Thus, the Meaning Relationship of Balanced Comparison involves a comparison of *entire clauses.*

Note that the two compared ideas are equal in importance. Indeed, the order of the two clauses could be reversed readily: "The female wolf often woos the male by romping like a playful puppy and soliciting gifts of food. In similar fashion, the female English sparrow courts the male by fluttering her wings like a fledgling and begging him to feed her." Note also that the two ideas are expressed in balanced (or parallel) sentence structure.

In employing Balanced Comparison, you must make sure that the two ideas display *significant points of difference* as well as *significant points of similarity.* You can profitably compare the cratered surface of the moon with the cratered surface of the planet Mercury, or a robin's sense of possessing a territory with a wolf's sense of territory. But it would be a waste of time to compare the appearance of one piece of unused carbon paper with that of another unused piece of carbon paper from the same package, or the taste of one Milky Way candy bar with that of another Milky Way candy bar, for the two compared ideas would involve characteristics which lack significant points of difference and indeed are practically identical. On the other hand, it would also be a waste of time to compare the smell of a rosebud with that of a piece of rye bread (although both might be pleasant), for the two ideas would involve characteristics which lack significant points of similarity—and hence do not actually involve a comparison.

In the following example, note that the entire second clause is compared with the entire first clause and that the two clauses are parallel in structure:

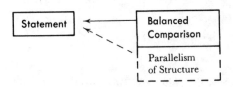

Although ultraviolet light speeds the healing of wounds, prolonged exposure to it can cause the destruction of body tissue. Similarly, although X-rays destroy cancer cells, prolonged exposure to them can produce malignant growths.
>(The entire second clause is compared with the entire first clause; the two clauses are linked by Parallelism of structure.)

Linking Devices are almost always present when two clauses interlock through Balanced Comparison. In addition to Parallelism of structure, several kinds of Meaning Links which point backward are often employed: the conjunctive adverbs *in similar fashion, in the same way, similarly*; the adverbs *comparably, likewise, similarly*; the adjectives *comparable, corresponding, like, parallel, related, similar*; and, less commonly, the nouns *comparison, resemblance, similarity*. Here is an example:

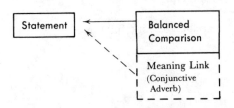

The angler fish lures prey to its enormous jaws by wiggling a fleshy "bait" which dangles in front of its mouth. *In similar fashion,* the alligator snapping turtle attracts unwary fish to its huge mouth by wiggling its large pink tongue, which resembles a lively worm.
>(The conjunctive adverb *in similar fashion* points back to the first clause and indicates the Meaning Relationship of Balanced Comparison between the clauses.)

DO EXERCISES 8 AND 9

4. RESULT

When two independent clauses are linked through *Result,* the second clause presents a consequence or effect of the situation or condition described in the first clause.

Suppose you have written the following sentence: "My sister has the annoying habit of using my jeans, sweaters, and skirts without asking permission." One way to continue would be to indicate the result: "Consequently, when I can't find something, I don't know whether it's lost, strayed, stolen—or borrowed again."

In other words, the second clause answers the question "What is (or was) the result of that?" with reference to the first clause.

Here is another example of Result:

The football team won only one of its games last fall. The coach is now looking for another job.
(The second clause answers the question "What was the result of that?" with reference to the first clause. Note that the Meaning Link *as a result* could be inserted at the beginning of the second clause. When this can be done appropriately, the Meaning Relationship between two clauses is always Result.)

Certain Linking Devices may help to join two clauses which have the Meaning Relationship of Result. Most of the Nouns Summarizing Previous Assertions can be used. Here is an example:

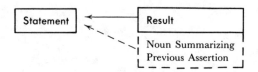

The football team won only one of its games last fall. That melancholy *fact* explains why the coach is now looking for another job.
(The noun *fact* summarizes the entire first clause.)

In addition, several kinds of Meaning Links which point backward are commonly employed: the conjunctive adverbs *accordingly, as a result, consequently, for this reason, hence, so, therefore, thus*; the adjectives *resultant, resulting*; and the nouns *consequence, effect, result*. Here is an example:

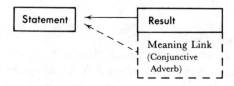

The football team won only one of its games last fall. *Consequently,* the coach is now looking for another job.
(The conjunctive adverb *consequently* links the clauses and indicates that the Meaning Relationship between them is Result.)

5. CAUSE

Cause is the opposite of Result. In this Meaning Relationship, the second clause presents a reason or cause for the situation or condition described in the first clause.

Suppose you have written this sentence: "Bill has dropped out of school and taken a job." Your reader will probably wonder what caused Bill to do this. You may therefore wish to give an explanation: "His father has been ill and unable to work." Your two statements are linked through the Meaning Relationship of Cause.

Actually, this Meaning Relationship includes a great many kinds of causation—reason, purpose, motive, occasion, and others; but such fine distinctions need not concern us here. As long as an independent clause answers the question "What is (or was) the cause of that or the reason for that?" with reference to the independent clause which precedes it, the Meaning Relationship between the clauses is some variety of Cause. Here is another example:

Nancy missed her eight o'clock class this morning. She overslept.
  (The second clause answers the question "What was the cause of that?")

To emphasize causation, the second clause often contains a Meaning Link which points backward. The Meaning Link most often employed for this purpose is the coordinating conjunction *for*. Also useful are the nouns *cause, explanation, motive, occasion, purpose, reason.* Here is an example of clauses joined by a Meaning Link indicating causation:

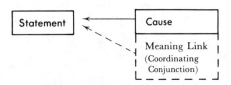

Bob's hands trembled violently, *for* he was badly frightened.
  (The coordinating conjunction *for* points back to the first clause and indicates the Meaning Relationship of Cause between the clauses. Note that without the Meaning Link one might interpret this passage as meaning that Bob was frightened *because* his hands trembled violently. Obviously, the Meaning Link *for* contributes greatly to the clarity of the passage.)

6. QUESTION

Sometimes a clause asks a *Question* suggested by the preceding statement.
  Suppose you have written this sentence: "Transistors and other solid-state devices have replaced tubes in modern radios, television sets, computers, and many other kinds of electronic equipment." You might then ask: "Is the tube, then, completely obsolete?" This is *not* an actual inquiry, seeking information from the reader; such a question would have no place in ordinary expository prose. Instead, it is a *rhetorical question,* inserted for the sake of emphasis. After posing such a question, you may then proceed to answer it yourself. This use of the Meaning Relationship of Question can be a decided asset to your prose, provided you do not use it too frequently. Here is another example:

Dutch elm disease is threatening the trees in our community. Is there anything we can do to combat this blight?
  (The second clause asks a question suggested by the first clause. The writer will presumably answer his own question in succeeding clauses.)

A pair of clauses having the Meaning Relationship of Question may also have a secondary Meaning Relationship, but Question will always be the overriding Meaning Relationship. Examine the following pair of clauses: "A blind date may be handsome, intelligent, and considerate. On the other hand, isn't it possible that he may turn out to be repulsive, moronic, and discourteous?" Obviously, the two clauses contain contrasting elements. Nevertheless, the primary Meaning Relationship is Question.

The Meaning Relationship of Question usually does not require that a Linking Device join the two clauses—the interrogative form of the second clause is sufficient. Sometimes, however, a Noun Summarizing a Previous Assertion is present:

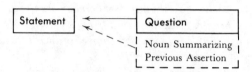

Dutch elm disease is threatening the trees in our community. Faced by such a *calamity*, what can we do to combat this blight?

(The noun *calamity* summarizes the entire first clause.)

In addition, when there is a secondary Meaning Relationship, the two clauses may be linked by one of the Meaning Links Pointing Backward which can indicate such a relationship: the coordinating conjunctions *and, but, or*; or a conjunctive adverb appropriate to the secondary Meaning Relationship. The example of Question dealing with blind dates contains the conjunctive adverb *on the other hand*; here is an example involving the use of a coordinating conjunction:

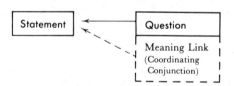

Russia says she desires world peace. *But* does she?

(The coordinating conjunction *but* links the two clauses. It indicates that the secondary Meaning Relationship is that of Contrast.)

7. ANSWER

If the first of two linked independent clauses asks a question, the second may present an *Answer.*

Suppose you have asked the following question: "In the whole animal kingdom, what is the greatest known difference in size between the female and the male of a species?" Having posed this question, you might then proceed to answer it: "According to the *Guinness Book of World Records,* the female of one variety of deep-sea angler fish may weigh up to 500,000 times as much as the male." This question-and-answer technique is much more dramatic and emphatic than the following conventional declarative presentation of the material: "According to the *Guinness Book of World Records,* the female of one variety of deep-sea angler fish may weigh up to 500,000 times as much as the male. In the whole animal kingdom, this is the greatest known difference in size between the female and the male of a species."

Used in moderation, the question-and-answer method can add variety and vigor to your prose style. Here is another example:

Why is a football field called a "gridiron"? The name has been applied because the rectangular playing field, with white lines painted across it at five-yard intervals, bears a fanciful resemblance to a real gridiron, a cooking utensil composed of parallel metal bars and used for broiling food over a flame.
(The second clause answers the question posed by the first clause.)

Although not indispensable, certain Meaning Links which point backward may help to join an answer clause to the preceding question clause. Especially useful are such conjunctive adverbs as these: *actually, all things considered, as a matter of fact, beyond doubt, beyond question, briefly, certainly, considering all things, for the most part, fortunately, indeed, in plain words, in reality, no doubt, obviously, of course, ordinarily, really, specifically, taking everything into account, taking everything into consideration, to be sure, typically, undoubtedly, unfortunately, unquestionably, without doubt.* Less common are the nouns *answer* and *explanation.* Here is an example of an answer joined to the preceding question clause by a Meaning Link:

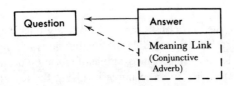

Why did the United States fight in Korea? *Without doubt,* we fought chiefly to defend our own interests.
(The conjunctive adverb *without doubt* links the two clauses.)

DO EXERCISES 10 AND 11

C. UNEQUAL MEANING RELATIONSHIPS

Sometimes the second of two linked independent clauses presents an idea which is both *unlike* that expressed by the first clause and also *unequal* to it in importance. In other words, the two ideas are of different types and possess different degrees of significance, and we may therefore say that the two clauses have an *Unequal Meaning Relationship.*

In some Unequal Meaning Relationships, the second clause simply increases our understanding of the first clause by offering us additional details or facts. Although the second clause is not grammatically subordinate to the first clause, its idea is *subsidiary* to the idea expressed by the first clause. Five important Unequal Meaning Relationships follow this pattern. They are *Definition, Amplification, Sample Item, Sample Fact,* and *Supporting Data.*

In a much smaller group of Unequal Meaning Relationships, the idea expressed by the second clause is more important than that expressed by the first clause. Although the first clause is not grammatically subordinate to the second clause, its idea is subsidiary, and that of the second clause is *dominant.* Two important Unequal Meaning Relationships follow this pattern. They are *Generalization* and *Inference.*

1. DEFINITION

When two independent clauses are linked through *Definition,* the second clause defines a term used in the first clause.

Suppose you have written this sentence: "Many midair collisions between airliners and private planes could be prevented if every private plane were required to carry a transponder." Feeling the need to explain that statement further, you might continue as follows: "This is an automatic radio device which detects the beam of a search radar and sends back a signal that registers as a special blip on the radar screen." In other words, you might use the second sentence to define the relatively unfamiliar term *transponder* in the first.

As the dictionary demonstrates, it is possible to define any word whatsoever. Moreover, definitions can take many forms. However, when the Meaning Relationship between two clauses is Definition, the term to be defined is ordinarily a noun, and the definition itself is usually either a *Formal Definition* or an *Informal Definition.* Let us see what is involved in each variety.

In *Formal Definition,* the second clause has a rigidly prescribed *form.* It is always based upon this formula: *Term = Class + Difference(s).* The *term* to be defined (either repeated from the first clause, or represented by a pronoun or a substitute expression) is first placed in the *class* to which it belongs. Then the term is distinguished from the other members of its class by the listing of one or more characteristics which it possesses but which the other members lack—in other words, its *difference* or *differences* from them. For example, if the term in the first clause needing definition is *transponder,* that term may be repeated in the second clause or else represented by a pronoun (*this* or *it*) or by a substitute expression such as *this instrument.* It is then placed in its class *automatic radio device* and, finally, distinguished from other kinds of automatic radio devices by the differences *which detects the beam of a search radar and sends back a signal that registers as a special blip on the radar screen.* Note how the following formal definitions also adhere to the prescribed formula:

TERM	=	CLASS	+	DIFFERENCE(S)
An acorn	is	the fruit		of the oak tree.
A square	is	a parallelogram		having four equal sides and four right angles.

Since no formal definition can be any better than its class and difference(s), you should therefore always choose these with care. Obviously, you must never use an *inaccurate* class or difference, for this would spoil your definition. For example, it would be wrong to define *acorn* as "the *leaf* of the oak tree" or "the fruit of the *maple* tree." Yet accuracy alone is not enough. You must also keep certain other qualities in mind.

The class must first of all be familiar to the reader. It would be unwise to define *abaptiston* as a "trephine used to cut out circular sections of the skull without penetrating the brain." There is little chance that a reader who is unfamiliar with the term *abaptiston* will know the meaning of the term *trephine.* A more familiar label for the class would be *surgical instrument.* In addition, the class must be the right size—the group it names should be neither too large nor too small. For example, if *eel* is the term being defined, *vertebrate* would be too generalized a class since eels would then need to be differentiated from all other animals with backbones. But *salt-water fish* would, on the other hand, be too restricted a class since some eels spend their adult lives in fresh water. Probably *bony fish* would be the best class to use. Then the definition of *eel* could be "a bony fish with an elongated snakelike body, smooth or slick skin, no pelvic fins, and no distinct tail fin."

Equally as important as the choice of the proper class is the selection of the difference(s) which will distinguish the term being defined from the other members of its class. First, the difference or differences must not be a mere repetition of the term itself. The reader will benefit very little from the explanation that a *mugger* is "a person who commits muggings" or that an *electric can opener* is "an electrically-powered device with which to open cans." In addition, the difference(s) should not include traits which the term being defined shares with the other members of its class—obviously, such traits would constitute similarities rather than differences and hence would not help to distinguish the term from other members of its group. Thus, if you should select the class *prose fiction* when defining *novel,* there would be no reason for the difference(s) to include the fact that the novel contains characters: so do other forms of fiction. Finally, the difference(s) must be familiar to the reader.

For example, it would be unwise to define *maggot* as "the legless larva of a dipteron." A reader who is unfamiliar with the term *maggot* will not know the meaning of the phrase *of a dipteron* and hence will not understand how maggots differ from other members of the class *legless larva*. It would be preferable to define *maggot* as "the legless larva of a two-winged insect."

Two clauses connected through Formal Definition usually do not require Linking Devices to make their Meaning Relationship clear:

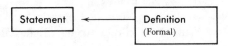

In fine perfume, an almost indispensable ingredient is ambergris. This is the grayish, waxy substance which forms in the body of a sick sperm whale.
(The second clause is a formal definition of the term *ambergris* used in the first clause.
The pronoun *this* replaces the term in the second clause.)

Sometimes, however, it is desirable to employ a Meaning Link, especially a conjunctive adverb. The Meaning Link usually implies either that the definition will be simple and easy (*briefly, in a few words, in plain words, in short, to be brief*), or else that the reader probably already knows the definition and needs only to have his memory refreshed a little (*incidentally, of course*). Although such Meaning Links tend to give a casual tone to the definition clause, it nevertheless remains a *formal* definition:

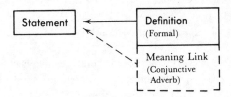

In fine perfume, an almost indispensable ingredient is ambergris. *Briefly,* this is the grayish, waxy substance which forms in the body of a sick sperm whale.
(The conjunctive adverb *briefly* points back to the first clause and implies that the definition in the second clause will be short and relatively simple.)

In *Informal Definition* the second clause always repeats the initial statement in different—and somewhat more specific—words. First of all, this repetition involves the *subject*—the word or word-group which names or indicates a person or a thing about which something is said. The second clause must have the same subject as the first clause (though a pronoun or synonym may be substituted for a noun appearing as the subject of the first clause). In addition, the repetition involves the *predicate*—the verb plus all elements directly connected with it (except the subject). The second clause must have essentially the same predicate as the first, but its predicate will be expressed in simpler and more specific terms than that of the first clause. In other words, the second clause is limited to a *restatement* of the original idea, but a term which occurs in the predicate of the first clause is replaced by other words in the second and is in this way defined:

The manufacturers favored a protective tariff. They wanted customs duties which would be high enough to eliminate foreign competition.

(The second clause is simply a restatement of the first one for the purpose of defining *protective tariff.*)

The second clause in Informal Definition is frequently introduced by one of the following conjunctive adverbs: *in a few words, in other words, in plain words, that is, that is to say.* The purpose of the conjunctive adverb is to indicate that the second clause is a restatement of the original idea:

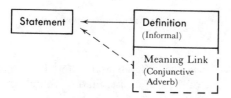

The manufacturers favored a protective tariff. *In other words,* they wanted customs duties which would be high enough to eliminate foreign competition.

(The conjunctive adverb *in other words* points back to the first clause by indicating that the second clause is a restatement of the original idea.)

Remember the following distinctions between the two kinds of Definition:

1. In Formal Definition, the second clause always has a prescribed *form* based upon this formula:

Term, Pronoun, or Substitute Expression + Form of *to be* (*is* or *are*) **+ Class and Difference(s)**

2. In Informal Definition, the second clause is always a *restatement* of the first. The subjects of the two clauses are identical (though a pronoun or synonym may be substituted in the second clause), and the predicates are equivalent—thus, a term which occurs in the predicate of the first clause is replaced by other words in the second clause and is in this way defined.

Review all of the examples of Definition in this section with these distinctions in mind.

2. AMPLIFICATION

When the Meaning Relationship between two clauses is *Amplification,* the second clause expands into an *assertion* some *anticipatory noun* which is contained in the first clause. Without this anticipatory noun, there can be no Amplification.

Suppose you have written this statement: "Then I made a startling discovery." The reader will sense that the noun *discovery* anticipates an explanatory assertion which will be made in the second clause. Therefore, he will expect you to amplify the anticipatory noun by expanding it into such an assertion—for example, "My credit cards were missing." In other words, you must amplify the anticipatory noun *discovery* if the reader is to understand your original statement.

The first clause in Amplification, then, always contains a *noun anticipating a following assertion,* and the second clause always presents the *anticipated assertion.* That assertion is usually made either by the *entire independent clause* or by a *dependent clause* or *verbal phrase* within the independent clause. (Both dependent clauses and verbal phrases are groups of words which function as subordinate elements within independent clauses; the major difference between them is that a dependent clause contains a subject and a verb but a verbal phrase does not.)

Here is an example of an anticipated assertion made by the *entire second independent clause*:

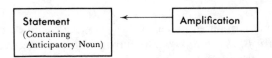

The two opposing lawyers had reached a satisfactory agreement: the suit would be dropped after the defendant had paid the plaintiff eight hundred dollars.
(The entire second clause is an assertion amplifying the anticipatory noun *agreement* in the first clause.)

Note the use of the colon between the two independent clauses. This punctuation is common when a complete independent clause amplifies an anticipatory noun coming at the end of the first clause. In this example the two clauses could also be set off as separate sentences: "The two opposing lawyers had reached a satisfactory agreement. The suit would be dropped after the defendant had paid the plaintiff eight hundred dollars."

The following is an example of an anticipated assertion made by a *noun clause*—a *dependent clause* used as a noun:

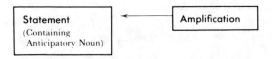

We heard an exciting rumor. It was that school would be dismissed during the basketball tournament.
(The noun clause *that school would be dismissed during the basketball tournament* is an assertion amplifying the anticipatory noun *rumor.*)

And here is an example of an anticipated assertion made by a *verbal phrase*:

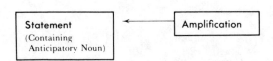

My brother has had one ambition ever since he was six years old. It is to learn to fly an airplane.
(The verbal phrase *to learn to fly an airplane* is an assertion amplifying the anticipatory noun *ambition.*)

A very large number of nouns can be used as anticipatory nouns. Of these, the most important are *advantage, agreement, arrangement, benefit, characteristic, concession, conclusion, consequence, decision, difficulty, disadvantage, discovery, fact, idea, lesson, mishap, mistake, objection, plan, problem, reason, request, result, rumor, statement, step,* and *suggestion.*

You can use a simple test to determine whether or not the Meaning Relationship between two clauses is Amplification. If it is, the anticipatory noun can be used as the subject of a form of the verb *to be,* and the anticipated assertion (rephrased, if necessary) can be used as a noun clause following the verb. Examine these sentences, which were derived from the examples of Amplification given earlier:

Anticipatory Noun + Form of *to be* **+ Noun Clause**

The *agreement* was *that the suit would be dropped after the defendant had paid the plaintiff eight hundred dollars.*

The *rumor* was *that school would be dismissed during the basketball tournament.*

The *ambition* was *that he would learn to fly an airplane.*

If you cannot form such a sentence from a pair of clauses, then you may be sure that the Meaning Relationship between them is *not* Amplification.

In addition to the indispensable anticipatory noun and anticipated assertion, two clauses linked through Amplification may also contain Meaning Links. Those occurring most frequently are certain conjunctive adverbs which point backward—*in a few words, in plain words, in substance,* and *specifically*:

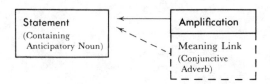

The two opposing lawyers had reached a satisfactory agreement: *specifically,* the suit would be dropped after the defendant had paid the plaintiff eight hundred dollars.

(The conjunctive adverb *specifically* points back to the first clause and implies that the amplification of *agreement* will be short and relatively simple.)

DO EXERCISES 12 AND 13

3. SAMPLE ITEM

When two clauses are linked through the Meaning Relationship of *Sample Item,* the first clause contains a word or word-group which names a class, and the second clause increases the reader's understanding of that class by giving one or more sample items which are members of the class.

Needless to say, the class named in the first clause must be large enough to contain other members which could be mentioned instead of—or in addition to—the members chosen for presentation as sample items. Here is an example:

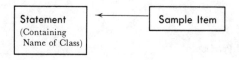

Many hardy birds remain in Indiana through the winter. One of these is the cardinal.

(The second clause gives a sample member of the class *hardy birds.*)

As the preceding passage demonstrates, when two clauses are linked through Sample Item, the second clause has one function only: that of presenting the sample item or items. Accordingly, its verb is usually a form of *to be;* and it often begins with a phrase such as *among these, one of these,* or *two of these.*

You can use a simple test to determine whether the Meaning Relationship between two clauses is Sample Item. If it is, you can always create a sentence with a meaning equivalent to that of the second clause by following this pattern:

_____ **is a sample (or are samples) of the class** _____ .

(The Item or   (The Class
Items Speci-   Named in the
fied in the   First Clause)
Second Clause)

The *cardinal* is a sample of the class *hardy birds.*

Among the Linking Devices associated with Sample Item, the most important are two Meaning Links which point backward—the noun *example* and the adjective *typical*:

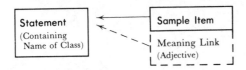

Many hardy birds remain in Indiana through the winter. *Typical* of these year-round songsters is the cardinal.

    (The adjective *typical* points back to the first clause, especially to the class *hardy birds,*
    and helps to indicate that the Meaning Relationship between the clauses is Sample Item.)

4. SAMPLE FACT

If the first of two linked clauses makes a generalization, the second may present a sample specific fact included within that general truth. This is the Meaning Relationship of *Sample Fact.*

Let us assume that you have written the following statement: "Many student organizations are involving themselves in significant community-service projects." Almost inevitably, you will wish to cite a specific instance: "Our Student Council is operating a program of work with retarded children in several schools and clinics." The Meaning Relationship of Sample Fact always follows this order: a *general assertion* plus a *sample fact* included within that assertion. Of course, the general assertion must be broad enough to include other specific facts which could be mentioned, even though the author may be content to offer only one sample.

When the Meaning Relationship between two clauses is Sample Fact, the first clause (the *generalization*) usually contains a class word or word-group as the general subject of a fairly general predicate, and the second clause (the *sample fact*) has a member of that class as a specific subject for a specific predicate which falls within the preceding general predicate. Here is an example:

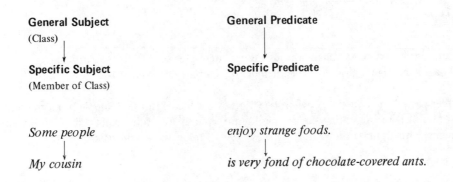

Sometimes the predicates follow this same pattern, but the subject of the first clause is repeated as the subject of the second. Here is an example:

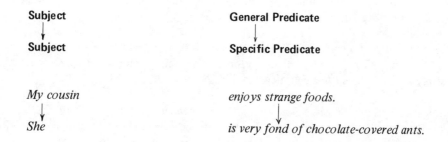

As you can see from the preceding examples, it is extremely important that you use parallel structure when you present a sample fact following a general assertion. The following clauses lack parallelism: "Some people enjoy strange foods. Chocolate-covered ants particularly appeal to my cousin." In this pair of clauses, the pattern of the second clause departs unnecessarily from the pattern set by the first clause, and the passage is therefore faulty.

Here is an additional pair of clauses which are linked through the Meaning Relationship of Sample Fact. Note the effective use of parallel structure:

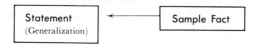

By following a strict diet, many overweight persons have shed their excess pounds. One former circus fat lady reduced from 555 pounds to 120 pounds in fourteen months.

> (The second clause presents a sample fact in order to increase the reader's understanding of the general assertion made by the first clause. The clauses exhibit parallel structure—the specific subject of the second clause is a member of the class which is named as the general subject of the first clause, and the specific predicate of the second clause falls within the general predicate of the first clause.)

A simple test will enable you to determine whether the Meaning Relationship between two clauses is Sample Fact. If it is, you can always create a meaningful sentence by following this pattern:

The specific fact that _____ **is a sample of the general truth that**
(Subject-Predicate from Second Clause)

_____ .
(Subject-Predicate from First Clause)

The specific fact that *my cousin is very fond of chocolate-covered ants* is a sample of the general truth that *some people enjoy strange foods.*

The specific fact that *one former circus fat lady reduced from 555 pounds to 120 pounds in fourteen months* is a sample of the general truth that, *by following a strict diet, many overweight persons have shed their excess pounds.*

A writer may employ the Meaning Relationship of Sample Fact for either of two purposes: (1) to make a non-controversial generalization more meaningful and interesting by giving a specific *example,* or (2) to convince the reader of the truth of a generalization by giving a sample fact as *evidence.* Often it is impossible to tell which purpose the author has in mind unless he employs a Meaning Link to make his intention clear. Note the role played by Meaning Links in the following pairs of clauses:

> Small foreign cars use little gas. The Renault gets up to forty miles per gallon.
> > (No Meaning Link is present, and the purpose of the sample fact is not clearly indicated, possibly because the author considers it unnecessary to do so.)

> Small foreign cars use little gas. *For example,* the Renault gets up to forty miles per gallon.
> > (The Meaning Link *for example* indicates that the purpose of the sample fact is to illustrate what the author presumes is a non-controversial generalization.)

> Small foreign cars use little gas. *Evidence* of this is the fact that the Renault gets up to forty miles per gallon.
> > (The Meaning Link *evidence* indicates that the purpose of the sample fact is to convince the reader of the truth of the generalization.)

As these examples demonstrate, the specific effect of a sample fact depends upon the Meaning Link used—if any. Nevertheless, in each pair of clauses the broad, over-all Meaning Relationship is the same—that of Sample Fact.

The Meaning Links most commonly used to indicate that a sample fact is being presented as an example or illustration are the conjunctive adverbs *for example, for instance, in fact, typically*; the adjective *typical*; and the nouns *case, example, illustration, instance.* The Meaning Links most commonly used to indicate that a sample fact is being presented as evidence are the nouns *evidence, proof.* Examine the following examples carefully:

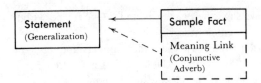

> My cousin enjoys strange foods. *For instance,* she is very fond of chocolate-covered ants.
> > (The conjunctive adverb *for instance* points back to the first clause and shows that the purpose of the sample fact is to furnish an example.)

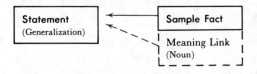

> By following a strict diet, many overweight persons have shed their excess pounds. *Evidence* of this is the fact that one former circus fat lady reduced from 555 pounds to 120 pounds in fourteen months.
> > (The noun *evidence* points back to the first clause and shows that the purpose of the sample fact is to furnish evidence.)

One final word of caution is necessary concerning the use of sample facts which furnish examples. You should not attempt to give an example of a *state of being* unless that state reveals itself through *action.* If you write "Mary is beautiful" or "Mary is ugly," you cannot logically present a specific illustration of her beauty or ugliness. The thought contained in your initial statement is not general enough or broad enough to cover more than one instance. On the other hand, if a state of being reveals itself through characteristic action, you can offer an example of such action. If you write "Mary is very hot-tempered" or "Mary has a nasty disposition," you can furnish a specific illustration of her hot temper or nasty disposition as it is revealed through her behavior: "For instance, she frequently swears at her bridge partner." Here is another instance of a state of being which could be exhibited through a number of different actions: "My cousin is excessively polite." From the various possible examples, you can select the one which you wish to present: "For instance, when visiting our home, he stands up every time my mother enters the room, even though she has asked him not to do so."

5. SUPPORTING DATA

Sometimes it is desirable to offer *Supporting Data* for a previous statement.

Suppose you have written this sentence: "Someone must have read the top-secret document." Since the reader may be inclined to doubt your assertion, you may decide to add the following: "The seal across the flap of the envelope has been broken." In this way, you have made your original statement more convincing. The clause presenting the supporting data answers the reader's question, "Why should I believe that?"

When two independent clauses are linked through Supporting Data, the first clause is a *hypothesis,* or theory, rather than an absolutely provable statement, and it therefore should contain a verb beginning with *may* or *must* or a Meaning Link like *probably* or *apparently* to show that it is a hypothesis. The second clause then offers data to support that hypothesis. For example, you may have written this statement: "The skin-diver was apparently killed by a shark." In the absence of absolute proof, you must be content to offer partial proof—one or more pieces of information which can be accounted for by your hypothesis and which therefore help to establish its validity. If you choose this supporting data well, you will convince the reader that your hypothesis is the simplest and best explanation of the available information. To support the theory that the skin-diver was killed by a shark, you may state: "A fragment of a shark's tooth was found embedded in a wound on the victim's hip." Note that this supporting data does *not* constitute absolute proof, since the shark might have attacked after the diver was already dead from some other cause. However, the supporting data is sufficiently convincing to make the hypothesis seem quite reasonable.

Here is another example of this Meaning Relationship:

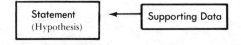

It was probably a fox that disturbed his chickens last night. Its tracks were plentiful in the soft mud near the hen house.

(The second clause offers data to support the hypothesis contained in the first clause.)

In this example, note the use of *probably* in the first clause to indicate that the clause is presenting a hypothesis.

Besides the words *may, must, probably,* and *apparently,* such Meaning Links as *beyond doubt, beyond question, obviously, undoubtedly, unquestionably,* and *without doubt* may also indicate that a statement is a hypothesis:

George obviously intends to leave town immediately after class. He has a suitcase with him.

Even though the first clause is expressed quite positively, it is still only a hypothesis, and there are other hypotheses which could equally well explain the second clause—for example, George could have arranged to let a friend borrow the suitcase.

Usually two independent clauses interlocking through Supporting Data do not require a Linking Device in the second clause to clarify the Meaning Relationship between them. Sometimes, however, a Meaning Link which points backward is present, usually a conjunctive adverb such as *actually, as a matter of fact, indeed,* or *in fact*:

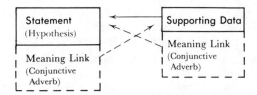

The skin-diver was *apparently* killed by a shark. *As a matter of fact,* a fragment of a shark's tooth was found embedded in a wound on the victim's hip.

> (The conjunctive adverb *apparently* in the first clause indicates that the statement is a hypothesis. The conjunctive adverb *as a matter of fact* in the second clause points back to the first clause and helps to indicate the Meaning Relationship of Supporting Data between the two clauses.)

DO EXERCISES 14 AND 15

6. GENERALIZATION

Generalization is the opposite of Sample Fact. The second clause in this Meaning Relationship sets forth a general idea which includes the specific fact given in the first clause.

Suppose you have written this sentence: "Beethoven composed some of his greatest music when totally deaf." You might then wish to offer the reader a general idea which includes the instance of Beethoven: "Geniuses have often triumphed over handicaps which would defeat lesser men." Thus, Generalization involves a new and broader idea based upon some specific fact cited earlier. It always follows this order of presentation: a specific fact, then the general idea which includes the specific fact and is more important than the specific fact. Here is an example:

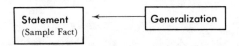

One former circus fat lady reduced from 555 pounds to 120 pounds in fourteen months. By following a strict diet, many overweight persons have shed their excess pounds.

> (The second clause presents a generalization based upon the specific fact in the first clause.)

Note that the pattern of subjects and predicates in Generalization is the reverse of that used in Sample Fact:

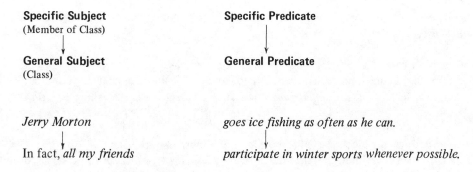

Here are the same sentences rearranged as Sample Fact:

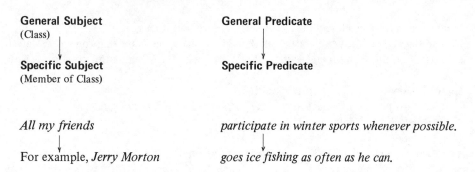

As we have already seen, a sample fact may be intended either as example or as evidence. Thus, in Generalization the first clause may be considered either as a concrete, specific fact leading up to a non-controversial general idea or as evidence attempting to convince the reader of the validity of the generalization. If you intend to convince your reader, you must be careful to avoid *hasty generalizations.* In this chapter, since we are examining pairs of clauses, we have looked at one clause expressing a general idea linked with a preceding clause giving one specific fact. Later, when you write fully developed paragraphs, you will ordinarily wish to base each generalization upon *several* specific facts. Otherwise, there is always the danger that you will present insufficient or unrepresentative instances. Let us assume that you have written the following statement: "Our cocker spaniel Laddie cannot learn even how to sit up and beg." Perhaps you then add, "Cocker spaniels are incapable of mastering even the simplest tricks." At this point the reader can raise a legitimate objection: Laddie's inability to learn tricks does not by itself indicate that *all* cocker spaniels have this difficulty. Unless you can present several additional instances, you have no right to make a statement concerning the breed as a whole.

Two clauses joined through Generalization do not ordinarily require the use of Linking Devices to make their Meaning Relationship clear. Occasionally they do employ a Meaning Link which points backward—a conjunctive adverb such as *certainly, in fact* or *obviously.*

7. INFERENCE

Inference is the opposite of Supporting Data. As we have seen, in Supporting Data the *first* clause presents a hypothesis. In Inference, on the other hand, the *second* clause sets forth a hypothesis, or conclusion, derived from the data presented in the first clause.

Suppose you have written this sentence: "Kowalsky's fingerprints were found on the murder weapon." You might then present an inference based on that statement: "He must have been involved in the crime." As this example demonstrates, Inference always follows this order of presentation: first the supporting data, then the hypothesis.

The hypothesis in Inference is usually a *hypothetical cause*. Note the difference between an *actual cause* and a *hypothetical cause*:

> Nancy missed her 8 o'clock class this morning. She overslept.
>> (The flat, unqualified declaration of the second clause indicates that the writer definitely knows that this is the *actual cause* of Nancy's absence. The Meaning Relationship is Cause.)

> Nancy missed her 8 o'clock class this morning. She must have overslept.
>> (The word *must* indicates that the second clause is a *hypothetical cause*. The Meaning Relationship is Inference.)

Occasionally the hypothesis is a *hypothetical result*. Note the difference between an *actual result* and a *hypothetical result*:

> Carl moved heavy boxes all day yesterday. He is very sore today.
>> (The flat, unqualified declaration of the second clause indicates that the writer definitely knows that this is the *actual result* of Carl's actions. The Meaning Relationship is Result.)

> Carl moved heavy boxes all day yesterday. He is probably very sore today.
>> (The word *probably* indicates that the second clause is a *hypothetical result*. The Meaning Relationship is Inference.)

Here is another example of the Meaning Relationship of Inference:

> The seal across the flap of the envelope has been broken. Someone must have read the top-secret document.
>> (The second clause presents a hypothesis based on the data given in the first clause.)

Of course, it is often possible to derive more than one plausible hypothesis from an item of supporting data. The example just given might have read as follows: "The seal across the flap of the envelope has been broken. The document must have received rough handling in the mail."

Certain Linking Devices may help to join two clauses which have the Meaning Relationship of Inference. Most of the Nouns Summarizing Previous Assertions can function in this way. Here is an example:

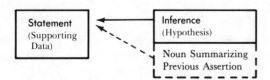

The seal across the flap of the envelope has been broken. That *fact* suggests that someone has read the top-secret document.

>   (The noun *fact* in the second clause links the clauses by summarizing the entire first clause.)

In addition, several kinds of Meaning Links which point backward are useful: the conjunctive adverbs *apparently, beyond doubt, beyond question, in all probability, obviously, probably, undoubtedly, unquestionably, without doubt*; the nouns *conclusion, deduction, inference*; the verbs *conclude, deduce, infer*; and the auxiliary verbs *may, must.* Here is an example:

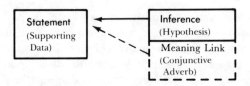

The seal across the flap of the envelope has been broken. *Obviously,* someone has read the top-secret document.

>   (The conjunctive adverb *obviously* links the two clauses and helps to indicate the Meaning Relationship of Inference between them. The use of the word *obviously* shows that the writer is convinced of the validity of the inference, but this is still only a hypothesis, not a proven fact.)

One final word of caution is necessary concerning the use of Inference. You must be careful to avoid *unwarranted inferences.* In this chapter, since we are examining pairs of clauses, we have looked at inferences based upon a single item of supporting data in the preceding clause. Later, when you write fully developed paragraphs, you will often wish to base an inference upon more data than can be contained in a single clause. Of course, one item of supporting data is sometimes sufficient. Suppose you have written this sentence: "Saying not a word, Gertrude marched up to me and slapped my face as hard as she could." The reader will not object to the following inference: "She apparently was very angry with me." On the other hand, one or two items of supporting data are often insufficient to warrant a sound inference: (1) You may find that you have treated a mere possibility as though it were a certainty: "He failed the examination. He obviously hadn't studied for it." Such an inference ignores the possibility that he might have been ill at the time of the examination or that he might have studied the wrong things. (2) You may find that you have arrived at a wholly unjustified inference based upon insufficient data: "I fished for three hours and never had a nibble. There certainly must not be any fish in that lake." Such an inference is unwarranted unless the writer has additional data to support his conclusion. A fisherman visiting the lake several days later might have come away with a full creel and therefore might have decided that he had discovered an angler's paradise.

DO EXERCISES 16 AND 17

D. COORDINATION VERSUS SUBORDINATION

In Chapter 1 you learned the necessity of avoiding *False Parallelism*, the use of parallel constructions to express ideas which are not truly similar or equivalent:

>   Laura Hunt is a psychology major, and she is the newly-elected president of the student council.
>   (The two independent clauses are linked by Parallel Idea but exhibit False Parallelism since the ideas they express are not truly equivalent.)

Subordinating the idea which is of lesser importance makes clear the writer's feeling about the relative significance of the two ideas:

> Laura Hunt, a psychology major, is the newly-elected president of the student council.
>   (There is only one independent clause; its main idea is that Laura Hunt is the newly-elected president of the student council.)

> Laura Hunt, the newly-elected president of the student council, is a psychology major.
>   (There is only one independent clause; its main idea is that Laura Hunt is a psychology major.)

False Parallelism is one aspect of the problem of *coordination versus subordination.* As the revisions of the "Laura Hunt" passage demonstrate, *subordination* occurs when one group of related words is of a lesser grammatical rank than another group of related words. *Coordination* occurs when two groups of related words are of equal grammatical rank. Every sample pair of linked clauses illustrating a Meaning Relationship in the earlier sections of this chapter is an example of coordination. This is true even in those instances where the clauses are joined by an Unequal Meaning Relationship; for, although the ideas of the two clauses have different degrees of significance, each is nevertheless sufficiently important to merit expression by an independent clause.

Our study of the Meaning Relationships between independent clauses should not lead you to write a string of independent clauses without stopping to consider whether each presents a major or a minor idea. For example, consider the following:

> Chester Greenwood was a native of Farmington, Maine, and he invented earmuffs in 1877.

This passage consists of two coordinate independent clauses linked by Parallel Idea. But it needs revision, for the ideas are not truly parallel. The writer's actual meaning is probably best expressed through subordination of the first clause:

> Chester Greenwood, a native of Farmington, Maine, invented earmuffs in 1877.

It is obvious that the passage has been improved by the elimination of False Parallelism.

Failure to subordinate those ideas which he considers minor weakens a student's writing in two ways. First, it blurs the meaning—since it does not distinguish between what is important and what is not. Second, it produces an extremely immature prose style—especially in long passages. Examine the following:

> I have a cat whose name is Fred. The cat has a bad habit. He brings live mice into the house. Then he turns them loose.

Such a series of short simple sentences sounds like something intended for very young children. The passage can be greatly improved through appropriate subordination:

> My cat Fred has a bad habit. He brings live mice into the house and then turns them loose.

As you can see, combining the ideas produces a much more mature form of expression than the original version. The four independent clauses have been reduced to two independent clauses, the second of which amplifies the anticipatory noun *habit* in the first one.

Clearly, then, part of your ability to write good prose depends upon your skill in employing subordination. When you wish to subordinate, you will find the following grammatical constructions especially useful: *appositives, adjective clauses, adverb clauses, phrases,* and *compound predicates.* If you convert an independent clause to one of these lesser grammatical constructions, it becomes part of another independent clause, and the complete independent clause thus formed may link in normal fashion with another clause through a Meaning Relationship. We have just seen this happen in the passage about the cat.

Appositives. The most common sort of *appositive* is a noun (plus its modifiers) following another noun or pronoun and providing a supplementary explanation of that noun or pronoun (my son, *the doctor*; Laura Hunt, *the newly-elected president of the student council*; my cat *Fred*; the stolen car, *a Chevrolet hardtop*; we, *the people*).

If the Meaning Relationship between two independent clauses is Parallel Idea or Definition, subordination of a minor idea can usually be achieved by turning its independent clause into an appositive. The "Laura Hunt" and "Chester Greenwood" passages you have already examined (pages 39-40) are examples of such revision when the Meaning Relationship is Parallel Idea. Here are two independent clauses linked through Definition:

> The biologist was studying the behavior of elvers. These are young eels that migrate upstream from the sea.

The second clause can easily be turned into an appositive:

> The biologist was studying the behavior of elvers, *young eels that migrate upstream from the sea.*

Notice that the complete appositive contains an adjective clause modifying the "core" appositive *eels*.

Adjective Clauses. As its name indicates, an *adjective clause* is a dependent clause which modifies a noun or pronoun (the man *who robbed the bank*; our team, *which was undefeated last year*; something *that he told me*).

If the Meaning Relationship between two independent clauses is Parallel Idea or Definition and you do not wish to subordinate by using an appositive, you will usually find it possible to change one independent clause to an adjective clause modifying a noun or pronoun in the other clause. Compare the following passages with earlier versions employing appositives:

> Chester Greenwood, *who was a native of Farmington, Maine,* invented earmuffs in 1877.

> The biologist was studying the behavior of elvers, *which are young eels that migrate upstream from the sea.*

Adverb Clauses. As its name indicates, an *adverb clause* is a dependent clause which modifies a verb (we shouted *when the team scored*), an adjective (she is smarter *than I thought*), or another adverb (they worked faster *than we did*).

If the Meaning Relationship between two independent clauses is Related Action, Contrast, or Cause, you can usually subordinate one independent clause by turning it into an adverb clause. In each of the following examples the first passage presents two ideas in two independent clauses, and the second illustrates the use of an adverb clause to achieve subordination:

Related Action

> The python swallowed the wild pig. Then it slept for several days while digesting its meal.

> *After it swallowed the wild pig,* the python slept for several days while digesting its meal.

Contrast

> The fox is usually considered sly and crafty, but it is actually rather stupid.

> *Although the fox is usually considered sly and crafty,* it is actually rather stupid.

Cause

> We left the football game early, for we got cold.

> We left the football game early *because we got cold.*

Phrases.   A *phrase* is a group of related words which does not have a subject and verb and which functions in an independent clause as a single unit.   Of the various kinds of phrases, the one most often used to achieve subordination is the *participial phrase.*   A participle is a verb-form (not a verb) which can function as an adjective (the *damaged* package).   A participial phrase is composed of a participle plus words which complete its meaning or modify it (my brother, *lost in the woods*).

If the Meaning Relationship between two independent clauses is Related Action, Contrast, or Cause and you do not wish to subordinate by using an adverb clause, you can subordinate even more drastically by using a participial phrase since the participial phrase has a lesser grammatical rank than an adverb clause has. Compare the following passages with the earlier versions employing adverb clauses:

> *Having swallowed the wild pig,* the python slept for several days while digesting its meal.

> *Usually considered sly and crafty,* the fox is actually rather stupid.

> *Getting cold,* we left the football game early.

Compound Predicates.   As we have seen, the predicate of a clause is composed of the verb plus all elements directly connected with it (except the subject).   A *compound predicate* consists of two or more predicates containing parallel verbs (the frightened burglar *dropped his gun* and *ran*; the photographer *inserted the holder, focused the camera,* and *took the picture*).

If the Meaning Relationship between two independent clauses is Related Action, Contrast, Alternative, or Result, the two clauses can usually be turned into one clause with a compound predicate made up of two elements. In each of the following examples the first passage presents two ideas in two independent clauses, and the second illustrates the use of a compound predicate to achieve subordination:

Related Action

> The dog gulped down its food. Then it begged for more.

> The dog *gulped down its food* and then *begged for more.*

Contrast

> He studied hard, but he failed the course.

> He *studied hard* but *failed the course.*

Alternative

> My sister may have forgotten the meeting, or she may have missed the bus.

> My sister either *forgot the meeting* or *missed the bus.*

Result

I forgot to set my alarm clock; therefore, I was late getting to work.

I *forgot to set my alarm clock* and therefore *was late getting to work.*

Revision through the use of compound predicates differs from other forms of subordination in one r   ct. It does not occur because a writer feels that the idea expressed by one independent clause is major and   idea of the other clause is minor. Instead, it occurs because he wishes to link two ideas more closely. He   s so by combining them to produce a single clause, an action which somewhat reduces the emphasis on, or the   portance of, both ideas since they no longer have separate independent clauses for their expression.

When should you subordinate, and when should you not? As was indicated earlier, yo   .ould subordinate (1) when it will help to clarify your meaning by indicating which ideas are important and   :h are not, (2) when it will make your style more mature and sophisticated, and (3) when it will add neede   .riety of expression to your prose and thus help you avoid monotonous writing. Obviously, there is n   .ason to subordinate in instances when you will not gain any of these benefits.

Sometimes it is not possible to subordinate because a pair of independent   .uses already contains subordinate elements that get in the way of revision. Examine the following:

Cockroaches secrete a sticky, bad-smelling fluid which may be depo   .d on anything they touch. Consequently, if they gain access to food, they may render it   .it for human consumption.

Perhaps a writer would like to turn the first independent clause into an   .erb clause: "Since cockroaches secrete a sticky, bad-smelling fluid which may be deposited on anything they   .ach"; but he cannot do so because of the adverb clause (introduced by *if*) which is already present in the se   .d independent clause. The result would be clumsy and confusing:

Since cockroaches secrete a sticky, bad-smelling fluid   .nich may be deposited on anything they touch, if they gain access to food, they may render it unfit for human consumption.

Obviously, a writer should never try to force subordination where he cannot employ it naturally and effectively.

DO EXERCISES 18 AND 19

3

The Five Patterns of Prose

Thus far, we have been studying the ways in which independent clauses are connected by the "thought links" of Meaning Relationships and the "word links" of Linking Devices. To do this, we have examined pairs of interlocking independent clauses.

Although some passages of prose are brief and contain only two linked independent clauses, most of them are longer and contain three or more linked clauses. Whatever the length of a passage, its clauses must fall into one of five patterns. That is to say, *any unified, coherent passage of prose containing two or more independent clauses must have as its over-all structural framework one of only five basic patterns.*

These patterns are *Enumeration, Equal Pair, Unequal Pair, Chain,* and *Leapfrog.*

In this chapter, we shall examine short passages of prose in which individual independent clauses are the units in the five patterns. Later, when we study full-length essays, we shall see groups of clauses, paragraphs, and even groups of paragraphs used as the units in the same five patterns. No matter how large the units are, one of the five patterns always provides the over-all structural framework.

Let us see, then, what each of the five patterns involves.

A. THE FIVE BASIC PATTERNS

As already indicated, the five basic patterns are *Enumeration, Equal Pair, Unequal Pair, Chain,* and *Leapfrog.*

As their names make clear, the first three patterns are closely related to the three classes of Meaning Relationships which we examined in Chapter 2. In fact, each sample passage illustrating a Meaning Relationship which you studied in Chapter 2 is also an example of one of the first three patterns. Thus, two clauses linked by an Enumerative Meaning Relationship follow the pattern of Enumeration, two clauses linked by an Equal Meaning Relationship follow the pattern of Equal Pair, and two clauses linked by an Unequal Meaning Relationship follow the pattern of Unequal Pair.

The final two patterns, Chain and Leapfrog, are more complicated than the others. Each always involves at least three units, and a great deal of variation is possible in the specific Meaning Relationships used.

1. ENUMERATION

The first basic pattern, *Enumeration*, consists of clauses connected by one of the two Enumerative Meaning Relationships—Related Action and Parallel Idea. In Chapter 2 we saw that pairs of clauses linked by these relationships may be diagrammed as follows:

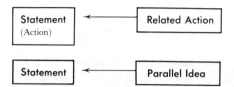

With both Related Action and Parallel Idea, the second clause *duplicates* the type of thought expressed by the first clause. With Related Action, the first clause presents an action, and the second presents another action related to that indicated in the first clause:

The squirrel reached doubtfully for the nut. Then, retreating several feet, he cracked the shell in order to get at the kernel.

    (The first clause presents an action, and the second presents a related action. Although the diagram does not show Linking Devices, notice the Meaning Link *then*.)

With Parallel Idea, the first clause presents an idea, and the second presents an idea of the same type:

After the school officials decided to place less emphasis on the "three R's," some of the students did not learn how to read. In addition, some of them did not learn how to write.

    (The first clause presents an idea, and the second presents an idea of the same type. Although the diagram does not show Linking Devices, notice the Meaning Link *in addition*.)

Of course, the sequence involving Related Action could be extended to include three or more related actions, and the sequence involving Parallel Idea could be extended to include three or more ideas of the same type. Here is an example of each:

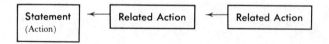

The squirrel reached doubtfully for the nut. Retreating several feet, he cracked the shell in order to get at the kernel. Then, apparently satisfied that I could be trusted, he scrambled to my shoulder to beg for more.

    (Observing chronological order, the second and third independent clauses present actions related to the one expressed by the first independent clause. Although the diagram does not show Linking Devices, notice the Meaning Link *then* in the final independent clause.)

After the school officials decided to place less emphasis on the "three R's," some of the students did not learn how to read. In addition, some of them did not learn how to write. Finally, some of them did not learn how to work simple problems in arithmetic.

> (The first clause presents an idea, and the second and third clauses present additional ideas of the same type. Although the diagram does not show Linking Devices, notice the Parallelism of structure and the Meaning Links *in addition* and *finally*.)

In the examples just given, note that each item could be numbered and would then form part of a *numbered listing*. The first basic pattern always involves *Enumeration*—a listing of two or more related actions or parallel ideas. The various possibilities are shown in the following diagrams:

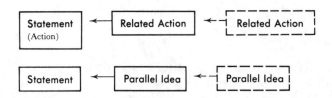

The arrows and boxes formed with broken lines indicate that *three or more* clauses may be present in Enumeration, even though *two* clauses are sufficient to constitute an Enumeration pattern.

2. EQUAL PAIR

In Chapter 2 we saw that two independent clauses may be linked by an Equal Meaning Relationship—Contrast, Alternative, Balanced Comparison, Result, Cause, Question, or Answer. Two clauses linked by any of these relationships form an *Equal Pair*, the second basic pattern. The two clauses present ideas which are of different types but which are equal in importance. This pattern may be diagrammed as follows:

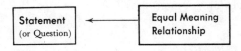

We have, of course, already examined this structural pattern in considerable detail. Here is an additional example:

During the past few years, many scholars have predicted that the world will soon starve to death because of the population explosion. However, Professor Snyder insists that this gloomy prophecy will not come true.

  (The idea expressed by the second independent clause contrasts with that expressed by the first one. Although the diagram does not show Linking Devices, notice the Meaning Link *however* and the Noun Summarizing a Previous Assertion *prophecy*.)

3. UNEQUAL PAIR

  In Chapter 2 we saw that two independent clauses may be linked by an Unequal Meaning Relationship— Definition, Amplification, Sample Item, Sample Fact, Supporting Data, Generalization, or Inference. Two clauses joined through one of these Meaning Relationships form an *Unequal Pair*, the third basic pattern. The two clauses present ideas which are unequal in importance. In Definition, Amplification, Sample Item, Sample Fact, and Supporting Data, the idea expressed by the second clause is *less significant* than that expressed by the first clause. In Generalization and Inference, the idea expressed by the second clause is *more significant* than that expressed by the first clause. The pattern involving an Unequal Pair of clauses may be diagrammed as follows:

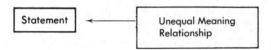

  We have, of course, already examined this structural pattern in considerable detail. Here are two additional examples:

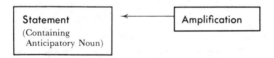

The sand tiger shark has a unique characteristic. It practices cannibalism even before it is born.

  (The entire second clause is an assertion amplifying the anticipatory noun *characteristic*. The idea of the second clause is *less significant* than that of the first.)

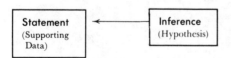

While inspecting the burned-out drug store, the insurance investigators found two gasoline cans near the prescription counter. The fire must have been deliberately set.

  (The second clause presents a hypothesis based on the data given in the first clause. The idea of the second clause is *more significant* than that of the first.)

4. CHAIN

The fourth basic pattern, *Chain*, must be distinguished from the second basic pattern, Equal Pair. As you know, the Equal Meaning Relationships are Contrast, Alternative, Balanced Comparison, Result, Cause, Question, and Answer. *Two* independent clauses linked by an Equal Meaning Relationship form an Equal Pair; *three or more* independent clauses linked by Equal Meaning Relationships form a Chain.

In the Chain pattern, the independent clauses present ideas which are of different types but which are equal in importance. The pattern may be diagrammed as follows:

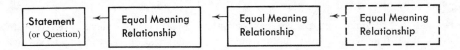

The arrow and box formed with broken lines indicate that *four or more* independent clauses may be present in a Chain, even though *three* are sufficient to establish the pattern.

Even in the basic three-unit form of the Chain pattern, many different combinations of the seven Equal Meaning Relationships are possible. Moreover, a writer can add extra clauses to the series, producing further combinations. Of course, there are some limitations on the specific sequences of Meaning Relationships which can occur in this pattern. For example, the Meaning Relationship of Answer is possible only if the preceding clause is a question. Nevertheless, the Chain pattern does possess great flexibility.

Obviously, we cannot examine here all the combinations of Equal Meaning Relationships which can occur in a Chain. Nor is such an undertaking necessary. By studying a few typical examples, we can sufficiently familiarize ourselves with this basic pattern:

My sister failed to have the filling-station attendant check the water in the radiator before she left. As a result, the engine became overheated during her trip to Chicago. Fortunately, though, no serious damage was done to the car.

> (The second independent clause gives a result of the circumstance indicated in the first independent clause, and the third independent clause presents an idea which contrasts with the idea expressed by the second independent clause. Although the diagram does not show Linking Devices, notice the Meaning Link *as a result* in the second clause and the Meaning Link *though* in the third clause.)

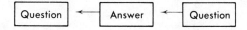

What did the great nineteenth-century scientist Thomas Huxley consider the most valuable result of all education? It was, he said, "the ability to make yourself do the thing you have to do, when it ought to be done, whether you like it or not." Is not modern man desperately in need of this very trait of self-discipline?

> (The second independent clause answers the question posed by the first independent clause, and the third independent clause asks a question suggested by the second independent clause.)

The female English sparrow courts the male by fluttering her wings like a fledgling and begging him to feed her. In similar fashion, the female wolf often woos the male by romping like a playful puppy and soliciting gifts of food. However, she quickly discards this behavior when her pups are born and need care that is altogether adult.

> (The entire second independent clause is compared with the entire first independent clause, and the third independent clause presents an idea which contrasts with that expressed by the second independent clause. Although the diagram does not show Linking Devices, notice the Meaning Link *in similar fashion* in the second independent clause, and the Meaning Link *however* and the Noun Summarizing a Previous Assertion *behavior* in the third independent clause.)

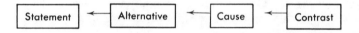

When threatened by danger, the hog-nosed snake may puff itself up and hiss fiercely. Or it may roll over on its back, go completely limp, and lie motionless. The cause of this deathlike state is a condition resembling shock which renders the animal unconscious. However, unlike shock in human beings, it is not harmful to the snake.

> (The second independent clause presents an alternative to the idea expressed by the first independent clause, the third independent clause presents the reason for the situation described in the second independent clause, and the fourth independent clause presents an idea which contrasts with the idea expressed by the third independent clause. Although the diagram does not show Linking Devices, notice the Meaning Link *or* in the second clause, the Meaning Link *cause* in the third clause, and the Meaning Link *however* in the fourth clause.)

5. LEAPFROG

The *Leapfrog* pattern, the least common of the five patterns, has an unusual arrangement of clauses.

In the first four basic patterns, the arrangement of the independent clauses is *sequential*. That is, each independent clause has a Meaning Relationship with the independent clause *immediately preceding it*, and all of the Meaning Relationships are arranged in a single unbroken sequence. In the Leapfrog pattern, the arrangement of the independent clauses is *non-sequential*. That is, one clause has a Meaning Relationship with a clause *other than the one immediately preceding it*. Thus, the Leapfrog pattern always contains *three or more* independent clauses, and *two* of those clauses are linked with the *same* earlier clause.

For example, the second independent clause may be linked with the first independent clause, and the third independent clause may skip back over the second independent clause and also be linked with the first independent clause. This Leapfrog series may be diagrammed as follows:

Occasionally, though, a Leapfrog series is composed of four or more clauses. The pattern may therefore be diagrammed as follows:

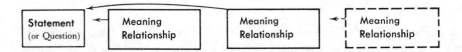

The arrow and box formed with broken lines indicate that *four or more* independent clauses may be present in a Leapfrog series, even though *three* are sufficient to establish the pattern.

Here are four examples of the Leapfrog pattern:

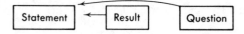

My cousin has gained nine pounds in four weeks. As a result, she now finds her dresses too snug. Could her increase in weight be due to her ignoring her diet and treating herself to candy bars, chocolate malts, and other between-meal snacks?

>   (The second independent clause gives a result of the circumstance stated in the first independent clause, and the third independent clause skips back to the first independent clause and asks a question suggested by the first independent clause. Although the diagram does not show Linking Devices, notice the Meaning Link *as a result* in the second clause.)

The salesman kept trying to interest me in "borax," but I preferred quality merchandise. In the language of the furniture industry, "borax" is flashy, shoddily constructed furniture masquerading as a bargain.

>   (The second independent clause presents an idea which contrasts with the idea expressed by the first independent clause, and the third independent clause skips back to the first independent clause and defines the term *borax* used there. Although the diagram does not show Linking Devices, notice the Meaning Link *but* in the second clause.)

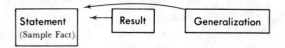

One former circus fat lady reduced from 555 pounds to 120 pounds in fourteen months; and, as a result, she was able to enter upon a new career as a buyer for a large department store. By following a strict diet, many overweight persons have shed their excess pounds.

>   (The second independent clause gives a result of the circumstance stated in the first independent clause, and the third independent clause skips back to the first independent clause and presents a generalization based upon the specific fact given in the first clause. Although the diagram does not show Linking Devices, notice the Meaning Links *and* and *as a result* in the second clause.)

Bill Smoot, our star quarterback, will not be able to play for the rest of the season. According to the team physician, he has a torn cartilage in his right knee. Consequently, the coach is planning to shift a halfback, Jud Branson, to the quarterback position. However, this change will give us less depth at halfback.

> (The second independent clause presents the reason for the situation described in the first independent clause, and the third independent clause gives a result of the situation described in the first independent clause. The fourth independent clause presents an idea which contrasts with the idea expressed by the third independent clause. Although the diagram does not show Linking Devices, notice the Meaning Link *consequently* in the third clause and the Meaning Link *however* in the fourth clause.)

B. REVIEW OF THE FIVE BASIC PATTERNS

1. ENUMERATION

The first basic pattern, *Enumeration*, consists of two or more units which are linked through one of the Enumerative Meaning Relationships (Related Action, Parallel Idea):

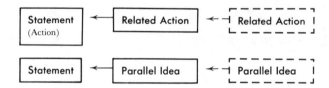

2. EQUAL PAIR

The second basic pattern, *Equal Pair*, consists of two units which are linked through one of the Equal Meaning Relationships (Contrast, Alternative, Balanced Comparison, Result, Cause, Question, Answer):

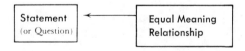

3. UNEQUAL PAIR

The third basic pattern, *Unequal Pair*, consists of two units which are linked through one of the Unequal Meaning Relationships (Definition, Amplification, Sample Item, Sample Fact, Supporting Data, Generalization, Inference):

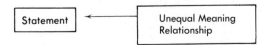

4. CHAIN

The fourth basic pattern, *Chain*, consists of three or more units which are linked through Equal Meaning Relationships (Contrast, Alternative, Balanced Comparison, Result, Cause, Question, Answer):

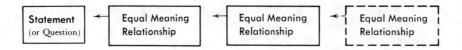

5. LEAPFROG

The fifth basic pattern, *Leapfrog*, consists of a non-sequential series of three or more units, with one of the units skipping back to link with a unit other than the one immediately preceding it:

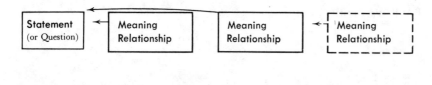

Throughout this chapter we have used independent clauses as the units in the five patterns. Remember that we shall later see groups of clauses, paragraphs, and even groups of paragraphs used as the units in these same five patterns.

DO EXERCISES 20 AND 21

4

The Cluster

Up to this point, we have studied the ways in which the independent clause functions as a unit in each of the five basic patterns of prose. Now we shall see that any structural function which can be performed by an independent clause can also be performed by a *cluster*—two or more independent clauses operating together *as a single unit.*

In Chapter 2 we examined the following example of the Meaning Relationship of Amplification: "Then I made a startling discovery. My credit cards were missing." In this passage, the second independent clause amplifies the anticipatory noun *discovery* in the first independent clause. Now let us change the initial statement in this fashion: "Then I made two startling discoveries." After this change it may be necessary to offer the reader more than a single clause of amplification since the anticipatory noun *discoveries* is plural. Thus, the complete passage might read as follows: "Then I made two startling discoveries. My motel room had been thoroughly ransacked, and my credit cards were missing." Note that, considered as a single unit, the two parallel clauses amplifying *discoveries* function in precisely the same way as did the single clause amplifying *discovery*. These parallel clauses constitute a *cluster*.

We can diagram this last example as follows:

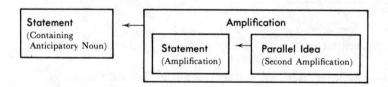

Then I made two startling discoveries. My motel room had been thoroughly ransacked, and my credit cards were missing.

As previously indicated, the second and third independent clauses in this passage form a cluster which amplifies the anticipatory noun *discoveries* in the first independent clause. Note that in the diagram the boxes representing the second and third clauses are enclosed by a larger box. That larger box represents the cluster and is labeled "Amplification" to show the Meaning Relationship of the cluster to the preceding independent clause. Within the cluster, the two clauses of amplification are linked through the Meaning Relationship of Parallel Idea.

In any of the five basic patterns of prose, a cluster of linked clauses can function as if it were a single clause. It may serve as the initial statement in a pattern and have a following element linked to it through a Meaning Relationship. Or it may itself be linked to a preceding element through a Meaning Relationship. Or it may be linked to a preceding element and have a following element linked to it. Thus, a cluster can be defined as *two or more independent clauses which function as a unit in relation to at least one other independent clause or cluster.*

Within the cluster, the individual clauses are connected by Meaning Relationships which are entirely independent of the function of the cluster as a unit. Thus, a cluster which as a unit is presenting a result can be made up of two clauses which are in contrast with each other.

A. VARIETIES OF CLUSTERS

There are five classes of clusters. As their names indicate, they have the same structure as the basic patterns we studied in Chapter 3: the *Enumerative Cluster,* the *Equal-Pair Cluster,* the *Unequal-Pair Cluster,* the *Chain Cluster,* and the *Leapfrog Cluster.*

As we examine the five kind of clusters, you should pay close attention to the way in which the various sample passages containing clusters are punctuated. And, in your own writing, you should make certain that you use punctuation which is in harmony with the Meaning Relationships among the various independent clauses. We shall go into this matter in considerable detail in the final section of this chapter.

1. THE ENUMERATIVE CLUSTER

Perhaps the simplest variety of cluster is the *Enumerative Cluster.* It consists of two or more independent clauses which are linked through either Related Action or Parallel Idea.

As we have already learned, a cluster and an independent clause can be linked through a Meaning Relationship, no matter which comes first. Below are two passages containing Enumerative Clusters which involve the Meaning Relationship of Related Action. In the first example, the cluster comes at the end and is linked with the preceding independent clause. In the second example, the cluster functions as the initial statement, and the following independent clause is linked with it. Here are the two passages:

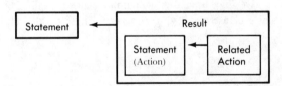

Maxine realized that her boss was having a heart attack. Therefore, she helped him into a comfortable position and loosened his collar; then, after assuring him that he would be all right, she telephoned for an ambulance.

(The second and third independent clauses form a cluster of related actions. The cluster has the Meaning Relationship of Result to the first independent clause.)

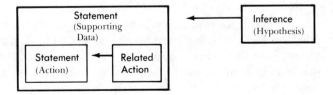

My tomcat Felix sniffed the unfamiliar catfood thoughtfully for several moments, the tip of his tail twitching slowly. Then he carried the stuff outdoors and buried it. Obviously, he was not wildly enthusiastic about this new product.

> (The first and second independent clauses present related actions. Together, they form a cluster which serves as the initial statement and gives supporting data. The third clause presents a hypothesis based on that data.)

In similar fashion, an Enumerative Cluster involving Parallel Idea may either follow or precede the independent clause with which it is connected. Here are two examples:

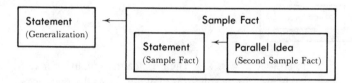

In increasing numbers, American youngsters are behaving like hard-riding, bow-legged, straight-shooting hombres from somewhere near the Rio Grande. For instance, my three-year-old nephew will not venture out of the house without his trusty six-shooter, and my neighbor's little boy even wears his spurs to bed.

> (The second and third independent clauses form a cluster of parallel sample facts. The cluster has the Meaning Relationship of Sample Fact to the first independent clause.)

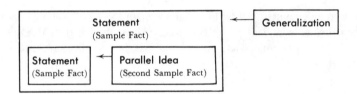

My three-year-old nephew will not venture out of the house without his trusty six-shooter. My neighbor's little boy even wears his spurs to bed. In increasing numbers, American youngsters are behaving like hard-riding, bow-legged, straight-shooting hombres from somewhere near the Rio Grande.

> (The first and second clauses form a cluster of parallel sample facts, and the third independent clause presents a generalization based upon the cluster.)

2. THE EQUAL-PAIR CLUSTER

The *Equal-Pair Cluster* occurs when two independent clauses linked through an Equal Meaning Relationship function as a unit in relation to some other independent clause or cluster. The Meaning Relationships occurring most often in this construction are Contrast and Alternative:

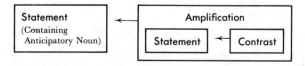

The cause of such economic strife is obvious. The consumer wants lower prices; the manufacturer wants bigger profits.

(The second and third independent clauses form a cluster which amplifies the anticipatory noun *cause* in the first independent clause. Within the cluster, the initial clause presents an idea, and the following clause presents a contrasting idea. Note that both parts of the cluster are necessary to produce "economic strife"; it is the cluster as a whole that amplifies the word *cause*.)

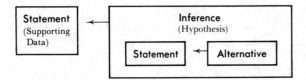

The tomato plants in my brother's garden are stunted and sickly. Their unhealthy condition may be due to the absence of certain necessary trace elements in the soil, or it may be due to the presence of toxic substances produced by a nearby grove of black-walnut trees.

(The second and third independent clauses form a cluster which presents an inference based on the data contained in the first independent clause. Within the cluster, the initial clause makes a statement, and the following clause presents an alternative to the idea expressed by the initial clause.)

3. THE UNEQUAL-PAIR CLUSTER

The *Unequal-Pair Cluster* occurs when two independent clauses linked through an Unequal Meaning Relationship function as a unit in relation to some other independent clause or cluster. All of the Unequal Meaning Relationships—Definition, Amplification, Sample Item, Sample Fact, Supporting Data, Generalization, and Inference—appear frequently in this construction. Here are two examples:

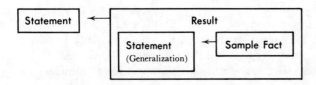

The president of the club did not attend more than half of the meetings. Therefore, several of the members thought that the club should take some sort of official action. The secretary, for instance, believed that the president should be impeached for failure to carry out the duties of his office.

(The second and third independent clauses form a cluster which gives the result of the circumstance indicated in the first independent clause. Within the cluster, the initial clause makes a general statement, and the following clause presents a sample fact illustrating that general statement and included within it.)

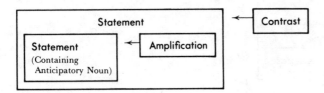

The editor discovered a grave mistake in the news story: the wrong man had been listed as the murderer of three children. Unfortunately, however, it was too late to correct the error before the paper was printed.

> (The first and second independent clauses form a cluster which serves as the initial statement for the whole passage. Within the cluster, the second clause amplifies the anticipatory noun *mistake* in the first clause. The third clause presents an idea which is in contrast with the ideas expressed by the cluster.)

4. THE CHAIN CLUSTER

In Chapter 3 we learned that two independent clauses linked through an Equal Meaning Relationship form an Equal Pair, while three or more such clauses form a Chain. This same distinction exists with regard to clusters. As we have seen, an Equal-Pair Cluster occurs when two independent clauses linked through an Equal Meaning Relationship function as a unit in relation to some other independent clause or cluster. A *Chain Cluster* occurs when *three or more* independent clauses linked through Equal Meaning Relationships function as a unit in relation to some other clause or cluster. Here are two examples:

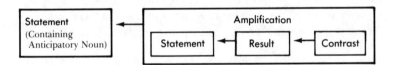

There is much recent news concerning multiple sclerosis. Scientists now have evidence that the disease is caused by a filterable virus. Consequently, they are making an intensive effort to isolate and identify that virus. A successful vaccine, however, is still a long way off.

> (The second, third, and fourth independent clauses form a cluster which amplifies the anticipatory noun *news* in the first independent clause. Within the cluster, the initial clause makes a statement, the second clause gives a result of the circumstance indicated in the initial clause, and the final clause presents an idea which is in contrast with that expressed by the second clause.)

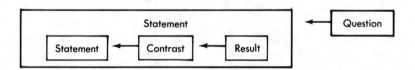

Last fall the student council tried to start a tutoring program to help inner-city high-school pupils with their studies. However, a call for volunteers to do the tutoring produced no results. Therefore, the program never got off the ground and eventually was canceled. Why does the student council find it so hard to get the student body interested in community-service projects?

> (The first, second, and third independent clauses form a cluster, and the fourth independent clause asks a question suggested by the cluster. Within the cluster, the initial independent clause makes a statement, the next independent clause presents a contrasting idea, and the final clause gives a result of the circumstance indicated in the preceding clause.)

5. THE LEAPFROG CLUSTER

In Chapter 3 we became familiar with the Leapfrog Pattern, a non-sequential series of three or more independent clauses, with one clause linked to an earlier clause rather than to the preceding one. If three or more clauses following the Leapfrog Pattern function as a unit in relation to some other independent clause or cluster, the clauses become a *Leapfrog Cluster*. Here is an example:

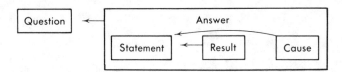

Why has the bald eagle suddenly become almost extinct throughout most of the continental United States? The female eagles have been laying eggs with paper-thin shells that break in the nest—or even eggs with no shells at all. Consequently, very few eaglets have been hatched in recent years. The defective eggs have been caused by the DDT which was deposited in a female eagle's body whenever she ate a contaminated fish.

(The second, third, and fourth independent clauses form a cluster which answers the question posed by the first independent clause. Within the cluster, the initial clause makes a statement, the next clause gives a result of the circumstance stated in the initial clause, and the final independent clause skips back to the initial clause and presents the cause of the circumstance stated there.)

B. A SPECIAL NOTE ON THE ENUMERATIVE CLUSTER

We have already studied the Enumerative Cluster, but there is a construction involving this cluster which is so important that it deserves additional treatment. This is the *Statement Plus an Enumerative Cluster Involving Parallel Idea.*

Usually in this construction the Enumerative Cluster is linked to the preceding Statement by one of the following Meaning Relationships: Result, Cause, Amplification, Sample Fact, or Supporting Data. Thus, the cluster could be an enumeration of two or more results, causes, amplifications, sample facts, or items of supporting data.

We have previously examined examples of this construction with a two-unit cluster of amplifications (page 53) and with a two-unit cluster of sample facts (page 55). Here are two additional examples of this pattern with a two-unit cluster:

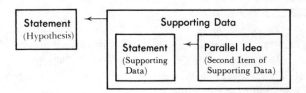

The new color television set our family got for Christmas must be defective. When we turn it on, the entire picture is blurred, and objects which should be green are bright blue.

(The second and third independent clauses form a cluster of parallel items to support the hypothesis presented by the first independent clause.)

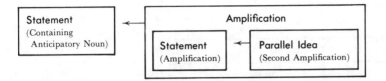

From the standpoint of the male of the species, the courtship of the praying mantis has both attractive and unattractive aspects. He is, obviously, a mate to the female; in addition, he is likely to be the main course in her bridal dinner.

(The second and third independent clauses form a cluster which amplifies the plural anticipatory noun *aspects* in the first independent clause.)

Frequently the Enumerative Cluster in this construction consists of three or more units. Here are two examples of this pattern with a three-unit cluster:

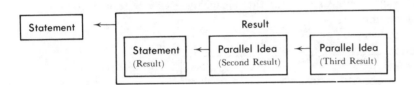

Feeling sorry for a stray tomcat, my sister brought it home with her. As a result, our furniture is covered with cat hair, our bird-loving neighbor is mad at us, and our venerable dachshund seems to be having a nervous breakdown.

(The second, third, and fourth independent clauses form a cluster of parallel results of the situation described in the first independent clause.)

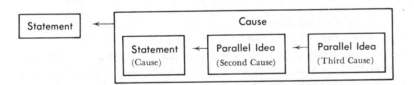

My brother was an hour late for work yesterday. His alarm clock failed to go off, then his electric razor wouldn't work, and finally his car refused to start.

(The second, third, and fourth independent clauses form a cluster of parallel causes of the situation described in the first independent clause.)

When presenting a series of parallel results or causes, a writer will usually find it desirable to list them in the order of their increasing importance, the order of their decreasing importance, or the order of their occurrence. In the sample passages just given, the parallel results are listed in the order of their increasing importance, the parallel causes in the order of their occurrence.

C. CLUSTERS WITHIN CLUSTERS

As we have just seen, a cluster may perform the various functions ordinarily performed by an individual independent clause in one of the five basic patterns. In addition, a cluster frequently occurs *within another cluster*.

A cluster within another cluster functions *as a unit* in relation to some other independent clause (or cluster) within the larger cluster. Any of the five varieties of cluster can function within any of the varieties of cluster, although the use of Leapfrog Clusters in this way is rare.

Here are two examples of a cluster within a cluster:

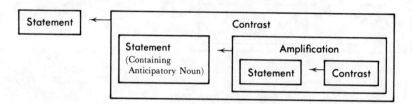

My brother greatly enjoys being a sophomore at the state university. However, he has a difficult problem to solve. He needs to work in order to pay his expenses, but working interferes seriously with his studying and may even cause him to fail some of his courses.

(The third independent clause and the fourth independent clause, which contrasts with the third, form a cluster which amplifies the anticipatory noun *problem* in the second independent clause. The second independent clause and the cluster of contrasting clauses form a large cluster which contrasts with the first independent clause. Thus, there is a cluster within a cluster in this passage.)

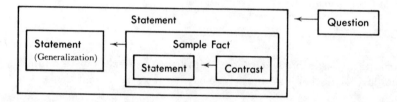

My brother and I continually disagree about TV programs. For example, last night I wanted to watch a basketball game, but he insisted on watching two second-rate wrestlers. Is a second television set the only solution?

(The second independent clause and the third independent clause, which contrasts with the second, form a cluster which gives a sample fact to increase the reader's understanding of a general assertion made by the first independent clause. The fourth independent clause asks a question suggested by the large cluster formed by the first three clauses. Thus, there is a cluster within a cluster in this passage.)

DO EXERCISES 22 AND 23

D. CLUSTERS RELATING TO CLUSTERS

A cluster often has a Meaning Relationship *to another cluster*. Each cluster functions as a unit, and the two cluster units are linked in the same way that two independent clauses would be. Here is an example:

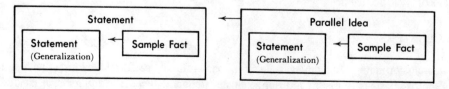

When the teachers all raised their grading standards, we began to study harder. My friend Tom, for example, visited the school library for the first time. Furthermore, we engaged in fewer social activities. In fact, I didn't even have a date or go to a movie on a school night during the rest of the term.

> (Each cluster serves as a unit in an Enumeration involving Parallel Idea. Within each cluster, the first clause makes a general assertion, and the second clause gives a sample fact to increase the reader's understanding of the general assertion.)

Note that the two *clusters* are linked in exactly the same way that these *clauses* are:

When the teachers all raised their grading standards, we began to study harder. Furthermore, we engaged in fewer social activities.

> (Each clause serves as a unit in an Enumeration involving Parallel Idea.)

Here are three additional examples of one cluster linked with another cluster:

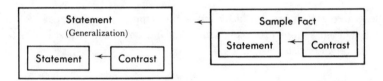

To get pollinated, some flowers attract several kinds of creatures; other flowers require one specific kind. For example, morning glories lure bees, butterflies, and hummingbirds; but certain European daisies depend upon snails alone.

> (The first cluster presents contrasting general assertions, and the second cluster presents contrasting sample facts to illustrate those general assertions.)

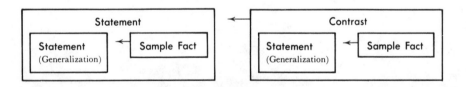

Some beetles are impressively large; for example, the goliath beetles of Africa are bigger than a mouse. Other beetles, however, are unbelievably tiny; for example, some hairy-winged beetles are smaller than an amoeba.

> (Within each of the contrasting clusters, the first clause makes a general statement, and the second clause presents a sample fact illustrating that general statement.)

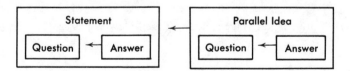

Can the nations of the world—including Russia and China—agree upon a program of disarmament to eliminate nuclear weapons? This seems highly unlikely. Can we, then, avoid a full-scale, all-out nuclear war if the arms race continues? This seems not only unlikely but practically impossible.

> (Each of the parallel clusters consists of a question and an answer.)

E. GROUPING AND PUNCTUATION OF CLAUSES IN PATTERNS CONTAINING CLUSTERS

When you write a passage which contains clusters, it is especially important to group your clauses logically and to punctuate them appropriately.

For instance, you should never break up a cluster by putting a clause from inside the cluster in the same sentence with a clause from outside the cluster and then putting the rest of the cluster in a separate sentence. Here is a passage containing this sort of *incorrect* grouping and punctuation:

CAP _____ ; _____ .

CAP _____ .

Mark has a problem; his girl friend's birthday is next week. But he doesn't have enough money to buy her a present.

As it stands, this passage seems to indicate that Mark's problem is his girl friend's approaching birthday. Actually, of course, the problem involves both of the contrasting ideas expressed by the cluster—namely, that her birthday is next week and that Mark lacks money to buy a present.

The passage can be revised as follows:

CAP _____ : _____ ,

but _____ .

Mark has a problem: his girl friend's birthday is next week, but he doesn't have enough money to buy her a present.

Or it can be revised by placing the *entire* cluster in a separate sentence:

CAP _____ . **CAP** _____ ,

but _____ .

Mark has a problem. His girl friend's birthday is next week, but he doesn't have enough money to buy her a present.

Each of these revisions makes the writer's meaning clear by showing that the clauses of the cluster are linked together closely and function as a single unit.

Here is another example. At the beginning of this chapter you encountered the following passage:

CAP _____ . **CAP** _____ ,

and _____ .

Then I made two startling discoveries. My motel room had been thoroughly ransacked, and my credit cards were missing.

Note how the punctuation helps to show the relationships among the ideas expressed by the three clauses. The first clause, standing alone as a separate sentence, is the first unit in the pattern, and the other two clauses go together to form the second unit, a cluster.

Suppose that the passage were punctuated as follows:

CAP _____ .   CAP _____ .

CAP _____ .

Then I made two startling discoveries. My motel room had been thoroughly ransacked. And my credit cards were missing.

Now each independent clause stands alone as a separate sentence. Such punctuation is acceptable, but it is certainly less helpful in indicating the relationships among the ideas expressed by the clauses than was the original punctuation.

Now suppose that the passage were punctuated as follows:

CAP _____ ;   _____ .

CAP _____ .

Then I made two startling discoveries; my motel room had been thoroughly ransacked. And my credit cards were missing.

This punctuation is obviously unacceptable, for it suggests that the second clause is more closely connected with the first clause than the third clause is. Such, of course, is not the case. As we have already seen, the second and third clauses form a cluster, and that cluster *as a unit* has a Meaning Relationship with the first clause. You must be careful to avoid punctuation which, as in this last example, misleads the reader concerning your meaning.

To help you understand the appropriate grouping and punctuation of clauses in patterns containing clusters, we shall re-examine several additional passages containing clusters which you have already encountered in this chapter. We shall accompany each passage with a diagram indicating the kind of grouping and punctuation which has been employed. Then we shall consider other kinds of grouping and punctuation which might have been used instead. Finally, we shall consider kinds of grouping and punctuation which would be ineffective or unacceptable.

If you are uncertain about how the clauses in any passage are grouped, review the boxes-and-arrows diagram and the explanatory material in parentheses which accompanied the passage when it was presented earlier in this chapter.

Examine this sample passage carefully:

CAP _____ .   CAP _____ ;

_____ .

Maxine realized that her boss was having a heart attack. Therefore, she helped him into a comfortable position and loosened his collar; then, after assuring him that he would be all right, she telephoned for an ambulance.

The following grouping and punctuation would also be acceptable:

CAP_____ . CAP_____ .

CAP_____ .

Maxine realized that her boss was having a heart attack. Therefore, she helped him into a comfortable position and loosened his collar. Then, after assuring him that he would be all right, she telephoned for an ambulance.

The following grouping and punctuation would be unacceptable since they produce a false impression of the relationships among the ideas expressed by the clauses:

CAP_____ ; _____ .

CAP_____ .

Maxine realized that her boss was having a heart attack; therefore, she helped him into a comfortable position and loosened his collar. Then, after assuring him that he would be all right, she telephoned for an ambulance.

Here is another sample passage:

CAP_____ . CAP_____ .

CAP_____ .

My tomcat Felix sniffed the unfamiliar catfood thoughtfully for several moments, the tip of his tail twitching slowly. Then he carried the stuff outdoors and buried it. Obviously, he was not wildly enthusiastic about this new product.

Although not entirely unacceptable, the following grouping and punctuation would be less desirable (even though they make the relationships among the clauses clear) because they would produce an overly long and complicated first sentence:

CAP_____ ; _____ .

CAP_____ .

My tomcat Felix sniffed the unfamiliar catfood thoughtfully for several moments, the tip of his tail twitching slowly; then he carried the stuff outdoors and buried it. Obviously, he was not wildly enthusiastic about this new product.

The following grouping and punctuation would be unacceptable since they produce a false impression of the relationships among the ideas expressed by the clauses:

CAP _____ . CAP _____ ;

_____ .

My tomcat Felix sniffed the unfamiliar catfood thoughtfully for several moments, the tip of his tail twitching slowly. Then he carried the stuff outdoors and buried it; obviously, he was not wildly enthusiastic about this new product.

Here is another sample passage:

CAP _____ . CAP _____ ,

_____ , and _____ .

My brother was an hour late for work yesterday. His alarm clock failed to go off, then his electric razor wouldn't work, and finally his car refused to start.

The following grouping and punctuation would be less desirable because they are less helpful in indicating the relationships among the ideas expressed by the clauses:

CAP _____ . CAP _____ .

CAP _____ . CAP _____ .

My brother was an hour late for work yesterday. His alarm clock failed to go off. Then his electric razor wouldn't work. And finally his car refused to start.

The following grouping and punctuation would be unacceptable since they produce a false impression of the relationships among the ideas expressed by the clauses:

CAP _____ ; _____ .

CAP _____ , and _____ .

My brother was an hour late for work yesterday; his alarm clock failed to go off. Then his electric razor wouldn't work, and finally his car refused to start.

The following grouping and punctuation would be unacceptable since they obscure the relationships among the ideas expressed by the clauses and produce too long a sentence:

CAP _____ ; _____ ;

_____ ; _____ .

My brother was an hour late for work yesterday; his alarm clock failed to go off; then his electric razor wouldn't work; and finally his car refused to start.

Here is another sample passage:

CAP _____ . CAP _____ .

CAP _____ . CAP _____ ?

Last fall the student council started a tutoring program to help inner-city high-school pupils with their studies. However, a call for volunteers to do the tutoring produced no results. Therefore, the program never got off the ground and eventually was canceled. Why does the student council find it so hard to get the students interested in community-service projects?

The following grouping and punctuation would be unacceptable since they produce an overly long and complicated first sentence:

CAP _____ ; _____ ;

_____ . **CAP** _____ ?

Last fall the student council started a tutoring program to help inner-city high-school pupils with their studies; however, a call for volunteers to do the tutoring produced no results; therefore, the program never got off the ground and eventually was canceled. Why does the student council find it so hard to get the students interested in community-service projects?

The following grouping and punctuation would be unacceptable since they produce a false impression of the relationships among the ideas expressed by the clauses:

CAP _____ . **CAP** _____ ;

_____ . **CAP** _____ ?

Last fall the student council started a tutoring program to help inner-city high-school pupils with their studies. However, a call for volunteers to do the tutoring produced no results; therefore, the program never got off the ground and eventually was canceled. Why does the student council find it so hard to get the students interested in community-service projects?

Here is another sample passage:

CAP _____ . **CAP** _____ ,

but _____ . **CAP** _____ ?

My brother and I continually disagree about TV programs. For example, last night I wanted to watch a basketball game, but he insisted on watching two second-rate wrestlers. Is a second television set the only solution?

The following grouping and punctuation would be unacceptable since they produce a false impression of the relationships among the ideas expressed by the clauses:

CAP _____ ; _____ ;

but _____ . **CAP** _____ ?

My brother and I continually disagree about TV programs; for example, last night I wanted to watch a basketball game; but he insisted on watching two second-rate wrestlers. Is a second television set the only solution?

The following grouping and punctuation would be unacceptable since they produce a false impression of the relationships among the ideas expressed by the clauses:

CAP _____ ; _____ .

CAP _____ . CAP _____ ?

My brother and I continually disagree about TV programs; for example, last night I wanted to watch a basketball game. But he insisted on watching two second-rate wrestlers. Is a second television set the only solution?

As these examples demonstrate, effective grouping and punctuation allow the writer's ideas to flow easily and accurately into the reader's mind by making clear the relationships among the various ideas. On the other hand, ineffective grouping and punctuation make the writer's ideas difficult to absorb by obscuring the relationships among them.

DO EXERCISES 24 AND 25

5

The Paragraph

The most obvious thing about the appearance of a page of printed prose in a book or magazine is, of course, that it is divided into blocks of sentences. Each block begins with an indented first line and constitutes what is called a *paragraph*.

When you read, you complete one paragraph, pause for an instant, and then move on to the next paragraph. Every prose composition—whether it is a student essay of 300 words or a published volume of 100,000 words or more—is basically an arrangement of paragraphs.

Occasionally a paragraph stands by itself, fulfilling a limited communication function halfway between that of an isolated sentence and that of a short essay. You can find such solitary paragraphs used as short filler items in *Reader's Digest* and other magazines.

Usually, however, a paragraph serves as part of a longer composition, such as an essay. In this function, a normal paragraph can be said to be *a group of related independent clauses which constitute a distinct unit of thought in the development of the subject of the complete composition.* Any of the sample passages which you examined while studying the first four chapters of this book could be a paragraph from a longer essay. All it would need is an indented first line to show that the writer means it to be a distinct unit of thought.

Sometimes a specialized paragraph—for example, an introductory or concluding paragraph—is nothing more than the bare statement of a particular idea or point and therefore is composed of only a single independent clause. In most paragraphs, however, one clause states the *central idea,* and one or more additional clauses supply whatever *further information* the reader needs in order to understand that central idea.

Perhaps the central idea is simple. If so, the paragraph will be short, a series of two or three linked clauses. For instance, suppose you have written this sentence: "Stamp collectors are often willing to pay high prices for 'inverts,' two-colored stamps with the central design printed upside down by mistake." A single example might be sufficient to develop this central idea, and the resulting paragraph could therefore be quite brief:

> Stamp collectors are often willing to pay high prices for "inverts," two-colored stamps with the central design printed upside down by mistake. For example, one collector recently gave $4,500 for a United States airmail issue of 1918, a twenty-four cent stamp in carmine rose and blue with the center airplane inverted.

On the other hand, a central idea might be understandable only if discussed at length. Then the paragraph might require five, ten, or even more additional independent clauses. For instance, suppose you have written this sentence: "When experimenting with model rockets, you must observe certain safety precautions." Such a statement will become truly meaningful only if you explain what the precautions are. The result might be a rather lengthy paragraph:

> When experimenting with model rockets, you must observe certain safety precautions. First, you should do library research into the principles of rocketry and also obtain advice from scientists, engineers, teachers, and other informed persons. Second, you should not make a rocket out of metal. If it exploded, "shrapnel" would fly in all directions. Third, you should avoid liquid propellants, which are difficult to control and also frequently toxic. Fourth, you should avoid those solid propellants which are unstable or which ignite too rapidly. For example, you should not use chlorates, chemicals of the picrate family, fulminates, iodate compounds, metallic dusts, or any high explosives—especially blasting caps. Fifth, you should handle the propellant (or the loaded rocket) with great care, shield it from temperatures above 125 degrees Fahrenheit, and protect it from sparks and static electricity. Sixth, you should wear protective clothing and a shatter-proof face shield when working with the fuel or the loaded rocket. Seventh, you should choose a non-populated area in which to fire your rocket— a spot away from houses, other buildings, and airports. Eighth, you should set your rocket to fly vertically and then use an electrical remote-control firing system. Ninth, as a final precaution you should stay away from your rocket for at least 30 minutes if it has failed to fire, for such "misfires" have been known to explode without warning.

Of course, the preceding paragraph is probably longer than most of the paragraphs which you will write. Nevertheless, it does demonstrate that a writer must sometimes offer a great deal of further information in order to develop a central idea.

Obviously, the two sample paragraphs just given differ markedly in length. The first paragraph contains only two linked clauses, while the second paragraph contains thirteen. Yet the same principle applies to both of them: a paragraph must be long enough to present its central idea satisfactorily.

A. BASIC PATTERNS OF PARAGRAPH DEVELOPMENT

As we have noted, a specialized paragraph—such as an introductory or concluding paragraph—may sometimes consist of nothing more than a single independent clause functioning as a sentence. We shall examine such paragraphs in Chapter 6.

Much more common is the paragraph which consists of two or more linked independent clauses. A paragraph of this kind is a unified, coherent passage of prose, and we learned in Chapter 3 that any such passage containing two or more independent clauses must have as its over-all structural framework one of the five basic patterns of prose.

Accordingly, with reference to structure, there are five types of paragraphs composed of two or more independent clauses: the *Enumerative Paragraph,* the *Equal-Pair Paragraph,* the *Unequal-Pair Paragraph,* the *Chain Paragraph*, and the *Leapfrog Paragraph.* All of these types of paragraphs can, of course, contain clusters and clusters within clusters. Let us examine each type briefly.

1. THE ENUMERATIVE PARAGRAPH

The *Enumerative Paragraph* may be based upon either Related Action or Parallel Idea. Such a paragraph has a distinctive structure. There is no single clause which expresses the central idea of the paragraph. Instead, the enumerated clauses or clusters present ideas which are equal in importance, with the central idea of the paragraph being merely implied.

The Enumerative Paragraph involving Related Action presents a series of actions. Here is an example:

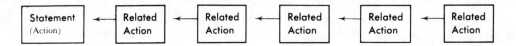

A troop of baboons moved slowly across the sun-baked plain. Suddenly a sharp bleat came from the tall grass. A large male baboon stood rigidly still for a moment and then pounced on a baby gazelle that was lying hidden in the grass. Holding his prey to the ground, the baboon ripped it apart with his teeth and started to feed. Then, realizing that the rest of the troop was hurrying toward him, he picked up the body in his powerful jaws and scampered away. The other baboons pursued him eagerly.

The preceding paragraph is part of a narrative essay about the behavior of baboons. All narrative writing consists mainly of such Enumerative Paragraphs involving Related Action.

The Enumerative Paragraph involving Parallel Idea presents a series of ideas or concepts. For reasons which we shall examine later, such a paragraph is usually brief. Here is an example:

We must maintain close ties with our Latin American neighbors. In addition, we must establish friendly relations with the new African nations.

This paragraph could *introduce* a discussion of the reasons for the two assertions. On the other hand, with a slight modification it could *conclude* a discussion of our nation's relationships with Latin America and Africa:

In short, we must maintain close ties with our Latin American neighbors, and we must establish friendly relations with the new African nations.

Of course, there are similar paragraphs containing *clusters* in an enumerative series. Here is an example:

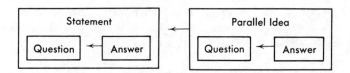

Can the nations of the world—including Russia and China—agree upon a program of nuclear disarmament? This seems highly unlikely. Can the human race, then, avoid a full-scale, all-out nuclear war if the missile race continues? This seems not only unlikely but almost impossible.

This paragraph could serve to introduce other paragraphs developing the ideas presented in it.

2. THE EQUAL-PAIR PARAGRAPH

The *Equal-Pair Paragraph* consists of two independent clauses or clusters which are linked through one of the Equal Meaning Relationships (Contrast, Alternative, Balanced Comparison, Result, Cause, Question, or Answer). Often one or both of the elements in this pattern will be clusters rather than clauses, and the resulting paragraph may be quite lengthy.

Note that in the following example the initial clause expresses the central idea of the paragraph and the following cluster of three clauses develops that idea by giving the results of the situation described in the first clause. In the diagram a *double box* is used to indicate the central idea:

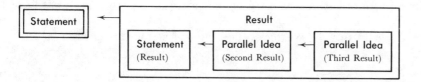

My brother bought a second-hand Stingray just before returning to college last September. The first result was that he immediately became popular with a lot of girls, since coeds prefer to date fellows with automobiles. The second result was that he was soon broke, since girls and cars are expensive luxuries. The third result was that he eventually found himself on academic probation, since he had been neglecting his studies during his wild pursuit of happiness.

3. THE UNEQUAL-PAIR PARAGRAPH

The *Unequal-Pair Paragraph* consists of two independent clauses or clusters which are linked through one of the Unequal Meaning Relationships (Definition, Amplification, Sample Item, Sample Fact, Supporting Data, Generalization, or Inference). Often one or both of the elements in this pattern will be clusters rather than clauses, and the resulting paragraph may be quite lengthy. The long paragraph dealing with model rockets which you encountered earlier in this chapter (page 69) is an Unequal-Pair Paragraph.

In this example the first clause presents the central idea of the paragraph, and the following cluster of two clauses amplifies the anticipatory noun *shortcomings* in the first clause:

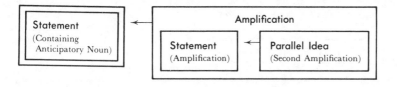

As a candidate for president of the student body, Kevin Simpson has two serious shortcomings. He is too lazy to complete any project he undertakes, and he is unable to get along with other students.

In this next example the initial cluster presents several parallel sample facts, and the final clause offers a generalization based upon those sample facts. That generalization is the central idea of the paragraph:

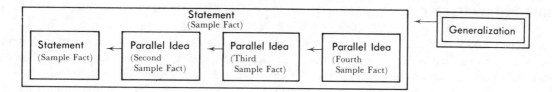

Alexander Hamilton exerted great influence upon George Washington when the latter was President. Colonel Edwin M. House made policy during the Wilson administration. Harry Hopkins, in effect, served as "Assistant President" under Franklin D. Roosevelt. And, during his years with Eisenhower, Sherman Adams ran the White House with an iron hand. As history clearly shows, presidential assistants and confidants have frequently wielded vast powers behind the scenes.

4. THE CHAIN PARAGRAPH

The *Chain Paragraph* consists of three or more independent clauses or clusters which are linked through Equal Meaning Relationships (Contrast, Alternative, Balanced Comparison, Result, Cause, Question, or Answer). Such paragraphs are usually of medium length or less. A long paragraph developed in this way tends to be loose and rambling.

Note that in the following example the first clause expresses the central idea of the paragraph:

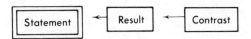

The federal Food and Drug Administration recently discovered that 90 per cent of the restaurants in nine major cities were dangerously unsanitary. Consequently, the FDA has been urging state and local health departments to enforce sanitary regulations more vigorously. So far, however, there has been very little concrete action to remedy the situation.

5. THE LEAPFROG PARAGRAPH

In Chapter 3 we learned that the Leapfrog Pattern is the least common of the five basic patterns of prose. Therefore, as you might suspect, the *Leapfrog Paragraph* is the least common kind of paragraph.

The Leapfrog Paragraph consists of three or more clauses or clusters arranged in a non-sequential series. That is, at least one element of the series has a Meaning Relationship with a *previous* element rather than with the element *immediately preceding it*. The Leapfrog Paragraph is usually of medium length or less. A long paragraph developed in this way is likely to wander aimlessly.

Note that in the following example the first clause expresses the central idea of the paragraph, an arrangement which is typical of most Leapfrog paragraphs:

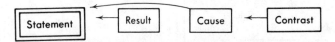

Many visitors to the Great Smoky Mountains National Park insist on trying to feed or even pet the black bears. Consequently, every year several persons get hurt, some seriously. The bears seem tame and "cute" to the tourists, but they are actually wild and potentially dangerous.

DO EXERCISE 26

B. THE TOPIC STATEMENT

As we have seen, a paragraph always has a central idea, usually expressed by one specific clause or cluster but at times (as in the Enumerative Paragraph) merely implied. That central idea is the "topic" (or subject) of the paragraph, and the clause or cluster which expresses it is known as the *topic statement* of the paragraph.

Sometimes the idea expressed by the topic statement is so broad that it includes everything in the paragraph. For instance, suppose a paragraph begins with the following statement: "My brother has several annoying habits." The rest of the paragraph would then be devoted to an explanation of what those habits are. Thus, everything in the paragraph would be included within the central idea as expressed by the topic statement.

On the other hand, sometimes the topic statement is not all-inclusive but is simply the most important of several ideas in the paragraph. In the paragraph which you have just examined about the park visitors and the bears, the first sentence is the topic statement: "Many visitors to the Great Smoky Mountains National Park insist on trying to feed or even pet the black bears." Note that this statement does *not* include the additional ideas that visitors get hurt and that their beliefs concerning the bears are incorrect.

Various options are open to the writer with respect to the location of the topic statement in a paragraph. As we shall see, he can place it at the beginning, at the end, or in the middle—or he can omit it altogether.

To make it easier for you to understand paragraph structure, we shall italicize the topic statement in each of the examples which follow. In addition, when we diagram a paragraph, we shall continue to use a *double box* to indicate the central idea and the topic statement which expresses that idea:

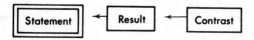

1. TOPIC STATEMENT AT BEGINNING

When writing an expository paragraph, you will usually find it desirable not only to include a topic statement but also to place it *at the beginning* of the paragraph.

Such an arrangement enables the reader to grasp the meaning of the paragraph with a minimum of effort. Here is an example of a paragraph organized in this fashion:

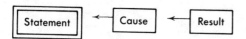

A factory doesn't necessarily avoid air pollution by using low-sulfur coal. Some low-sulfur varieties give off so little heat that a plant would have to burn twice as much in order to produce the same amount of heat as could be obtained from high-sulfur coal. In actual use, therefore, the "clean" coal would cause as much air pollution as the "dirty" coal.

A very common and important kind of paragraph organized in this fashion begins with a topic statement which is developed by an enumerative sequence. The pattern is thus *Topic Statement plus Enumerative Cluster.* Here is an example:

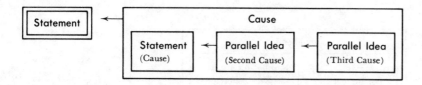

I like crows. They are intelligent and resourceful, cheerfully scrounging a living from rural barn-yard or city parking lot. They are brave and loyal, defending other crows which are in danger or even feeding their injured comrades. Finally, they display a raffish sense of humor—teasing owls, plucking hairs from a horse's mane, or dive-bombing a sleeping tomcat.

Most *really* long paragraphs are organized in this manner. For example, here is a diagram of the long paragraph about model rockets which you encountered earlier in this chapter (p. 69):

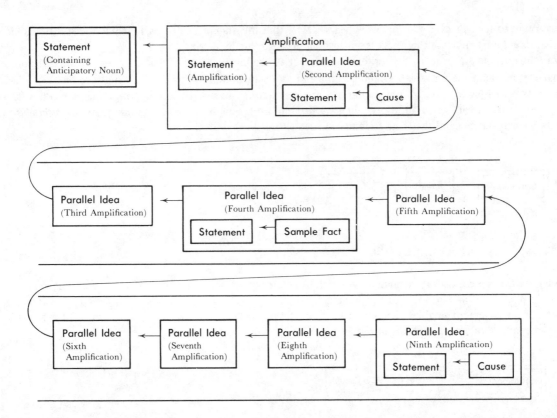

As the diagram shows, the "model rockets" paragraph has a very complicated structure. If the topic statement were not located at the very beginning, the reader would probably have difficulty in absorbing all of the information contained in the paragraph. But since the topic statement comes first, the reader quickly grasps the central idea of the paragraph and consequently understands the purpose of the further information which follows it. In other words, the long cluster of amplification unfolds logically from the central idea expressed in the initial topic statement, and the structure of the paragraph is therefore clear.

Of course, you will rarely wish to compose such a long paragraph. But the paragraph pattern of *Topic Statement plus Enumerative Cluster* is one which you will find very useful in your own writing. Here are two additional examples:

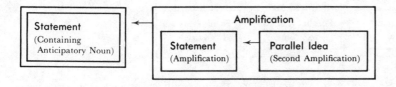

From the standpoint of the male of the species, the courtship of the praying mantis has both attractive and unattractive aspects. He is, obviously, a mate to the female; in addition, he is likely to be the main course in her bridal dinner.

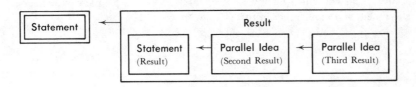

In increasing numbers, American families are pulling up stakes and moving to distant parts of the country in a search for the "good life." As a result, scores of once-proud cities are declining, some of them deteriorating rapidly. In addition, hundreds of small communities are expanding rapidly, some of them experiencing severe growing pains. Finally, many remote and formerly sparsely-populated areas are filling up, some of them fast turning into what might be called orphan suburbs without cities.

2. TOPIC STATEMENT AT END

In an Equal-Pair or Unequal-Pair Paragraph, the topic statement may come *at the end* of the paragraph. This is almost always true when the subject is developed by Answer, Generalization, or Inference, and it is often true when it is developed by Contrast, Result, or Question.

If the Paragraph is relatively brief, placing the topic statement at the end may be an effective arrangement, since it produces a sense of climax. On the other hand, if the paragraph is long, the reader may lose interest or become confused before he gets to the topic statement and learns what the central idea of the paragraph is.

Here are two paragraphs with their topic statements at the end:

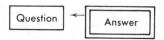

What may be the most serious result of air pollution? *Some scientists feel that, by drastically reducing the amount of sunlight reaching the earth, air pollution will lower the earth's temperature enough to cause a new ice age.*

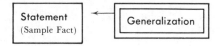

Although Sir William Crookes was a world-famous physicist, he was violently attacked for asserting that the medium Daniel D. Home was not a fraud. *During the past century, many distinguished persons have been bitterly ridiculed for expressing a belief in any form of extrasensory perception.*

In a paragraph of medium length with the topic statement at the end, the clauses preceding the topic statement are usually organized in the form of an Enumerative Cluster. The parallelism of the clauses makes it easier for the reader to grasp their meaning and their relationship to the topic statement than would otherwise be the case. Here is an example:

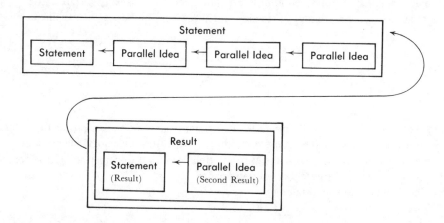

Our star center tore the ligaments in his right knee during our first game and has been unable to play ever since. Our highest-scoring guard of last year failed two of his courses and is therefore academically ineligible this year. Our tallest forward transferred to another school when his family moved out of the state last summer. Our most valuable substitute player broke his wrist in December and still has it in a cast. *As a result of all these disasters, our basketball team has been unable to win a single game all season, and the coach is reportedly planning to emigrate to Australia and become a sheepherder.*

3. TOPIC STATEMENT IN MIDDLE

Occasionally you may be dealing with a subject which can best be handled by building up to the central idea and then following it with some further explanatory or illustrative material. In such a paragraph, the topic statement is *in the middle.*

Here is an example of a paragraph with the topic statement in the middle. Note, however, that the clause functioning as the topic statement of the paragraph is a part of the first element in the Equal-Pair Paragraph pattern:

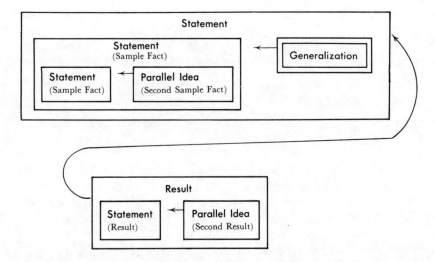

A small girl in Maryland was put in a coma by the English ivy berries she had eaten. A young boy in California was killed by toxic substances in the oleander branch he used to roast hotdogs over a backyard campfire. *Thousands of youngsters are poisoned every year by popular house and garden plants.* Consequently, many parents of young children have eliminated all such leafy hazards from their homes, and medical authorities are attempting to acquaint the general public with this all-too-present danger.

4. NO TOPIC STATEMENT

As we have already seen, the central idea of an Enumerative Paragraph is always implied rather than stated specifically. Therefore, an Enumerative Paragraph has *no topic statement.* Moreover, the central idea of an Equal-Pair Paragraph is sometimes merely implied, especially if the Meaning Relationship is Contrast or Alternative and the two contrasting or alternative ideas are of absolutely equal significance.

Here are two paragraphs which contain no topic statements:

Keeping in the shadow of the building, he crept slowly and stealthily to a point just beneath the bedroom window. Once there, he waited patiently, listening for any sounds from inside.

The Legislature may find it necessary to increase the state sales tax. Or it may add a surcharge to the state income tax.

Note that the preceding sample paragraphs are quite brief. An Enumerative Paragraph developed through Parallel Idea is almost always short. A long one would usually prove unsatisfactory because it would have no topic statement to make clear the writer's central idea. The reader would be forced to grope his way through the paragraph—without guidance at the beginning or confirmation of the writer's meaning at the end.

On the other hand, an Enumerative Paragraph developed through Related Action need not be particularly short:

While picking wild blueberries last summer, I rounded a clump of sumac and came face to face with an enormous black bear. He gave a startled "Whoof!" and reared up on his hind legs. I gave a frightened yelp and dropped my bucket, spilling blueberries all over the ground. Wheeling about, I fled to my car. The bear dropped down on all fours and lumbered off just as rapidly in the opposite direction.

Such narrative paragraphs are effective without any topic statement. The first independent clause relates the initial happening in the series, and each successive independent clause presents an additional happening. In other words, the paragraph resembles a miniature dramatic scene, and the happenings making up that scene are presented in the order of their occurrence. Even if the paragraph should be quite long, the reader will have no difficulty following the progression of actions.

DO EXERCISE 27

C. THE "LAWS" OF THE PARAGRAPH

After you have written a paragraph, you should ask yourself what you can do to improve it. Merely composing the paragraph is not enough. You must analyze it thoroughly, determine its virtues and shortcomings, and then revise it to the very best of your ability. No one is able to produce a flawless first draft; effective prose is always the result of careful rewriting and polishing.

Of course, we cannot hope to deal here with all of the characteristics of a well-written paragraph. Such a paragraph is a blend of many things. And some of them, although important, lie outside the main purpose of the present study: for example, proper word choice, correct grammar, accurate punctuation, and faultless spelling.

Instead, we are here concerned with those qualities which reflect good organization and development of ideas. Writers of textbooks often refer to certain principles of paragraphing as the "laws" of the paragraph. Since it may suggest arbitrary rules, the term "laws" is somewhat misleading. Nevertheless, it does indicate the importance which many persons attach to these five principles: *unity, coherence, completeness, emphasis,* and *variety*. As we shall see, all are essential to good prose.

1. UNITY

A paragraph which has *unity* confines itself to the development of one central idea and contains nothing which does not contribute to the understanding of that central idea. A paragraph utterly lacking in unity would have no central idea and no true Meaning Relationships between the clauses or clusters making up the paragraph:

> Nearly a billion meteors enter the earth's atmosphere every day. The collapsible opera hat was invented by a Parisian hatter. Before seceding from Colombia in 1903, Panama was considered a part of South America.

It is obvious that none of these statements has any connection with the others. Instead of being a meaningful sequence of related ideas, the paragraph is mere nonsense.

Admittedly, the sample paragraph just given is an extreme example of lack of unity. More typical would be a faulty paragraph like the following:

> The poinsettia plant can be dangerous in two ways to small children. Widely used as a Christmas decoration, it is named after its discoverer, J. R. Poinsett. If chewed or eaten, the poinsettia's stem and leaves cause abdominal cramps, diarrhea, and delirium. In addition, its sap can cause severe skin irritation and, if rubbed in the eyes, blindness.

In this example, the second sentence does not contribute to the reader's understanding of the central idea of the paragraph—obviously, references to the poinsettia's use at Christmas and the origin of its name have nothing to do with an explanation of its dangerous characteristics. Note the improvement when we eliminate the irrelevant material and thus produce a paragraph which has unity:

> The poinsettia plant can be dangerous in two ways to small children. If chewed or eaten, the poinsettia's stem and leaves cause abdominal cramps, diarrhea, and delirium. In addition, its sap can cause severe skin irritation and, if rubbed in the eyes, blindness.

Note that in the revised version the structure of the paragraph is clear: two parallel clauses amplifying the anticipatory noun *ways* in the initial topic statement. Although this same basic structure was present in the original version, it was somewhat obscured by the irrelevant clause.

Whenever you compose a paragraph, you should ask yourself this question: "Just what point am I trying to make in this paragraph?" That point is the central idea. And, after you have decided what it is, you should eliminate everything unrelated to it.

2. COHERENCE

A paragraph has *coherence* when its central idea is developed in a logical, orderly fashion. Good prose is never a mere jumble of statements. Instead, it is a series of ideas which are linked through Meaning Relationships to produce a clear and effective discussion of the subject the writer has chosen. Indeed, the main purpose of this book is to assist you in writing coherently.

When you have written a paragraph, read it over carefully. If it does not seem to "hang together," make sure that its clauses present a logical, orderly progression of ideas and that the Meaning Relationships between the clauses are made clear by Linking Devices. If necessary, revise the clauses and add appropriate Meaning Links. You will be gratified to discover that you can usually transform a "problem" paragraph into a well-organized treatment of a central idea.

If you examine the following paragraph, you will find that the Meaning Relationships among its independent clauses are not very clear, and the paragraph does not hang together well. In other words, it lacks coherence:

Count Dracula must certainly have been a bloodthirsty sadist. He lived in Transylvania during the fifteenth century. He derived great pleasure from torturing and murdering hundreds of persons. We learn this from historical records from that period. He was, of course, no vampire. He often dined outdoors amid the dying screams of his victims, who were impaled on stakes arranged in a circle around the dining table.

The paragraph has unity—every statement in it deals with Count Dracula. But it is an incoherent series of ideas which the reader is bound to find a bit irritating. The writer can convert it into an effective, coherent paragraph by subordinating some of the statements, rearranging the order of others so that the clauses are joined securely, and adding appropriate Linking Devices:

Although he was no vampire, Count Dracula of Transylvania must certainly have been a bloodthirsty sadist. According to fifteenth-century records, he derived great pleasure from torturing and murdering hundreds of persons. For instance, he often dined outdoors amid the dying screams of his victims, who were impaled on stakes arranged in a circle around his dining table.

The revised paragraph can be diagrammed as follows:

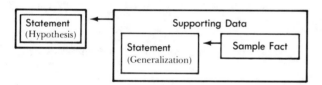

3. COMPLETENESS

A paragraph obeys the principle of *completeness* when it develops the full implications of the central idea. As we have already seen, a simple central idea may require only a clause or two of further information, while a complicated central idea may be understandable only if discussed at greater length. There is an easy way to determine whether or not a specific paragraph is complete. When judging your own work, ask yourself these two questions: "Have I covered the topic thoroughly? If I were the reader, would I be able really to understand the central idea?"

Some incomplete paragraphs result from a writer's ignorance of paragraph structure. Instead of composing well-developed paragraphs, a beginning writer may produce a series of paragraph fragments. Here is an example:

Every student should take at least one course in public speaking.
Such a course will teach him to organize his ideas and hence to think more clearly.
It will also give him practice in communicating those ideas to other persons—with the opportunity to receive expert criticism of his speaking techniques, and helpful suggestions for their improvement.
Finally, the course will help him to develop poise, self-confidence, and any latent capacity for leadership.

It is obvious that these fragments should be combined into one well-developed paragraph:

Every student should take at least one course in public speaking. Such a course will teach him to organize his ideas and hence to think more clearly. It will also give him practice in communicating those ideas to other persons—with the opportunity to receive expert criticism of his speaking techniques, and helpful suggestions for their improvement. Finally, the course will help him to develop poise, self-confidence, and any latent capacity for leadership.

Now the paragraph structure is clear and mature: a topic statement plus a cluster of three parallel clauses giving reasons. Such organization is much more effective than the series of paragraph fragments it replaces.

Other incomplete paragraphs result from a writer's failure to develop their central ideas. Note the following:

> The Honorable Buford H. Crookston, one of the senior members of the Senate, has cheated the taxpayers of this country in many ways.
>
> Moreover, as the news media have recently revealed, he has accepted improper—if not illegal—gifts from a number of special-interest groups.

Each of these paragraphs is incomplete. It presents a central idea but does not develop it. The reader is therefore left wondering, "In what ways did the Senator cheat the taxpayer, and from whom did he accept what improper gifts?"

The incomplete paragraphs could serve as the topic statements for two well-developed paragraphs:

> The Honorable Buford H. Crookston, one of the senior members of the Senate, has cheated the taxpayers of this country in many ways. For instance, he has taken European vacations at public expense by calling them "fact-finding missions," and he has submitted requests for reimbursement of "travel expenses" for periods when he actually never left Washington.
>
> Moreover, as the news media have recently revealed, he has accepted improper—if not illegal—gifts from a number of special-interest groups. For example, he has received secret "campaign contributions" in cash from aerospace companies seeking government contracts, and he has enjoyed free airline tickets, superbowl tickets, and hotel accommodations furnished by lobbyists representing trucking companies, food-processing companies, and major oil companies.

Now the paragraphs are complete. Each consists of a generalized central idea plus two examples which increase the reader's understanding of that central idea.

4. EMPHASIS

According to the principle of *emphasis*, the relative importance of an idea or fact should determine the amount of attention it receives. Such stress can be achieved in several ways. First, the amount of space devoted to an idea helps to indicate its significance. It is illogical to discuss a minor idea more fully than a major one. Second, expressions such as *chiefly, especially, most important, primarily, secondarily,* and *less important* help to indicate the importance of the idea so labeled. Third, the position of an idea in a paragraph helps to indicate its significance. This is especially true if it is located at the beginning or at the end, since these are the two most emphatic positions in a paragraph.

In a short paragraph, improper emphasis usually results from a failure to understand the problem of *coordination versus subordination* which we studied earlier. Often the writer is guilty of False Parallelism, treating a minor idea as though it were equal in importance to a major idea. Here is an example:

> John House is a lawyer, and he is a confirmed bachelor. His brother Fred is a lumberjack, and he has been married eight times.

In this paragraph the ideas expressed by the first and third clauses are clearly less important than those expressed by the second and fourth clauses. To treat all of them as equally important ideas is to violate the principle of emphasis. Here is an appropriate revision:

> John House, a lawyer, is a confirmed bachelor. His brother Fred, a lumberjack, has been married eight times.

Turning the first and third clauses into appositives has eliminated the violation of emphasis.

In a long paragraph, also, improper emphasis may result from False Parallelism. In addition, it may result from any or all of the following: devoting too much space to the discussion of a relatively minor idea or too little space to the discussion of a major idea; failing to use labels like *chiefly* or other expressions listed on page 80; and placing items in the wrong locations.

Examine this faulty paragraph:

> Training the student for a profession is one of the important functions of a college or university. In the first place, professional training confers certain benefits upon the student himself. It enables him to enter a respected occupation and thus to have a high social standing in the community, and it usually assures him of a higher income than he could otherwise hope to receive, resulting in his being able to buy a nice home and car, to travel and enjoy many forms of recreation, and to provide the good things of life for his family. In the second place, professional training helps to safeguard our way of life. In the third place, professional training provides our complex society with the trained men and women it sorely needs.

You can best understand the shortcomings of the preceding paragraph by comparing it with a revised version which follows the principle of emphasis:

> Training the student for a profession is one of the important functions of a college or university. In the first place, professional training confers certain benefits upon the student himself, enabling him to enter a respected occupation and usually assuring him of a higher income than he could otherwise hope to receive. More important, professional training provides our complex society with the trained men and women it sorely needs. In an age of space flight, surgical transplants, automation, and nuclear research, there is an increasing need for highly skilled persons. Most important of all, professional training helps to safeguard our way of life. As Thomas Jefferson said long ago, "If a nation expects to be ignorant and free. . . it expects what never was and never will be." Today, when the world's democracies are threatened by the growing might of totalitarian regimes, Jefferson's words take on added significance.

In this revised paragraph, the three reasons for the importance of professional training are arranged in the order of increasing importance, their relative degrees of importance are indicated by the labels *more important* and *most important of all*, and the amount of discussion devoted to each is in keeping with its relative importance. The paragraph thus obeys the principle of emphasis.

When judging your own work, always ask the question, "Have I placed the proper amount of emphasis upon each element in the paragraph?" If you have not, rewrite your paragraph so that you will accomplish this. Clear and accurate emphasis is an important characteristic of good prose.

5. VARIETY

Good prose is characterized by *variety* of expression. After you have written a paragraph, you should check it carefully to make sure it contains no wearisome repetition of structure. This is especially important if the paragraph is lengthy; for the longer the paragraph, the greater the chance that it may be monotonous. Let us see what is involved in achieving variety.

Variety of Sentence Type. On the basis of the clauses they contain, we can distinguish four types of sentences: *simple, compound, complex,* and *compound-complex.*

A *simple sentence* is composed of a single independent clause and *never* contains a dependent clause. Here is an example: "Last week my dentist capped two of my front teeth."

A *compound sentence* is composed of two or more independent clauses and *never* contains a dependent clause. Here is an example: "The cockroach is a difficult pest to eradicate; for it reproduces rapidly, eats practically all organic substances, adapts to almost any environment, and quickly develops an immunity to insecticides."

A *complex sentence* is composed of a single independent clause plus one or more dependent clauses (that is, adjective clauses, adverb clauses, or noun clauses). Here is a complex sentence containing an adjective clause: "The Japanese have developed a new wine *which is made from watermelons*." Here is a complex sentence containing an adverb clause: "*When a boy loses his father*, he loses part of himself too." Here is a complex sentence containing a noun clause: "Industrialists report *that the price of coal burned under boilers has more than doubled in the past three years*."

A *compound-complex sentence* is composed of two or more independent clauses plus one or more dependent clauses. Here is an example containing both an adverb clause (at the beginning of the sentence) and an adjective clause (within the second independent clause): "*When I returned to my car*, the left front window was broken, and the citizens-band radio *which I had installed that morning* was missing."

When you compose a paragraph (especially a long one), you should strive for *variety of sentence type*. Is your paragraph composed almost entirely of simple sentences? Or of compound sentences? You can introduce a pleasing variety of structure by converting some of the independent clauses into appositives, adjective clauses, adverb clauses, phrases, or compound predicates.

Here is a paragraph in which all of the sentences are of the same type:

> Five kinds of spurious stamps can fool an unwary collector. The first class is composed of *fakes*. These are real stamps. However, their appearance has been altered to make them resemble more valuable issues. A second class of spurious stamps includes *forgeries* and *counterfeits*. These are fraudulent imitations of real issues. They are intended either to deceive the postal authorities or to cheat collectors. A third group is composed of *facsimiles*. These are outright imitations of real stamps. They are so represented to the original purchaser. A fourth group is made up of *bogus stamps*. These are printed labels or seals. They superficially resemble postage stamps. However, they have not been issued by a recognized government for postal purposes. Finally, there are *reprints*. These are stamps reprinted from old plates of discontinued issues. They are intended for direct sale to collectors. They are not valid for postage.

The chief shortcoming of this paragraph is that it is composed entirely of simple sentences. Properly revised, the paragraph contains a variety of sentence types and is therefore more effective:

> There are five kinds of spurious stamps which can fool an unwary collector. The first class is composed of *fakes*. These are real stamps whose appearance has been altered to make them resemble more valuable issues. A second class of spurious stamps includes *forgeries* and *counterfeits*. These are fraudulent imitations of real issues, intended either to deceive the postal authorities or to cheat collectors. A third group is composed of *facsimiles*. These are outright imitations of real stamps, and they are so represented to the original purchaser. A fourth group is made up of *bogus stamps*. These are printed labels or seals which superficially resemble postage stamps but which have not been issued by a recognized government for postal purposes. Finally, there are *reprints*. These are stamps which have been reprinted from old plates of discontinued issues; they are intended for direct sale to collectors and are not valid for postage.

Variety of Sentence Length. Monotony of sentence length often accompanies that of sentence type. When you compose a paragraph, you should strive for *variety of sentence length*. Are the sentences in your paragraph all the same length, like a series of prefabricated units moving down an assembly line? If they are, you should attempt to introduce variety by expanding some elements, shortening others, and perhaps combining others.

Here is a paragraph in which all of the sentences are about the same length:

> My brother Bill stomped angrily into the room. He slammed the door with all his strength. This made two pictures fall off the wall. Next, he hurled his books onto his desk. Then he flopped down heavily on his bed. He scowled at the ceiling for several minutes. He took Marlboros and matches from his pocket. Lighting a cigarette, he puffed on it glumly. I laid down my magazine and grinned at him. "What's the matter with you?" I asked him. "Was there another little misunderstanding with your girl friend?"

Composed entirely of short sentences, the preceding paragraph is very monotonous. Properly revised, the paragraph contains sentences of various lengths:

> My brother Bill stomped into the room, slamming the door so hard that two pictures fell off the wall. He hurled his books onto his desk and flopped heavily on his bed. After scowling at the ceiling for several minutes, he fished a pack of Marlboros and a book of matches from his shirt pocket. Then, still sprawled on his back, he lit a cigarette and puffed on it glumly. I laid down my magazine and grinned at him. "What's the matter—did you have another little misunderstanding with your girl friend?" I asked.

Variety of Sentence Organization. When you compose a paragraph, you should strive for *variety of sentence organization*. Do the sentences of your paragraph contain some noticeable grammatical construction which becomes irritating or boring through repetition? For example, do a majority of the sentences begin with a conjunctive adverb? Or with a participial phrase? Or an adverb clause? Do several sentences contain a series of appositives? Remember that it is *noticeable* repetition which becomes objectionable when it is overdone. In Chapter 1 you learned that Parallelism can be a useful Linking Device, but do not assume that the more you use, the better your prose will be. *Too much* Parallelism will make your writing dull and uninteresting.

Here is a paragraph in which the writer has employed Meaning Links too lavishly. Notice that almost every independent clause begins with a conjunctive adverb:

> Some species of bacteria are tiny, but potent, enemies of the human race. In the first place, they cause disease. Also, they destroy our livestock and crops. In addition, they pollute our streams. Moreover, they even collaborate with the termite to destroy our houses. Yet many bacteria are beneficial to man. Specifically, they play a crucial role in most sewage-disposal systems. Too, they enrich the soil through nitrogen fixation and the decomposition of organic material. In addition, they are essential to the production of cheese and vinegar. Also, when harnessed by modern technology, they manufacture great quantities of enzymes, vitamins, and industrial chemicals. Finally, they even carry on their useful activities inside us: for example, most of the vitamin K our bodies require is produced by microbes inhabiting our digestive tracts.

Properly revised, the paragraph avoids over-use of this construction:

> Some species of bacteria are tiny, but potent, enemies of the human race. They cause disease. They destroy our livestock and crops. They spoil our food. They pollute our streams. They even collaborate with the termite to destroy our houses. Yet many bacteria are beneficial to man. They play a crucial role in most sewage-disposal systems. They enrich the soil through nitrogen fixation and the decomposition of organic material. They are essential to the production of cheese and vinegar. When harnessed by modern technology, they manufacture great quantities of enzymes, vitamins, and industrial chemicals. Finally, they even carry on their useful activities inside us—a good example being the production, by the microbes inhabiting our digestive tracts, of most of the vitamin K our bodies require.

The difference between an ineffective paragraph and an effective one may be merely a matter of monotony. Always check carefully to make sure that your prose has variety. You may spend a great deal of time formulating a central idea, expressing it clearly in a topic statement, and developing it fully in the remainder of the paragraph. But if the paragraph is monotonous, your reader will be bored, and you will be unable to communicate your thoughts to him effectively.

DO EXERCISES 28 AND 29

6

The Essay:
Preliminary Considerations

Now that you have studied the paragraph, you are ready to learn how to write a full-length essay.

As we saw in Chapter 5, a paragraph functions as a distinct unit of thought in the development of the subject of an entire essay. Therefore, we may say that an essay is *a series of paragraphs appropriately arranged for the treatment of a subject.*

Most of the paragraphs in an essay combine to form the *body*. The rest function in either the *introduction* or the *conclusion*. Together, they provide the reader with a complete and coherent discussion of the particular subject which the writer wishes to discuss.

It is important that you learn to write good essays. These brief compositions will give you valuable practice in organizing your ideas and expressing them clearly and gracefully, and your ability to write essays will later assist you in writing longer compositions such as reports and term papers.

A. THE PARTS OF AN ESSAY

You have just learned that the three parts of an essay are the *introduction*, the *body*, and the *conclusion*. Let us see what each involves.

1. THE INTRODUCTION

As its name indicates, the *introduction* introduces the subject of the essay. In other words, it prepares the reader for the main discussion of the subject contained in the body.

The length of any specific introduction is determined partly by the over-all length of the whole composition and partly by the nature of the subject which is being discussed. In the essays which you will be writing, it will ordinarily be possible to limit the introduction to a single paragraph. But, whatever the length of the whole composition, the introduction should never be much longer than the treatment of any main topic of the body, and it will usually be shorter.

Occasionally the introduction of an essay is extremely short—perhaps a single independent clause set off as a separate paragraph. For example, an essay dealing with the rapid increase of violence during the present century might begin with this one-clause introductory paragraph:

Man is the most ferocious species of animal life ever to appear on this planet.

Or an essay dealing with poisons might begin as follows:

> The most powerful poison yet discovered, the toxin of one strain of botulism bacteria, is so deadly that a single ounce of it would be enough to kill every inhabitant of 3,000 planets like the earth.

Such extremely short paragraphs can be quite effective. Their very brevity makes them emphatic. If their subject matter is either very striking or very important, paragraphs like these catch the reader's attention with double force. Nevertheless, you should use such short paragraphs sparingly. Ordinarily you will find that you need more than one clause to present satisfactorily the central idea of your introductory paragraph.

Here is a paragraph which could serve as the introduction of an essay about modern trends in dentistry:

> When great-grandfather got dentures, he usually wanted them to be "perfect"—gleaming white, unblemished, and regular. Today, however, over one-third of all American dental patients gladly pay premium prices for false teeth with simulated stains, cracks, chips, and even fillings, since these carefully designed imperfections make the dentures look like real teeth.

Here is a paragraph which could serve as the introduction of an essay about air pollution in the nation's capital:

> According to recent newspaper stories, Washington, D. C., has been experiencing some of the worst smogs ever recorded there. Yet most other major cities are having at least modest success in reducing atmospheric pollution. What is so different about Washington? Why is it almost the sole exception to the general trend?

And here is a paragraph which could serve as the introduction of an essay about wind-generated electrical power:

> Modern civilization requires vast amounts of energy. But we will soon run out of fossil fuels, and nuclear power plants are both enormously expensive and also possibly dangerous. Where, then, can we turn? The answer is blowing in the wind.

A good introduction does two things. First, it catches the reader's interest and makes him want to read the rest of the composition. Second, it prepares him for what is to follow, so that he can better understand the writer's main discussion of his subject.

In order to be truly effective, an introduction must be *interesting, relevant,* and *concise.* If it is to hold the reader's attention, an introduction must be clearly organized and free from dull or pointless materials. In addition, it must be appropriate to the discussion it introduces. No matter how fascinating it may be, a description of the feeding habits of vampire bats will not suitably introduce a discussion of how radar works. Finally, the introduction should be no longer than is necessary to develop its central idea satisfactorily. Long-winded opening remarks mean that a writer is unable to come to the point. They may also mean that he cannot organize his ideas.

There is no magic formula for writing a good introduction. Every introduction is designed to fit its own special subject, and therefore no two are very much alike. Nevertheless, there are seven varieties of introductions which appear frequently in expository prose. Later in this chapter, we shall examine them in some detail.

2. THE BODY

In any prose composition, it is the body which presents a detailed discussion of the subject. We can therefore say, with only slight exaggeration, that the body *is* the composition. If we compare an essay to a pie, the introduction and conclusion are the pie crusts and the body is the filling. Obviously, good pie crusts are always desirable; still, it is the quality of the filling which chiefly determines the excellence of the pie. No essay, then, can be better than its body. Even a dazzling introduction and a brilliant conclusion cannot make up for an incoherent, rambling, and poorly organized body. Indeed, through contrast they will only further emphasize its inadequacy.

As we saw in Chapter 5, every paragraph deals with a central idea or "topic," and this topic is usually expressed by a topic statement. In the body of a short essay, each separate paragraph constitutes a main division of the body. Thus, the topic of each paragraph is also the topic of that main division, and the topic statement of the paragraph is the topic statement of the whole main division. In a longer or *expanded* essay, at least one main division of the body consists of two or more paragraphs. In such a pattern, there is a topic statement expressing the central idea of the main division, while the topic statements of the individual paragraphs serve as *subtopic statements* in relation to the main division.

In other words, each main division of an essay deals with a *topic*. If the main division is a single paragraph, the topic statement of the main division and the topic statement of the paragraph are the same. But, if the main division is made up of two or more paragraphs, the topic statement of the main division expresses the central idea (or topic) of the entire division, and the topic statements of the individual paragraphs express the ideas of these subdivisions and are called *subtopic statements*.

It is the relationships among the central ideas of its main divisions (or topics) which produce the basic organization of an essay body. Such relationships fall into patterns which we have already studied. Thus, there are the following classes of essay bodies: *Enumerative, Equal-Pair, Unequal-Pair, Chain,* and *Leapfrog.*

Here are two paragraphs which could serve as the body of a brief essay about wind-generated electrical power. Each paragraph is a separate main division (or topic) of the essay body, and its topic statement is therefore also the topic statement of the whole division in which it appears:

Incredible amounts of wind energy are potentially available for the production of electricity. More than twenty years ago, the World Meteorological Organization estimated that a total of 20 billion kilowatts of power could be generated at especially windy sites around the globe such as coastal promontories and mountain tops. One recent calculation, however, indicates that available wind energy might produce as much as 80 trillion kilowatts in the Northern Hemisphere alone. In contrast, the whole world currently has a total electrical generating capacity of under 2 billion kilowatts. Obviously, wind power offers great promise if it can be harnessed.

Consequently, many efforts are under way to develop efficient wind-energy systems. The old-fashioned farm windmill, once common in rural areas, could generate only 10 kilowatts. NASA, however, has developed a windmill that will generate up to 100 kilowatts. Moreover, plans are being made to build huge windmills that could produce up to thirty times as much power as the NASA device. By the year 2000, national networks of these gigantic structures could conceivably be supplying 1.5 trillion kilowatt hours annually, almost as much as the total amount of energy now being produced in the United States.

The Meaning Relationship between two main divisions of an essay body is the same as that between the two topic statements. Let us take the topic statements of the essay body you have just examined and consider them as a pair of linked clauses:

Incredible amounts of wind energy are potentially available for the production of electricity. Consequently, many efforts are under way to develop efficient wind-energy systems.

As you can see, the second clause presents a consequence of the condition described in the first clause. The Meaning Relationship between the clauses is, of course, Result, and this same relationship exists between the two divisions of the essay body.

In order to be truly effective, an essay body must conform to the principles of *unity, coherence, completeness,* and *emphasis.* In Chapter 5 we encountered them (along with *variety*) as "laws" of the paragraph, but they also apply to larger units of prose. A well-written essay body avoids irrelevant topics, is clearly organized, contains everything necessary to the satisfactory development of the subject, and allocates space to the discussion of its various topics in accordance with their relative importance.

In the essays which you will study, and also in those which you will write, the body will be organized independently of the introduction and the conclusion. This does not, of course, mean that the three parts of an essay are separate, unrelated entities. Rather, it means that a writer frequently has a choice concerning the kind of introduction and conclusion he will employ in conjunction with a particular essay body. For example, if the essay body is devoted to a discussion of automation, the introduction might give an example of automation, define the term, explain the reasons for its development, or discuss its effects on our society. It has sometimes been suggested that one should write the body of his essay first and then plan the introduction and conclusion. On the whole, this is probably *not* the best procedure. When actually composing an essay, most writers find it easier to start at the beginning and progress steadily towards the end. Nevertheless, when you are planning and outlining a proposed essay, you will usually find it desirable to consider the body first. Having determined what the main discussion of your subject will be, you can then decide what kind of introduction and conclusion would be the most effective.

3. THE CONCLUSION

The *conclusion* of an essay contains the writer's final remarks to the reader. The length of any specific conclusion is determined partly by the over-all length of the whole composition, and partly by the nature of the subject which is being discussed. In the essays which you will be writing, it will ordinarily be possible to limit the conclusion to a single paragraph.

Occasionally, the conclusion of an essay is extremely short—perhaps a single independent clause set off as a separate paragraph. For example, an essay dealing with the hijacking of airliners might end with this one-clause concluding paragraph:

> Clearly, the officials of all world airlines must begin working together to wipe out this most dangerous form of modern-day piracy—the "skyjacking" of airliners in flight.

Such extremely short paragraphs are sometimes effective, since their brevity makes them emphatic. As a general rule, however, you should avoid conclusions this short in the essays you write. And you should always keep in mind that every concluding paragraph you compose must be long enough to develop its central idea satisfactorily.

Here is a paragraph which could serve as the conclusion of an essay about prison reform:

> Obviously, more criminals would go to prison under this proposed system of prison reform, perhaps for longer terms. But they would serve their sentences in less crowded institutions, under more humane conditions, with a greater chance for effective rehabilitation.

Here is a paragraph which could serve as the conclusion of an essay about home stereo systems:

> Such evidence can lead to only one conclusion. Although dozens of different home stereo systems are advertised and sold as "high fidelity," most of them are unable to reproduce the sound of modern full-range recordings with even medium fidelity.

And here is a paragraph which could serve as the conclusion of an essay about wind-generated electrical power:

> As fossil fuels get scarce and electricity therefore gets increasingly expensive to produce by present-day methods, wind-generated power will become economically competitive. Moreover, such power will be pollution-free. Therefore, it seems certain that research and development efforts will continue and that our nation's energy problems will someday be gone with the wind.

A good conclusion performs two functions. First, it makes the essay seem complete. The reader feels that he has been transported to his final destination, not abandoned in mid-journey. Second, it allows the writer to re-emphasize his main idea or ideas. As his final word on the subject, the conclusion provides one last chance for him to hammer home his message.

To be truly effective, a conclusion must be *relevant, clear,* and *concise.* The conclusion must be based on what has preceded it. It should never present irrelevant or pointless materials, or offer entirely new ideas not previously implied in the body of the essay. Moreover, it must be clearly organized. For, if a writer's final comments on his subject are incoherent, the reader will end the essay in a state of confusion. Finally, although the conclusion should not be incomplete or unduly abrupt, it must never seem long-winded. The writer should make his final remarks concisely and emphatically, then quit.

Every conclusion must, of course, be designed to fit the writer's treatment of his particular subject, and therefore no two conclusions are very much alike. Nevertheless, there are ten varieties of conclusions which appear frequently in expository prose. Later in this chapter, we shall examine them in some detail.

DO EXERCISE 30

B. OUTLINING

As the first step in learning to write essays, you must become familiar with the techniques of *outlining*. You should carefully plan the organization of your essay before you start to write it. The best way of doing this is to construct an outline, a brief list of the topics which you plan to discuss in the essay. Such an outline will help you in two ways.

In the first place, constructing an outline will simplify the task of planning your essay. By deciding what goes where at the outline stage of your essay, you can avoid considerable wasted effort. It is much easier to correct a faulty outline than to revise a faulty essay. By preparing the outline carefully, you can make sure that your essay contains no irrelevant material, that its ideas are presented in logical, coherent fashion, that your discussion of the subject is complete, and that every part of the essay receives its proper amount of emphasis.

In the second place, the completed outline will serve as a sort of "blueprint" of your intended essay and will guide you as you write. Having already decided upon the structure of the essay, you will always know what topic comes next. A well-organized outline almost always leads to a well-organized essay.

1. THE STEPS IN OUTLINING

Before making your outline, you must know exactly what you intend to write about. In other words, you must select a subject for your essay. You can best accomplish this by composing a brief *statement of purpose*. Preparing such a statement will force you to crystallize your thinking.

Selecting a subject means more than merely choosing some vague generality like "Pollution." Instead, you must ask yourself what *specific aspect* of pollution you wish to discuss. For example, you might decide that it would be worthwhile to write about "Air Pollution Caused by the Automobile." Although this is much more specific than "Pollution," it may still be too broad a subject for you to handle in an essay of the length you intend to write. Therefore, you may decide on an even more limited subject such as "How the Automobile Causes Air Pollution" or "How We Can End Air Pollution Caused by the Automobile." Then you can write an appropriate statement of purpose such as the following: "My purpose will be to explain, in approximately 500 words, the ways in which the automobile causes air pollution."

Having composed your statement of purpose, you are ready to construct an outline of your essay. This is a simple process involving the following steps:

1. As they occur to you, make a list of your ideas on the general subject of your essay.
2. Delete any item which is irrelevant or unimportant.
3. Decide on a small number of main "points" which you wish to cover, and determine the order in which they can be discussed most effectively.
4. Assign each individual item to one of the main "points," and arrange the material under each main "point" in logical, coherent fashion.
5. Study the completed outline, and make any revisions that seem desirable. Do any of the items need to be rearranged? Should anything be deleted? Do you need additional supporting material?

6. As a final check, prepare a generalized, one-sentence summary of the outline for your proposed essay. Ignore your original statement of purpose while preparing the summary. However, after completing the summary, compare it with the statement of purpose. There should be no conflict between the two items. For example, you might compose the following summary: "The automobile causes two kinds of air pollution."

If you follow the preceding steps carefully, you will produce a satisfactory outline for your essay. With an outline, you will always know where you are going as you write, and can concentrate upon the best way to get there.

2. THE FORMAL OUTLINE

Although there are several varieties of outline, it will be best for you to construct a *formal outline* when planning your essay. Such an outline is well worth the time required to prepare it, for it will give you tight control over your essay during every stage of its composition. The formal outline gives you a comprehensive view of your subject—that is, it shows all the ideas you intend to discuss and their exact relationships with one another. Therefore, we shall confine our discussion of outlining to the formal outline.

A well-organized formal outline displays the following characteristics:

1. Parallel items are indented equally.
2. Parallel items bear parallel labels (numerals or letters). The main divisions of the body are labelled with capital Roman numerals: I, II, III, *etc.* Each class of lesser subdivision has its own variety of label. In the order of decreasing importance, these labels are as follows: A, B, C; 1, 2, 3; a, b, c; (1), (2), (3); (a), (b), (c); [1], [2], [3]; [a], [b], [c].
3. Parallel items are expressed in parallel phrasing—that is, in parallel grammatical form.

Wrong:	**Right:**
I. Origin of pollutants	I. Origin of pollutants
A. Exhaust emissions	A. Exhaust emissions
B. From the crankcase	B. Crankcase emissions
C. Engine	C. Engine emissions

4. The body contains a comparatively small number of main divisions. In an essay, the usual number is from two to four main divisions. In a book-length work, each chapter constitutes a main division.
5. The divisions of an outline are mutually exclusive. In other words, the divisions do not overlap.

Wrong:	**Right:**
II. Varieties of pollutants	II. Varieties of pollutants
A. Particles	A. Particles
1. Carbon	1. Hydrocarbons
2. Lead	2. Carbon
B. Gases	3. Lead
1. Carbon monoxide	B. Gases
2. Carbon dioxide	1. Hydrocarbons
3. Oxides of nitrogen	2. Carbon monoxide
4. Oxides of sulphur	3. Carbon dioxide
C. Hydrocarbons	4. Oxides of nitrogen
	5. Oxides of sulphur

6. Each item in the outline is listed under the correct heading.

Wrong:	Right:
A. Particles	A. Particles
1. Hydrocarbons	1. Hydrocarbons
2. Carbon	2. Carbon
B. Gases	3. Lead
1. Lead	B. Gases
2. Hydrocarbons	1. Hydrocarbons
3. Carbon monoxide	2. Carbon monoxide
4. Carbon dioxide	3. Carbon dioxide
5. Oxides of nitrogen	4. Oxides of nitrogen
6. Oxides of sulphur	5. Oxides of sulphur

7. If subdivided, a division has at least two subdivisions. A single subdivision would be illogical, since it is impossible to divide anything into one piece.

Wrong:	Right:
3. Carbon dioxide	3. Carbon dioxide
a. Often not classed as pollutant, but possibly eventually most harmful of all	a. Often not classed as pollutant
	b. Possibly eventually most harmful of all

Here is a formal outline for an essay dealing with the kinds of air pollution caused by the automobile. Note that it displays all of the characteristics just listed.

HOW THE AUTOMOBILE CAUSES AIR POLLUTION

Introduction. Problem of air pollution caused by automobile extremely serious

I. Origin of pollutants
  A. Exhaust emissions
  B. Crankcase emissions
  C. Engine emissions
II. Varieties of pollutants
  A. Particles
    1. Hydrocarbons
    2. Carbon
    3. Lead
  B. Gases
    1. Hydrocarbons
    2. Carbon monoxide
    3. Carbon dioxide
      a. Often not classed as pollutant
      b. Possibly eventually most harmful of all
    4. Oxides of nitrogen
    5. Oxides of sulphur
Conclusion. Elimination of air pollution caused by automobile absolutely necessary

Examine the above outline carefully. All of its entries are phrases or sentence fragments, and it is therefore known as a *topic outline*. If each entry were a complete sentence, it would be a *sentence outline*. Here are equivalent sections of a topic outline and a sentence outline which demonstrate the differences between these two kinds of outlines:

Topic Outline:	Sentence Outline:
3. Carbon dioxide	3. Carbon dioxide is a third
a. Often not classed	variety of gaseous pollutant.
as pollutant	a. Often it is not classed as
b. Possibly eventually	a pollutant.
most harmful of all	b. It may eventually be shown to
	be the most harmful pollutant
	produced by the automobile.

As a rule, it takes longer to prepare a sentence outline than it does a topic outline. Therefore, the sentence outline is less common than the other type. It has, however, one great value: the meaning of each item is unmistakable. For this reason, a writer who wishes to furnish the reader with an outline of his work will often find it wise to prepare a sentence outline, especially if the work to be outlined is quite long.

Of course, even a topic outline must be tailored to fit the work it summarizes. The full-length topic outline presented earlier would be appropriate for an essay of from 500 to 800 words. For a shorter essay of 200 or 300 words, an abbreviated topic outline like the following would be sufficient:

HOW THE AUTOMOBILE CAUSES AIR POLLUTION

Introduction. Problem of pollution serious
I. Origin of pollutants
II. Varieties of pollutants
  A. Particles
  B. Gases
Conclusion. Elimination of pollution necessary

This brief outline should offer a writer adequate guidance in composing a short essay. However, there is a definite limit to the brevity which is permissible in a formal outline for an essay. *There must be at least one entry in the outline for every paragraph in the essay*, although a long paragraph may be further subdivided, with each of its subordinate elements appearing as a subordinate entry in the outline.

3. DIAGRAMMING ESSAY STRUCTURE

In earlier sections of this chapter, you encountered various parts of a brief essay about wind-generated electrical power. That essay can be outlined as follows (with paragraph designations and with a bracket enclosing the body entries to help you understand the relationship between the outline and the essay itself):

WIND-GENERATED ELECTRICAL POWER

B   ¶1   Introduction. New source of energy needed
O   ¶2   I. Amount of available wind energy enormous
D   ¶3   II. Development of efficient wind-energy systems under way
Y   ¶4   Conclusion. Future of such systems promising

The structural relationships among the four paragraphs in the essay can be diagrammed as follows:

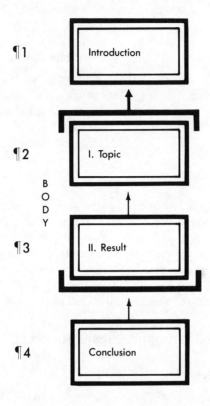

As the diagram shows, the body *as a unit* has a relationship to the introduction: the relationship of *that which is introduced* to the *introductory material*. Furthermore, the conclusion has a relationship to the body *as a unit*: the relationship of *concluding material* to *that which is concluded*. These are the only possible relationships among the major parts of the essay. The diagram also shows that the topics of the essay body are linked through the Meaning Relationship of Result.

Here is the actual essay, with the body enclosed by a heavy-line bracket:

Modern civilization requires vast amounts of energy. But we will soon run out of fossil fuels, and nuclear power plants are both enormously expensive and also possibly dangerous. Where, then, can we turn? The answer is blowing in the wind.

Incredible amounts of wind energy are potentially available for the production of electricity. More than twenty years ago, the World Meteorological Organization estimated that a total of 20 billion kilowatts of power could be generated at especially windy sites around the globe such as coastal promontories and mountain tops. One recent calculation, however, indicates that available wind energy might produce as much as 80 trillion kilowatts in the Northern Hemisphere alone. In contrast, the whole world currently has a total electrical generating capacity of under 2 billion kilowatts. Obviously, wind power offers great promise if it can be harnessed.

Consequently, many efforts are under way to develop efficient wind-energy systems. The old-fashioned farm windmill, once common in rural areas, could generate only 10 kilowatts. NASA, however, has developed a windmill that will generate up to 100 kilowatts. Moreover, plans are being made to build huge windmills that could produce up to thirty times as much power as the NASA device. By the year 2000, national networks of these gigantic structures could conceivably be supplying 1.5 trillion kilowatt hours annually, almost as much as the total amount of energy now being produced in the United States.

As fossil fuels get scarce and electricity therefore gets increasingly expensive to produce by present-day methods, wind-generated power will become economically competitive. Moreover, such power will be pollution-free. Therefore, it seems certain that research and development efforts will continue and that our nation's energy problems will someday be gone with the wind.

Throughout the remainder of this book, we shall use the diagramming devices employed with this sample essay. We shall use a *double box* to indicate each paragraph and a *heavy-line outer box* to indicate the introduction, the conclusion, and each main division (or topic) of the essay body. Thus, if an introduction, a conclusion, or a main division of the body consists of only one paragraph, the double box indicating such a paragraph will have a heavy outer line, as in the diagram just given. On the other hand, in an expanded essay pattern, if an introduction, a conclusion, or a main division of the body consists of two or more paragraphs, those paragraphs will be enclosed by a heavy-line box, as in this example:

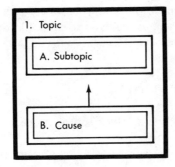

Finally, we shall use a heavy-line bracket to enclose all of the elements constituting the body of the essay.

DO EXERCISE 31

C. VARIETIES OF INTRODUCTIONS

As was stated earlier, there are seven varieties of introductions which appear frequently in expository prose. They are those presenting (1) *a general explanation of the subject,* (2) *an example,* (3) *a definition,* (4) *cause and result,* (5) *comparison and contrast,* (6) *a question,* (7) *narrative materials.*

1. INTRODUCTIONS PRESENTING A GENERAL EXPLANATION OF THE SUBJECT

Many introductions are devoted to a *general explanation of the subject.*

Such introductions usually stress the importance of the subject and state the writer's purpose in dealing with it. In addition, they indicate the general organization of the essay, offering what is sometimes called an "anticipatory summary." Obviously, an introduction of this sort is primarily concerned with preparing the reader for what is to follow.

A writer using this sort of introduction must strive to make it as interesting as possible, for the chief shortcoming of this variety is that it may be dull.

Here is an example of an introduction which presents a general explanation of the subject. Note that its final three independent clauses clearly indicate the nature of the three main topics in the essay body which will follow:

Astronauts have visited the moon, physicists are studying a growing number of subatomic particles, and biologists are discovering the innermost secrets of the living cell. Obviously, we are living in a scientific age, and no one can hope to understand our complex society unless he has some knowledge of science. Therefore, we shall examine three important aspects of present-day science education in the United States. First, we shall become familiar with the methods of teaching science which are in most widespread use in American high schools and colleges. Second, we shall look at certain serious shortcomings in those methods of instruction. And, finally, we shall consider some suggestions for improving the teaching of science.

2. INTRODUCTIONS PRESENTING AN EXAMPLE

Another common variety of introduction is that which gives one or more *examples* of the subject, usually followed by a generalization.

Such introductions are designed primarily to arouse the reader's interest so that he will wish to read the whole composition. The examples must be truly representative of the subject, but they must also be striking—presenting dull examples is an almost certain method of discouraging the reader from proceeding further.

Here is an introductory paragraph which makes effective use of striking examples:

> For many years automatic vending machines have dispensed such products as cigarettes, soft drinks, and candy bars. Now these robot salesmen are becoming more versatile. The simple act of inserting a coin in the appropriate slot can now get you a toothbrush impregnated with toothpaste, a spray of French perfume, underwear, a cup of hot chicken soup, a live lobster, or an insurance policy. There are other machines which will shine your shoes, wash your car, take your blood pressure, give you a whiff of pure oxygen, or rock you to sleep. Clearly, the once-humble dispenser of cigarettes has become one of America's star salesmen.

3. INTRODUCTIONS PRESENTING A DEFINITION

When the subject of an essay involves a term which is likely to be unfamiliar to the reader, the introduction often contains a *definition* of the unfamiliar term.

Such a definition prepares the reader for what is to follow. Nevertheless, there is always a danger that this variety of introduction will discourage the reader by making the subject seem dull or overly difficult. Therefore, introductions presenting a definition often combine that definition with a statement stressing the importance of the subject. In this way they attempt to hold the reader's interest.

Here is an introductory paragraph presenting a definition:

> Many manufacturers are following a policy of planned obsolescence. Briefly, this may be defined as the practice of designing a product in such a way that it will need to be replaced in a short time. Every consumer needs to be on guard against companies which make frequent radical changes in the styling of their products so that the customer will be dissatisfied with the "old model," companies which lower the quality of their products so that they will wear out rapidly, and companies which even deliberately produce defective products that are useless when brand-new.

4. INTRODUCTIONS PRESENTING CAUSE AND RESULT

Some introductions present one or more *causes* of a situation. Others present one or more *results*. Still others present both *causes and results*.

By presenting causes, a writer can improve the reader's understanding of the subject and hence prepare him for what is to follow. For example, an essay describing Carlsbad Caverns might be introduced by a brief discussion of those natural forces which produced the caverns.

By presenting results, a writer can stress the importance of the subject, thereby arousing the reader's interest. For example, an essay tracing the life cycle of the Japanese beetle might be introduced by a brief discussion of the effect this insect pest has had upon American agriculture.

Finally, by presenting causes and results, a writer can both increase the reader's understanding of the subject and also arouse his interest by showing its importance. For example, an essay describing a typical suburban shopping center might be introduced by an explanation of why such shopping centers have sprung up rapidly during the past quarter century and also what effect their development has had upon our national economy. Of course, an introduction presenting both causes and results is likely to be rather long; therefore, it can be used appropriately only if the essay body itself will be quite lengthy.

Here are two introductory paragraphs; the first presents causes, the second results:

> According to the Coast Guard, motorboating accidents have increased rapidly in recent years. In part, this increase has been caused by the crowding of our nation's waterways, since more than forty million Americans have taken up boating. In addition, it has been caused by poorly-trained and sometimes careless or reckless operators, unseaworthy boats, and inadequate safety equipment.

> For the past two summers, my father has covered the soil in his vegetable garden with long strips of black polyethylene film, slit every few inches to let the growing plants poke through. The results have been amazing. The soil stays moist, and there are almost no weeds. Strawberries and tomatoes are free from the rotting that occurs if fruit touches the ground. And all of the berries and vegetables get bigger, stay healthier, and mature sooner than any my father ever raised before using the film.

5. INTRODUCTIONS PRESENTING COMPARISON AND CONTRAST

Many introductions make use of *comparison* and *contrast* to increase the reader's understanding of the subject and also to arouse his interest. Some introductions present similarities only, others present differences only, and some longer introductions present both.

Here are two introductory paragraphs, the first using comparison, the second using contrast:

> Bees, butterflies, and hummingbirds feed on nectar and in doing so carry pollen from flower to flower. In similar fashion, certain tropical bats feed on nectar and pollinate hundreds of species of plants, including the trees from which we obtain kapok and balsa wood.

> The differences between my sister Beth and me are as great (if I may borrow Mark Twain's phrase) as those between the lightning and the lightning bug. She bounds gaily from her bed at 6:30 a.m., eager to greet the new day; I burrow my head deep into the pillow until the alarm clock runs down and then drift blissfully back to sleep. She is always orderly and neat; I always look as if I had just gone through a tornado. Finally, Beth is always poised and tactful, but I was practically born with my foot in my mouth.

6. INTRODUCTIONS PRESENTING A QUESTION

When a writer is especially desirous of gaining the reader's attention, he may compose an introduction which centers around one or more rhetorical *questions*. Of course, any introduction may contain the Meaning Relationship of Question, but the variety which we are considering makes one or more questions the very heart of the introduction. Since each question theoretically requires an answer, the reader is forced to think about the subject.

Here is an introductory paragraph which asks a series of questions:

> A discussion of cats is likely to produce a great many questions. Is the cat an affectionate pet, or does it merely tolerate the person who feeds it? Is its failure to learn tricks the result of sturdy independence or simple stupidity? Why does a well-fed cat continue to stalk and kill birds? Can a cat really see in the dark? And does it always land on its feet after a fall?

7. INTRODUCTIONS PRESENTING NARRATIVE MATERIALS

Introductions which present *narrative materials* can be extremely effective in arousing the reader's interest. For narration is potentially the most vivid and dynamic form of prose, offering the reader movement, action, and sometimes dialogue.

If the whole essay is based on narration, the narrative introduction "sets the scene," and the body then presents the main incidents or happenings which constitute the "story." For example, an essay dealing with the writer's experiences during a tornado might start with a brief account of what he was doing just before the tornado occurred.

But narrative introductions may also be used with other kinds of subjects. For example, an essay dealing with college football might start with a humorous anecdote about one of Knute Rockne's half-time pep talks.

A narrative introduction has one potential drawback: it is usually rather long—especially if it involves the telling of an anecdote. A writer needs a great deal of space to present the specific happenings which make up a narrative incident. Therefore, an introduction presenting narrative materials can be used appropriately only if the essay body will be rather lengthy. In fact, one common mistake made by beginning writers is to compose a narrative introduction which is too long in relation to the rest of the essay in which it appears.

Here are two narrative introductions. The first presents the opening incident in a narrative essay, setting the scene and preparing the reader for the main happenings which will be recounted in the body. The second begins a discussion of amateur authorship by offering an appropriate anecdote. Note that these introductions are comparatively long:

One warm afternoon last May, our English literature class was drowsily plodding its way through "Lycidas." Professor Huggins was reading the poem aloud in a soft hypnotic monotone, and more than one head was beginning to nod. "Next, Camus, reverend sire, went footing slow," he intoned, "His mantle hairy, and . . . ." Abruptly, Professor Huggins stopped reading and stared at the open doorway. There stood the Sigma Kappa fraternity mascot, a huge Saint Bernard named Tiny. Ordinarily a lumbering, good-natured beast, Tiny was growling softly and swinging his head from side to side, as if annoyed. His eyes seemed unusually bright. "Hey," said someone in a startled tone, "what's wrong with that dog?"

A New York editor was once cornered in his office by a determined matron who wanted to discuss a first novel she was writing. "How long should a novel be?" she demanded. The editor squirmed. "That's an impossible question to answer," he explained. "Some novels, like *Ethan Frome,* are only about 40,000 words long. Others—*Gone with the Wind*, for instance—may run to 300,000." The lady frowned. "But what is the average length of the ordinary novel?" she asked. "Oh, I'd say about 80,000 words," said the editor. With a cry of triumph, the lady jumped to her feet. "Thank heaven!" she exclaimed, "my book is finished."

DO EXERCISE 32

D. VARIETIES OF CONCLUSIONS

As was pointed out earlier, there are ten varieties of conclusions which appear frequently in expository prose. The ten include those presenting (1) *a summary*, (2) *a final generalization*, (3) *a final inference*, (4) *a striking example,* (5) *an analogy*, (6) *a parting question*, (7) *a call to action*, (8) *a forecast*, (9) *a denouement,* (10) *narrative materials.*

1. CONCLUSIONS PRESENTING A SUMMARY

A common variety of conclusion is that which presents a *summary* of the writer's main ideas. In addition, it often stresses the importance of those ideas.

Such a summary usually occurs in formal rather than informal compositions. This kind of conclusion is, perhaps, less interesting than the other types we shall study. Nevertheless, it does have the merit of emphasizing, through repetition, the chief points of the essay which it concludes.

Here is an example of a conclusion presenting a summary:

To summarize, our American system of higher education confers three benefits upon the individual student: it prepares him for a profession, it enables him to achieve a high standard of living, and it helps him to develop an appreciation of our cultural heritage. In addition, it supplies our nation with highly trained persons for business, industry, public service, and the learned professions, and it produces those broadly educated persons who are the true leaders of our society. Indeed, our system of higher education is truly one of our most important national assets.

2. CONCLUSIONS PRESENTING A FINAL GENERALIZATION

If the body of an essay has been devoted to a series of examples, the conclusion may present a *final generalization* based on those examples. For instance, an essay which has dealt with the pollutants found in a number of specific rivers might end with the observation that many American streams are disgracefully contaminated and need to be cleaned up.

Conclusions presenting a final generalization are usually rather brief and are therefore perhaps best suited to short essays.

Here is an example of a conclusion presenting a final generalization:

As these examples demonstrate, many American cities now find it necessary to get rid of their trash in unusual—and expensive—ways. Consequently, I shall not be really surprised when some desperate mayor attempts to buy some surplus rockets in order to shoot the stuff into outer space, for it is clear that we are rapidly running out of places to put it here on earth.

3. CONCLUSIONS PRESENTING A FINAL INFERENCE

Sometimes a conclusion presents a *final inference* or judgment based on the data offered in the body of the essay. This variety of conclusion is especially useful when a writer is dealing with a controversial topic, since it produces an air of fairness and objectivity.

Here is an example of a conclusion presenting a final inference:

Such evidence indicates that our school "honor code" is a failure. Cheating is widespread, and the present system merely serves to penalize the honest student. Obviously, the administration should act promptly to abolish the "honor code."

4. CONCLUSIONS PRESENTING A STRIKING EXAMPLE

A common variety of conclusion is that which presents a *striking example*. By ending with such an example, a writer effectively emphasizes the main idea of his essay.

Here is a conclusion which presents a striking example:

Obviously, one should never underestimate the resourcefulness of city dwellers in coping with problems created by strikes of municipal employees. A certain New York householder gift-wrapped the previous day's accumulation of garbage so that it made a very attractive package, set it on the subway seat beside him when he went to work, and then "forgot" to keep an eye on it while reading his newspaper. For eighteen consecutive mornings, by the time he reached his destination, someone had stolen the package. And the householder therefore arrived at the office empty-handed, happy in the knowledge that he had taught somebody that crime does not pay.

5. CONCLUSIONS PRESENTING AN ANALOGY

Sometimes an essay ends with an *analogy*.

An analogy is a comparison which attempts to increase the reader's understanding of some idea or concept by showing its resemblance to another idea or concept which is familiar to him. For example, suppose you wish the reader to visualize the specially-designed antenna which the astronauts erected on the moon in order to communicate with earth. Your reader probably knows little, if anything, about antennas for interplanetary radio systems. But if you tell him that it looks like a large open umbrella set upside down on a tripod, he will be able to visualize the antenna since an umbrella is a familiar object. This comparison of an antenna with an umbrella is an analogy.

If a final analogy is well-chosen, it strongly emphasizes the writer's main idea. In addition, it acts as a sort of final stylistic flourish which gives the essay a sense of completeness.

Here is an example of a conclusion presenting an analogy:

> In his quest for a drug which will cure cancer, the medical researcher may be compared to a botanist who is trying to develop a new weed killer. Although there are thousands of chemicals which completely destroy weeds, most of them are equally efficient in wiping out grass. So the botanist must look for a chemical which is selective in its action, killing the weeds but leaving the grass unharmed. In similar fashion, the medical researcher knows that there are many chemicals which will quickly destroy cancer cells in a test tube, but which are just as deadly to normal body cells. Therefore, he must hunt for a chemical which selectively kills the cancer cells but leaves the patient's healthy tissues uninjured.

6. CONCLUSIONS PRESENTING A PARTING QUESTION

Sometimes an essay ends with a *parting question*. Having completed his discussion of the subject, the writer poses one or more questions which invite the reader to ponder the matter further and thus to crystallize his own thinking.

Such a conclusion is especially effective when the essay has dealt with a "problem" subject—for example, crime, narcotics, defects in our educational system, corruption in government, unethical business practices, pollution, racial strife, or the possibility of worldwide warfare.

Here is an example of a conclusion presenting several parting questions. Although its subject is hardly of earthshaking significance, it is nevertheless one which the writer considers important:

> Without doubt, the present faculty disciplinary committee should be replaced by a student court. An overwhelming majority of the student body favors such a change. Why, then, are the officials of this school reluctant to take action? Are they unaware of the advantages of a student-court system? Or are they simply indifferent to student opinion?

7. CONCLUSIONS PRESENTING A CALL TO ACTION

If the essay deals with a "problem" subject, a writer may not wish to end with a parting question. Instead, he may prefer a conclusion which presents a *call to action*. Such a conclusion encourages the reader to pursue some desired course of action.

Here is an example of a conclusion presenting a call to action:

> Since the officials of this school seem reluctant to replace the present faculty disciplinary committee with a student court, we'll simply have to try to make them understand the great advantages of a student-court system. So let's form a committee of concerned students to meet with the faculty— and, if necessary, with the deans and president as well. And let's get the dialogue started right away. We students have a right to be heard on an issue of such importance to every one of us.

8. CONCLUSIONS PRESENTING A FORECAST

Sometimes an essay ends with a *forecast*. For instance, after discussing the development of the laser, a writer might prophesy its future use as a weapon. Such a conclusion can give added significance to the subject the writer has been discussing.

Here is an example of a conclusion presenting a forecast:

> Certainly, the available evidence suggests strongly that the major American political parties are currently in deep trouble. And their problems are quite likely to become even more severe in the future. The cost of electioneering will continue to skyrocket. Large numbers of young adults will either ignore politics altogether as a boring and dishonest activity, or at least refuse to wear a party label. And more and more voters of all ages will dismiss the major political parties as irrelevant and hopelessly out of tune with the realities of contemporary society. For these reasons, it seems very probable that our present political parties are destined to disappear in the near future.

9. CONCLUSIONS PRESENTING A DENOUEMENT

Sometimes the conclusion of a narrative essay presents a *denouement*. In other words, after the body of the essay relates the main series of happenings, the conclusion briefly explains what happened afterwards. For instance, if the body of the essay describes the frantic search made by police officers to locate a child bitten by a rabid dog, the conclusion might briefly explain that the child received the Pasteur treatment and did not contract the disease. Such an explanation would be a denouement.

After finishing the writer's account of the series of connected happenings which constitute the body of the essay, the reader may be inclined to ask, "Well, what were the consequences of those events? What was the final outcome?" By attempting to anticipate—and answer—such questions, the denouement can be very useful in "wrapping up" the subject. It makes the essay seem truly complete.

Here is an example of a conclusion presenting a denouement:

> Eventually, of course, my sister Janice became an excellent cook. She now has a bulging file of tasty recipes, and her delicious meals have earned the praise of the whole family. But none of us has ever quite forgotten the fiasco that occurred when Janice, then a recent bride, roasted a turkey without first removing its insides. And she herself blushed scarlet last Thanksgiving when a guest, in all innocence, asked the simple question, "What kind of stuffing did you have this year, my dear?"

10. CONCLUSIONS PRESENTING NARRATIVE MATERIALS

Often a conclusion presents *narrative materials*. If the writer finishes with an appropriate anecdote or an exciting incident, the reader will be likely to feel that the whole essay has been interesting and has ended on a "high note."

Such a conclusion is most effective when the essay body does *not* deal with a series of related happenings. In other words, a narrative essay usually does *not* have a separate narrative conclusion. Rather, as we shall see in Chapter 7, each body topic presents one of the related happenings, with the last topic giving the final climactic incident—and at that point the writer has finished telling his "story." If he adds a conclusion, it is ordinarily a forecast, a denouement, or some other non-narrative type. On the other hand, an essay made up of non-narrative body topics often has a narrative conclusion. For example, if the body of an essay lists the ways in which college basketball differs from professional basketball, the conclusion might present an anecdote about a former college star playing his first professional game.

Here is a conclusion which presents narrative materials:

> As these examples show, American parents used to name their offspring after "great" persons— Biblical figures, European monarchs, conquering generals, Presidents, and major writers. But I believe

that a new trend has developed. In recent years thousands of children have been given the names of television personalities. Chicago newspapermen tell the story of a housewife who asked her paper boy his name. "Walter," replied the youngster. "Walter Cronkite Smith." "My goodness," said the woman, "that's certainly a well-known name." The boy nodded. "Well, it sure as heck ought to be," he replied. "I've been delivering papers on this street for three years!"

DO EXERCISE 33

E. TRANSITIONAL ELEMENTS

In essays and other prose compositions more than one paragraph long, *Transitional Elements* play an important role. They are *specific word links between paragraphs or longer units of prose.*

We have already learned that every paragraph presents and explains a central idea and that an essay is essentially a series of paragraphs appropriately arranged for the treatment of a subject. Transitional Elements help the reader to understand precisely *how* these paragraphs are related. By connecting two paragraphs (or larger units of prose), Transitional Elements promote coherence and insure a sense of continuity which might otherwise be lacking.

In earlier chapters of this book, we became familiar with two kinds of Linking Devices which operate between clauses or clusters *within* a paragraph. Both *Automatic Linking Devices* and *Deliberate Linking Devices* can also serve as Transitional Elements linking paragraphs or even larger units. In addition, there are *Special Transitional Devices* which serve as Transitional Elements but which cannot perform a linking function *within* a paragraph.

1. AUTOMATIC LINKING DEVICES

Every essay, of course, contains *Automatic Linking Devices* connecting its paragraphs.

Any extended discussion of a subject is bound to involve *Repetition*, ordinarily both *word-form repetition* and the use of *synonyms*. For example, an essay dealing with "Homicide Investigation" must inevitably employ in most, if not all, of its paragraphs such words as *homicide, homicidal, murder,* and *killing.* An essay which divides its subject into varieties or types must necessarily deal with *class-member concepts.* For example, a discussion of "Kinds of Bacteria" will deal not only with the class ("bacteria") but also with the specific varieties which are members of that class (for instance, "bacilli" and "cocci"). And an essay which analyzes a subject into its component parts must necessarily deal with *whole-part concepts.* For example, a discussion of "The Parts of an Essay" will deal not only with the whole essay but also with its parts—the introduction, body, and conclusion. Repetition, then, occurs automatically in expository prose and often functions as a Transitional Element.

In addition, *Pronoun Reference* helps to connect related paragraphs. For example, a discussion of Shakespeare's sonnets will probably refer to the author by name in some paragraphs but use the personal pronouns *he, his,* and *him* in other paragraphs.

2. DELIBERATE LINKING DEVICES

Deliberate Linking Devices can also function as Transitional Elements linking paragraphs or larger units.

First, there can be *Parallelism*, which is especially effective when it is employed in topic statements located at the beginning of their respective paragraphs. For example, one paragraph might begin with this topic statement: "The cocci are bacteria which are spherical." And a second paragraph might begin: "The bacilli are bacteria which are rod-shaped." The parallel structure exhibited by these two topic statements would help to connect the two paragraphs in which they appear.

Second, there can be a *noun* in one paragraph which *summarizes an assertion* made in the preceding paragraph. As a matter of fact, the noun sometimes summarizes the entire preceding paragraph. For example, one paragraph might discuss the present shortage of water in many sections of the country, and a second paragraph might state, "As our population continues to grow, this problem will become increasingly serious." Note that the noun *problem* would summarize the entire preceding paragraph.

Third, there can be *Meaning Links* between related paragraphs. For example, a series of paragraphs might begin with the conjunctive adverbs *in the first place, in the second place*, and so on. One paragraph might refer to a "primary" reason for something, while another paragraph mentions a "secondary" reason. And a conjunctive adverb like *consequently, however,* or *similarly* at the beginning of a paragraph would clearly indicate the Meaning Relationship between that paragraph and the one preceding it. In addition, many other Meaning Links can help to connect paragraphs. In fact, of all Deliberate Linking Devices, it is the Meaning Links which function most frequently as Transitional Elements.

3. SPECIAL TRANSITIONAL DEVICES

In addition to the Transitional Elements which we have just examined, essays and other expository compositions more than one paragraph long may contain *Special Transitional Devices* which operate *only* between paragraphs. These are *transitional adverb phrases, transitional adverb clauses, transitional sentences,* and *transitional paragraphs.*

Transitional adverb phrases and transitional adverb clauses are especially useful when a writer is explaining the steps in a process. After concluding his discussion of Step "A," the writer may start a new paragraph by indicating that Step "B" follows Step "A"; then he discusses Step "B." For example, after describing the step of jacking up an automobile in order to change a flat tire, he may use a transitional phrase or clause to introduce the next step, the removing of the wheel:

> *After jacking up the car*, the motorist is ready to remove the wheel.
> (The initial adverb phrase functions as a Transitional Element.)

> *After he has jacked up the car*, the motorist is ready to remove the wheel.
> (The initial adverb clause functions as a Transitional Element.)

A more elaborate device is the *transitional sentence*, which can be very effective in creating a sense of continuity, especially between main divisions of a long essay body. In its commonest form, the transitional sentence fits the following pattern: "So far we have been considering 'A'; now let us consider 'B.'" By referring to the topic just concluded and then announcing the topic next to be considered, the writer makes his discussion seem thoroughly unified. Here are two examples:

> Thus far, we have been concerned with the symptoms of trichinosis; now we must consider the best means of controlling the disease.

> Now that you have studied paragraph structure, one task still remains: you must learn how to judge your own work so that you can then improve it.

When the "A plus B" pattern requires more discussion than it can receive in a transitional sentence, a writer may decide to employ a *transitional paragraph*. Here is an example:

> Up to this point, we have been discussing the causes of earthquakes. Now we shall briefly examine the efforts which are being made to forecast their occurrence. As we shall see, significant progress in earthquake prediction has recently been made in China, Russia, and the United States.

In Chapters 7 through 10, while becoming familiar with the patterns of essay-body development, you should also examine the specific Transitional Elements employed in each sample essay. In basic essay patterns, Transitional Elements are especially useful in indicating the relationships among the main divisions (or topics) of the body. In expanded essay patterns, they have the additional function of indicating the relationships among subtopics, or even among sub-subtopics. In both basic and expanded essay patterns, Transitional Elements can also help to bridge the gap between introduction and body or between body and conclusion. After studying the ways in which Transitional Elements are employed in the sample essays, you should be able to use them more effectively yourself. Then you will find that your prose flows more smoothly, with increased coherence and continuity.

DO EXERCISE 34

7

The Essay:
Types of Enumeration

Of all basic essay body patterns, those employing *Enumeration* are the most common.

As we have already seen, Enumeration always involves the multiplication of some item. More specifically, the pattern involves *the enumeration of related actions or equivalent ideas.* In Chapter 2 we learned that a pair of independent clauses may be linked through Related Action or Parallel Idea, and in Chapter 5 we saw that those same Meaning Relationships may be used to create an Enumerative Paragraph. Now we shall study essay bodies displaying the same kind of structure.

When a writer wishes to deal with two or more *topics* of the same kind, he will use an enumerative pattern, and the body of his essay will be *an enumeration of equivalent topics.*

The present chapter and the next one will acquaint you with several important kinds of essay bodies based on Enumeration. In this chapter we shall examine first the essay body involving *narration,* then the essay body presenting *process explanation,* and finally the essay body developed by *description.*

A. NARRATION

When we studied Related Action in Chapter 2, we learned that the proper use of this Meaning Relationship requires three things: (1) each clause must present an action, (2) each action must be a part of the same series of connected events, and (3) all of the actions in the series must be presented in chronological order (that is, in the order of their occurrence).

These same principles apply with equal force to a *narrative essay body* with its topics linked through Related Action. In such a narrative essay you are, in effect, telling the reader a "story"; so you must concentrate on what happened first, what happened second, what happened third, and so on, until you have finished recounting the entire series of connected events which constitutes the subject of your essay. Indeed, it is sometimes difficult to tell whether a particular composition is a narrative essay or a short story. The difference is that a narrative essay deals with *real* incidents, while a short story deals with *fictional* (that is, with *imaginary*) incidents.

If your narrative essay body builds up to an exciting climax, you may feel that your essay is complete and does not need a conclusion. On the other hand, you may wish to add a conclusion—for example, one presenting a forecast or a denouement. Which strategy you should follow will depend upon your subject and the way you have developed it in the body of your essay.

A well-written narrative essay must, of course, always be *clear;* the reader must always be able to visualize what is happening. In addition, the essay should be as *vivid* and *interesting* as possible. For a good narrative essay stimulates and entertains the reader even while it informs him.

Here is a narrative essay. Note that it does have a conclusion. The body entries in the outline and the body paragraphs in the essay itself are indicated by marginal brackets. Study the diagram and the outline carefully before reading the essay:

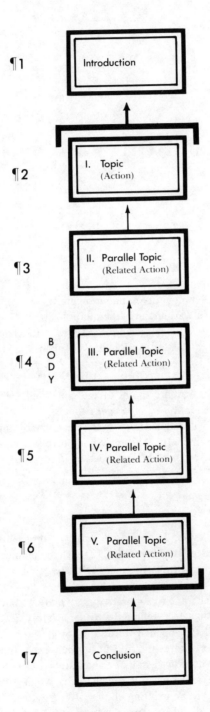

A CLOSE CALL

Sentence Summary:

Promptly administered first aid saved Harry Watson from choking to death.

Outline:

¶1   Introduction. Life of party

¶2   I. Symptoms of choking

¶3   II. Onset of unconsciousness

¶4   III. Failure of efforts

¶5   IV. Dislodging of food

¶6   V. Resumption of breathing

¶7   Conclusion. Comment of paramedic

(BODY — ¶1 through ¶7)

As usual, Harry Watson was being the life of the party. His voice boomed through the crowded restaurant as he entertained the rest of us with a steady flow of wisecracks and jokes, pausing only to pop an occasional bite of steak into his mouth.

Suddenly Harry became silent. Although his mouth was wide open, no sound came out. He looked alarmed, clutched his chest, and rose unsteadily to his feet. "Hey," Bill Anderson exclaimed, "something's wrong! Harry's having a heart attack!"

Harry staggered away from the table, his eyes staring wildly. His face was turning blue. After a few steps, he tottered and slumped to the floor unconscious. "He's choking to death!" somebody yelled. "He's got a piece of steak stuck in his windpipe! Call an ambulance quick!"

Bill knelt by Harry, rolled him on his side, and began pounding him between the shoulder blades. Nothing happened. So he pried open Harry's mouth, stuck in a couple of fingers, and tried to dislodge the piece of steak. "I think I'm touching it," he groaned, "but I can't budge it!" Pinching Harry's nostrils, he tried to give him artificial respiration by blowing into his mouth. But the piece of meat plugging Harry's windpipe kept any air from reaching his lungs.

"Let me try!" cried Fred Houck. "I know a way to help him!" Flopping on the floor behind Harry, he grabbed him in a "bear hug." Making a fist with his left hand, he grasped this fist with his right hand. Then he placed the fist against Harry's abdomen, just above the navel and below the rib cage. He pressed in hard and gave a quick upward thrust to push Harry's diaphragm up and expel the air from his lungs. Nothing happened; so he did it again. This time the piece of meat popped out of Harry's windpipe like a cork coming out of a bottle. Fred fished the meat from Harry's mouth and then started giving mouth-to-mouth resuscitation.

Gradually the blue faded from Harry's face. He shuddered and began to breathe again. His eyelids fluttered. "He's in shock," I said. "Cover him with my coat and keep him quiet until the ambulance gets here."

After the ambulance had arrived and Harry had been placed inside it on a stretcher, Fred Houck and I decided to accompany him to the hospital. During the ride, nobody had much to say. But just as the ambulance pulled into the hospital driveway, one of the paramedics patted Fred on the shoulder. "You guys saved his life," he said. "This man's had a close call, but I think he's going to be all right." Fred turned toward me. Though his face was still pale, it was covered by a big smile. "Whew!" was all he said.

In this essay, the introduction "sets the scene" for the incidents which follow, and the conclusion lets the reader know that everything will turn out all right for Harry. The parallel topics making up the body tell what happened while his friends were trying to save his life.

DO EXERCISE 35

B. PROCESS EXPLANATION

A rather specialized form of Enumeration is found in the *process-explanation essay body*. It is used when the writer wants to explain the steps in a process—for example, the steps in changing a tire, the steps in cleaning a hunting rifle, or the steps in refinishing a piece of furniture.

The introduction of a process-explanation essay may belong to any of the types of introductions we studied in Chapter 6. However, it often includes a brief explanation of what the process is and an indication of why and when it is performed.

The topics of a process-explanation essay body are, of course, presented in chronological order. Each topic deals with one of the main steps in the process. It explains what equipment or supplies are needed for the step and then offers a chronological list of the substeps making up the main step.

Although a process-explanation essay may sometimes have a conclusion, it often does not. The essay is finished when the writer has finished discussing the last main step. On the other hand, if the process results in some product or other physical object, a conclusion describing that product or object may be desirable.

A well-written process-explanation essay obeys the following principles:

1. The writer must make sure that his explanation of the process is complete and accurate. If he omits a step or substep, or if he presents it incorrectly, he may invalidate all subsequent steps. To avoid such an error, he usually lists all of the substeps in his outline even though they are merely sub-topics within paragraphs. The resulting outline, although long, is very useful to the writer in guiding him as he actually composes the process explanation.

2. The writer must preserve strict chronological order in presenting the actions making up the process. After the spice cake is in the oven, it is too late to tell the reader that the cake pans should be greased.

3. The writer must make sure that his discussion of each step is clear and concrete. If a person must perform an action in a certain way—for example, gently, vigorously, or slowly—the writer must make that fact evident. Similarly, if a person must avoid a certain action—for example, getting acid on his bare skin, allowing two uninsulated wires to touch, or scarring a polished surface—the writer must emphasize that fact.

4. The writer must always define or explain any technical terms which might be unfamiliar to the reader. For example, in a discussion of how to paint a house, he should not use the following sentence unless he intends to explain it: "In order to avoid alligatoring, allow the primer to dry thoroughly before applying the finish coat." The average reader will probably be familiar with "primer" and "finish coat," but he might be unfamiliar with "alligatoring" (development on a painted surface of cracks and ridges so that it resembles alligator hide).

5. The writer should maintain a consistent point of view in his process explanation. For example, he should not compose a sentence such as this: "The calibration screws are tightened; then the mechanic replaces the dial on the control at the 400-degree setting." Instead, he should be consistent: "The mechanic tightens the calibration screws and then replaces the dial on the control at the 400-degree setting." Nor should the writer use this sort of sentence: "Drop teaspoonfuls of batter, well apart, onto a greased and floured cookie sheet; the cookies are then baked in a moderate oven—325 degrees—for about 15 minutes." Instead, he should be consistent: "Drop teaspoonfuls of

batter, well apart, onto a greased and floured cookie sheet, and then bake the cookies in a moderate oven—325 degrees—for about 15 minutes."

Here is a process-explanation essay. As the diagram shows, the body is composed of a series of related actions, the steps in the process. Note that the essay lacks a conclusion:

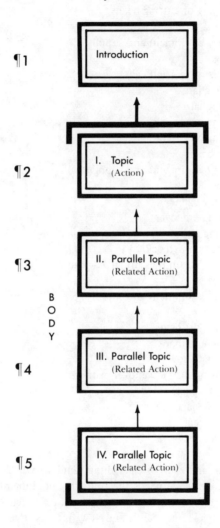

HOW TO COLD PACK SNAP BEANS

Sentence Summary:

The process of canning snap beans by the cold-pack method includes four main steps.

Outline:

¶1   Introduction. Brief explanation of process
        A. The process
        B. Necessary equipment and supplies
        C. Main steps

BODY

¶2 I. Preparing the beans
  A. Necessary equipment and supplies
  B. Substeps
    1. Washing beans
    2. Removing ends and "strings"
    3. Snapping or cutting beans
¶3 II. Filling the jars
  A. Necessary equipment and supplies
  B. Substeps
    1. Sterilizing jars and caps
    2. Packing jars
    3. Adding salt
    4. Adding water
    5. Putting on cap
¶4 III. Cooking the beans
  A. Necessary equipment and supplies
  B. Substeps
    1. Loading canner
    2. Locking on cover
    3. Turning on heat
    4. Tightening petcock
    5. Keeping steam pressure at 10 pounds
¶5 IV. Cooling the jars
  A. Necessary equipment and supplies
  B. Substeps
    1. Turning off heat
    2. Opening petcock
    3. Removing cover
    4. Throwing dish towel over canner
    5. Removing jars
    6. Covering jars
    7. Testing seal

A housewife finds it quick and easy to can young, tender snap beans by the cold-pack method. In order to carry out the process, she needs the following equipment: a pressure canner with wire basket, petcock, pressure gauge, and automatic air-vent plunger; clean canning jars in perfect condition; a supply of two-piece caps—screw bands and new flat lids; two pans; a pair of tongs; a paring knife; and several dish towels. Her supplies include the beans, a box of salt, and water. The main steps in cold packing snap beans are preparing the beans, filling the jars, cooking the beans, and cooling the jars.

The first step which the housewife must perform is preparing the beans for canning. To do this, she needs the two pans, the paring knife, some cold water, and the beans themselves. She washes the beans thoroughly in a pan of cold water to get rid of dirt, leaf fragments, and other impurities. Then she removes the stem and blossom ends of the beans, together with any "strings." Finally, using the paring knife, she cuts the beans into lengths of one inch or less and drops them into an empty pan.

Now the housewife is ready to fill the jars. To carry out this step, she needs the jars and two-piece caps, the tongs, a dish towel, the beans, the salt, and a quantity of boiling water. First, using the tongs, she sterilizes the jars and two-piece caps by dipping them into a pan of boiling water. Then she packs each jar tightly with beans up to one-half inch from the top. She adds salt to each jar—one-

**B
O
D
Y**

half teaspoonful of salt for a pint jar, or one teaspoonful for a quart jar; then she covers the beans with boiling water, making sure that she leaves one-half inch of space at the top of the jar. Wrapping a dish towel around a jar in order to keep from burning her hand on the hot glass, she places a flat metal lid on the jar and then adds the other part of the two-piece cap, the screw band. She turns the screw band until it is as tight as she can get it. In similar fashion, she puts a cap on each of the other jars.

Now the housewife is ready to cook the beans. To do so, she needs the filled jars, the pressure canner, and two quarts of hot water. After placing the pressure canner on the stove, she pours the hot water into it and then puts in as many jars as she can insert upright in the wire basket without having to force them in. When she has finished loading the canner, she locks the cover in place, opens the petcock, and turns the heat up high under the canner. Soon steam begins escaping from the open petcock, and she allows it to do so for ten minutes. In this way she makes sure that all the air has been exhausted from the canner. Next, she tightens the petcock and waits until the steam pressure inside the canner registers ten pounds on the pressure gauge. Then she reduces the heat until it is just sufficient to maintain the ten pounds of pressure while the beans cook. Proper cooking time is twenty minutes for pint jars of beans, twenty-five for quart jars.

After the beans have cooked, the housewife must perform one final step: cooling the jars. To do this, she needs several dish towels. She turns off the heat, waits until the pressure gauge drops to zero, and then gradually opens the petcock. After steam has ceased to issue from the petcock and the automatic air-vent plunger has dropped, she loosens and removes the cover, lifting it away from her in order to avoid being burned by any remaining steam. Then she immediately throws a dish towel over the canner so that cold air will not come into contact with the hot jars, causing them to crack. After waiting a minute or two, she removes the basket of jars from the canner and sets it on a folded dish towel, placing a towel over the jars to protect them from drafts of cold air. She does *not* attempt further to tighten the screw bands; instead, she simply allows the jars to cool for twenty-four hours. Then she tests each jar for proper vacuum seal by tapping the lid gently with a spoon. A clear, ringing sound indicates that a partial vacuum has formed inside, sealing the flat lid tightly to the jar; and the housewife can then remove the screw band, wipe the jar with a damp towel or dishcloth, and put it away. On the other hand, if the lid gives back only a dull "thud" when she taps it, the housewife knows that no vacuum has formed and that the beans will not keep in storage. She must therefore either use the beans promptly or else put a new lid on the jar and then recook them in the pressure canner.

DO EXERCISE 36

C. DESCRIPTION

The *descriptive essay body* describes the subject of the essay. In other words, it presents the significant characteristics of the subject. For example, a writer might wish to describe a hurricane, a tape-recorder cassette, a rattlesnake fang, a comet, a jet engine, or an ostrich egg.

Much description deals with sense impressions: a rose is red; ice is cold and slick; vinegar is sour; a scream is loud and shrill. Sometimes, however, description presents opinions and interpretations rather than data derived directly from the five senses: a man is stubborn; a lion is fierce; a sunset is beautiful; a remark is insulting.

A descriptive essay presents either *literary description* or *factual description,* but almost never both. Literary description is designed to make the reader respond *emotionally*—for example, the description of a spooky "haunted" house, the description of a picturesque view from a mountaintop, or the description of a serious automobile accident. Factual description, on the other hand, is designed to make the reader respond *intellectually.* It attempts to increase his understanding of the subject by presenting its chief attributes—as, for example, in the description of a new kind of highway surface or a certain brand of stereo speaker.

The arrangement of descriptive details in literary description is quite flexible. Often a writer will present such details in the order in which he feels they will have the greatest impact on the reader. Indeed, he is free to arrange literary descriptive details in just about any order he wishes. If the resulting description is vivid and has the emotional impact he intended, then the arrangement of details is a good one.

Since literary description is extremely subjective, we shall not study it in detail here. As a matter of fact, although the inclusion of some appropriate and vivid descriptive details can greatly enhance a narrative essay, a whole essay devoted solely to literary description can quickly tire—or even bore—the reader. It is like eating a whole box of candy at a single sitting: one can get too much of a good thing. Therefore, literary descriptive essays are relatively uncommon today.

On the other hand, the essay based on factual description is a useful and common kind of prose composition. A writer wishing to discuss the chief characteristics of his subject first analyzes that subject into its main parts and then devotes a body topic to the discussion of each main part. Since each topic presents an equivalent idea, the Meaning Relationship between the body topics is Parallel Idea.

In order to help the reader understand the subject, the writer of factual description always arranges the body topics in some logical order. The most commonly used order is that of *spatial arrangement.* In other words, the writer takes up the parts of his subject in an order based on their relative locations. For example, a factual description of the solar system would probably discuss the planets in the order of their increasing distance from the sun, a factual description of a golf ball might start with the outer covering and progress steadily inward toward the core (or *vice versa*), and a factual description of a typical insect might start with the head and progress steadily toward the rear end.

It is not enough, of course, for a writer of a factual description to employ a logical order in presenting his topics. In addition, he must try to make sure that his reader is aware of that logical order and thus understands the physical relationships among the parts of the subject. For example, if a reader does not realize that a factual description of the solar system is discussing the planets in the order of their distance from the sun, he will gain only a vague—and probably incorrect—idea of the solar system.

In addition to arranging his topics in some appropriate logical order, the writer of a factual description must obey the following principles:

1. The writer must present every main part of his subject. For example, it would be wrong for him to state that a baseball has two main parts—the core and the winding. A baseball also has a cover.

2. The writer must not treat a subpart as if it were a main part. For example, it would be incorrect for him to state that a baseball has four main parts—the core, the woolen-yarn winding, the cotton-thread winding, and the cover. The woolen yarn and the cotton thread are actually subparts of one main part—the winding.

3. The writer must make sure that the main parts are mutually exclusive, with no overlapping. For example, it would be wrong for him to state that a baseball has four main parts—the core, the winding, the cover, and the stitching. The stitching is a subpart of the cover.

If he obeys these three principles, the writer wishing to describe a baseball will state that it has three main parts—the core, the winding, and the cover.

Here is a factual-description essay employing spatial arrangement. As the diagram shows, the body of the essay consists of a series of parallel topics, each discussing a main part of the coffee cherry:

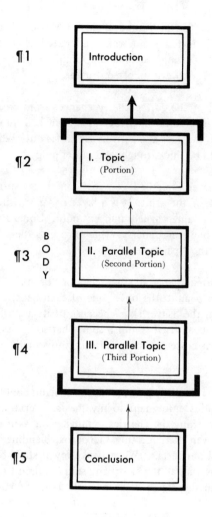

THE COFFEE CHERRY

Sentence Summary:

The coffee cherry is composed of three main parts.

Outline:

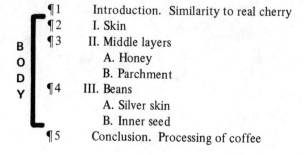

¶1 Introduction. Similarity to real cherry
¶2 I. Skin
¶3 II. Middle layers
    A. Honey
    B. Parchment
¶4 III. Beans
    A. Silver skin
    B. Inner seed
¶5 Conclusion. Processing of coffee

Last summer during a vacation trip in the mountains of Mexico, I saw coffee trees covered with fruit which resembled slightly elongated, somewhat undersized cherries. It is the seeds of these "coffee cherries" which, after processing, become the familiar coffee beans. The structure of this fruit should therefore be of interest to every coffee drinker.

B O D Y

The outside layer, or "skin," of the coffee cherry changes from green to yellow-brown and then to bright red as the fruit ripens. The coffee cherries which I saw had smooth skins, but my guide told me that the ripe fruit eventually wrinkles and shrivels as it dries out. When I cut into a coffee cherry with my knife, I found the skin to be thick, tough, and rather pulpy.

Inside the coffee cherry are several middle layers that completely surround the seeds. Immediately beneath the skin is the meat of the fruit. It is a layer of yellowish, jellylike substance that my guide called the "honey." It has a faint, vaguely pungent odor. Under the jelly layer is a tough membrane, corresponding to the "stone" in a cherry, which protects the seeds; since it becomes brittle when dry, coffee growers call it the "parchment."

At the heart of a typical coffee cherry are two seeds or "beans." They lie with their flat sides together like the two halves of a peanut; the outer side of each bean is rounded. Each bean has its own delicate seed-skin, known as the "silver skin" because of its grayish color. After removing the silver skin, I discovered that the bean itself is moist, somewhat soft, bluish-green in color, and almost odorless. My guide explained that coffee beans acquire their distinctive aroma and brown color only after they are roasted.

I found it hard to believe that the little green seeds in my hand could have any relationship to the steaming, fragrant coffee that adds enjoyment to my meals. Certainly, much skill is required in processing coffee—picking and washing the cherries; removing the skin and honey; drying the beans; removing the parchment and silver skin; roasting the beans; blending, grinding, and packaging the coffee. However, of one thing I am certain: When I take my first sip of breakfast coffee, the world seems brighter, and I am positive that all the effort and skill required to transform the humble coffee cherry into that brown nectar called coffee have been lavished on a worthwhile cause.

DO EXERCISE 37

8

The Essay:
Types of Enumeration (Continued)

If a writer wishes to present several equivalent "points" concerning a subject, he can employ an Enumerative essay body consisting of a series of parallel topics. This pattern is similar to those we studied in Chapter 7, but it involves an enumeration of *ideas* rather than actions or main parts. The parallel topics are, of course, linked through the Meaning Relationship of Parallel Idea.

There can be an enumeration of such topics as accomplishments, achievements, advantages, aims, alternatives, arguments, aspects, beliefs, benefits, causes, changes, characteristics, circumstances, classes, clues, concessions, contrasts, contributions, criteria, criticisms, dangers, demands, differences, difficulties, disadvantages, discoveries, effects, errors, examples, experiments, goals, hints, impressions, incidents, inferences, lessons, mistakes, objections, observations, opinions, pieces of evidence, points, portions, possibilities, predictions, problems, proverbs, purposes, qualities, reasons, requests, results, rewards, shortcomings, similarities, species, steps, suggestions, theories, things, traits, types, virtues, warnings, or weaknesses.

Indeed, most plural subjects can be developed in this fashion. There can be an enumerative discussion of poisonous plants, new inventions, insect pests, favorite television programs, movie monsters, famous bank robberies, childhood diseases, great English novels, or Amendments to the Constitution. It is this great flexibility which makes Enumeration important as a method of organizing an essay body.

In this chapter, we shall first study essay bodies which are simply a *listing of points.* Next, we shall study essay bodies which involve *point-by-point contrast.* Finally, we shall study essay bodies which make use of certain *special two-point patterns.*

A. LISTING OF POINTS

If a writer presents a *listing of points,* the body of his essay must contain as many topics as are necessary for the proper development of his subject. For example, let us suppose that he wishes to list difficulties. If there are only two difficulties, his essay body will consist of two topics. But if there are four difficulties, it will consist of four topics.

A typical two-point pattern for an essay body can be diagrammed as follows:

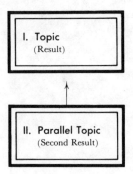

Of course, a three-point pattern is much more frequently used, since most subjects require more than two topics for full discussion:

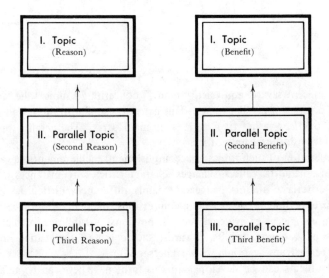

After you have analyzed your particular subject and selected the topics or points which you wish to list and discuss, you must decide in what order you can best present them to the reader. The possible patterns are *random order, chronological order, order of spatial arrangement, climactic order,* and *anticlimactic order.*

In general, *random order* is a pattern which you should avoid since it involves an arbitrary, rather than a logical, arrangement of topics. As we have seen, a reader will usually gain a fuller understanding of your subject if he grasps the logical relationships among the topics. Nevertheless, some subjects naturally lend themselves to a random-order presentation. For example, suppose you wish to discuss some common superstitions. You might decide to take them up in this order: A, B, C, D. But you might find it equally possible to take them up in some other sequence—B, C, A, D or A, C, D, B—since the arrangement is arbitrary and hence relatively unimportant. Other subjects lending themselves to random-order presentation might be discussions of several well-known rock groups, some popular sayings, four changes in the student honor code, or three words you have trouble spelling.

We have already seen that *chronological order* is necessary when you are presenting related actions. In addition, you will find it useful when you are listing a series of items which somehow involve a time scheme. For example, you might discuss Hemingway's novels in the order of their publication, great bank robberies in the order of their occurrence, or Presidents of the United States who died while in office in the order in which they occupied the Presidency.

Some listings of points follow the *order of spatial arrangement* even though no description is involved. For example, a discussion of the results of changing global weather patterns might present those results by geographical areas. Similarly, a discussion of the causes of water pollution might first take up pollution in Eastern industrial areas, then in Midwestern rural areas, and finally in Western areas.

Even more useful than the three preceding patterns are *climactic order* and *anticlimactic order.* If enumerated items differ in importance or in their inherent interest to the reader, that fact is likely to determine their order of presentation.

Usually *climactic order* is best. In following this arrangement, you begin with the least significant item and progress steadily toward the most significant one. In effect, you are continually implying, "If you thought *that* item was interesting, just wait until you get to the *next* one!"

The climactic-order pattern stimulates the reader's interest and gives him the satisfying feeling that the discussion is moving toward a "high point" or climax. You can use climactic order effectively in discussing such subjects as your embarrassing experiences as a camp counselor, new uses for the computer, or strange creatures of the ocean depths.

Here is an essay in which the body topics are listed in climactic order. Note that each mishap experienced by the writer is more serious than the one which precedes it:

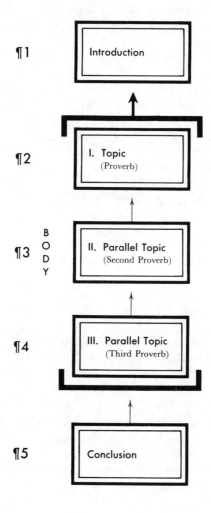

THE WISDOM OF THE AGES

Sentence Summary:

My personal experience indicates that proverbs are often based on truth.

Outline:

B
O   ¶1   Introduction. Proverbs worthy of respect
D   ¶2   I. My lawnmower and "Two heads are better than one"
Y   ¶3   II. My television set and "Look before you leap"
     ¶4   III. My driving mishaps and "Haste makes waste"
     ¶5   Conclusion. Proverbs certain of my respect

Those little gems of wisdom called proverbs are certainly not to be sneered at. The earliest collection of English sayings was printed in the sixteenth century, and we still repeat them: Look before you leap. Strike while the iron is hot. Two heads are better than one. A rolling stone gathers no moss. Haste makes waste. While such proverbs may sound quaint and old-fashioned, they are based on the experience of countless thousands. And I *know* that some of them are true.

Two heads frequently *are* better than one. I decided this after bungling a repair job on a power mower. For an hour I worked without tracing the source of the trouble, and my mower was rapidly disintegrating into a pile of loose lock washers, throttle nuts, bracket bolts, fuel lines, carburetor parts, and air-cleaner gaskets. Finally, I called my next-door neighbor. Together we located the difficulty in about five minutes. It seems that the spark plug was fouled by a carbon deposit.

How many of us have purchased a "bargain" without investigating the quality of the merchandise—have, in other words, leaped before looking? I wish I had not been so eager to leap for a used television set I bought last summer. Stroking the glossy wood cabinet, the salesman pointed out that it was still unscratched and new-looking. Somehow he neglected to mention the electronic and mechanical portions of the set, and I forgot to ask, especially after the salesman uttered the magic word "guarantee." As it turned out, the guarantee expired in sixty days, the picture tube in sixty-five. Then assorted rectifiers, condensers, and switches started going bad—some singly, others in groups. I now realize that a new set would have been cheaper in the long run.

That haste makes waste I have learned with a great deal of sorrow. One day last month, I was in a hurry to get to an important meeting. I was late getting started—my first mistake—and consequently drove too fast through a restricted speed zone. A motorcycle policeman crowded me to the curb, gave me a ticket, and not only hurt my pocketbook but made me later than ever for my appointment. So, when I saw a long line of traffic slowing down ahead of me, I had the bright idea of turning off onto a seldom-traveled side road which I knew rejoined the highway after a few miles. What I did not know was that a rainstorm had turned that country lane into a sea of muck. Instead of looking for a driveway that would allow me to turn around easily, I attempted a U-turn and slipped into a ditch, crumpling my right-front fender. Finally, I waded for help and called the garage to come after my car. The total bill was nearly three hundred dollars, and—needless to say—I missed my meeting altogether.

So I do not scorn proverbs. A stitch in time saves nine; time and tide wait for no man; and none are so deaf as those who will not hear. I believe a word to the wise should be sufficient.

In the preceding essay, the body lists a series of unhappy experiences which illustrate well-known proverbs. Those experiences are arranged climactically in the order of their increasing unpleasantness. A climactic arrangement is usually desirable when the items you wish to list are personal achievements, personal experiences, anecdotes, incidents, or examples.

Instead of climactic order, you may find it desirable to employ its opposite, *anticlimactic order*. In this pattern, the most significant item comes first, with subsequent items being arranged in the order of their decreasing significance.

Anticlimactic order is usually desirable when you wish to present a list of causes, reasons, or results. But it may also be effective when you are listing such items as benefits, dangers, demands, difficulties, disadvantages, inferences, objectives, pieces of evidence, possibilities, problems, shortcomings, virtues, warnings, or weaknesses. In adopting this arrangement, you are in effect stating, "I believe this first item to be especially important, but I also think that these other items are worthy of consideration."

You will find anticlimactic order effective in developing such subjects as these: why the postal system needs drastic overhauling, why we must continue to explore outer space, why personal bankruptcies are increasing, the effects of pollution of water by mercury, how to save money when buying food, or the results of the last election.

Here is an essay which lists three reasons in anticlimactic order:

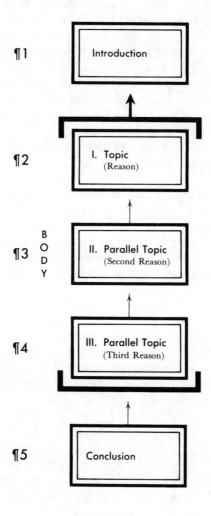

WHY I WANT TO BE A PHYSICIAN

Sentence Summary:

A career in medicine will enable me to serve mankind, to satisfy my love of science, and to enjoy a comfortable standard of living.

Outline:

B	¶1	Introduction. Since childhood, goal in life unchanged
O	¶2	I. Serve mankind
D	¶3	II. Satisfy love of science
Y	¶4	III. Enjoy comfortable standard of living
	¶5	Conclusion. Despite sacrifices, career in medicine rewarding

About the time I entered the second grade, I acquired a new mission in life. Previously I had been determined to become a fireman when I grew up, but at the age of seven I decided to become a doctor instead. Now, almost twelve years later, my goal remains unchanged. I am a first-year premedical student, and my highest ambition in life is to become a physician. For a number of reasons, I believe that no other career could possibly bring me as much satisfaction as one in medicine.

My chief reason for wishing to become a physician is that I shall then be able to serve mankind. Even in America there is a critical shortage of doctors; elsewhere, according to the World Health Organization, the situation is often desperate. Disease and injury strike everywhere; yet an overwhelming majority of the world's people must live or die without any doctor, nurse, hospital, or medicine—other than some folk remedy of little value. Such a lack of even rudimentary medical care is all the more tragic since it occurs in an age of "wonder drugs," new surgical techniques, and other dramatic advances in the healing arts. By entering the medical profession, I can do my part to lessen human suffering and make the world healthier and happier.

BODY

My second reason for choosing a career in medicine is that it will satisfy my love of science. As a small child, I made collections of insects, minerals, and fossils. As a teen-ager, I read and reread *Microbe Hunters, The Science of Life, Fabre's Book of Insects,* and the books of Willy Ley. In high school my favorite subjects were biology, chemistry, physics, and mathematics. I have always had, then, a real love of science; and as a doctor I shall be working in such areas of science as anatomy, physiology, embryology, bacteriology, and organic chemistry. I therefore expect always to love my work.

My final reason for wanting to be a physician is that I shall be able to enjoy a comfortable standard of living. Members of the medical profession have considerable social prestige and a relatively high income. As a doctor I should be able to provide my family with a good home, cultural and educational advantages, and opportunities for travel. While these material considerations would not by themselves have led me to choose a career in medicine, they do enhance the attractiveness of the profession.

Certainly, I feel that medicine is the right profession for me. I know, of course, that my goal will not be easy to reach. Seven more years of intensive training lie ahead of me—training that will put my determination and talent to the test. But when I think of the rewards—tangible and intangible—of a career in medicine, I know that my goal is well worth the time, effort, and money that it will cost me. When I have earned the right to add "M.D." after my name, that will be the proudest day of my life.

In the preceding essay, note the effective use of Transitional Elements: my *chief* reason, my *second* reason, my *final* reason.

DO EXERCISE 38

B. POINT-BY-POINT CONTRAST

If a writer wishes to contrast two or more subjects, he may use another kind of Enumeration—that involving *point-by-point contrast.* In this pattern, each enumerated item is an aspect or point upon which the subjects are contrasted. The pattern is, in effect, an *enumeration of contrasts.*

In discussing this type of essay, we shall consider how a writer goes about organizing his material in order to present it most effectively. As we shall see, he can choose any of the five plans of organization just studied.

Let us assume that a writer wishes to discuss the differences between a typical insect and a typical spider. Here is a skeleton outline for a point-by-point contrast essay. Note that the contrast occurs *within* each of the parallel topics:

    I. Trait "X"
     A. Insect
     B. Spider
   II. Trait "Y"
     A. Insect
     B. Spider
  III. Trait "Z"
     A. Insect
     B. Spider

The writer considers point-by-point contrast a suitable method of organization because it is clear and explicit and because he can discuss each crucial point or difference before passing on to the next. Let us assume that he has also decided that the specific differences meriting discussion are as follows: number of legs, number of body divisions, and the presence or absence of certain body structures such as wings or antennae. So far, so good. But in what order should he present these topics? Should he employ random order, chronological order, order of spatial arrangement, climactic order, or anticlimactic order? In other words, which plan of organization is most appropriate for his essay?

Depending upon the subject of a point-by-point contrast, any of the five types of organization might be used. Note the following examples:

1. *Random Order* in an essay dealing with "Vocabulary Differences Between Yankee and Southerner":
    I. Words related to weather
     A. Yankee
     B. Southerner
   II. Words related to agriculture and rural life
     A. Yankee
     B. Southerner
  III. Words related to food and eating
     A. Yankee
     B. Southerner
  IV. Words related to sports and recreation
     A. Yankee
     B. Southerner

2. *Chronological Order* in an essay dealing with "Two Famous Battles of World War II":
    I. Preliminary preparation
     A. Guadalcanal
     B. Tarawa

II. Landing operation
A. Guadalcanal
B. Tarawa
III. Mopping-up operation
A. Guadalcanal
B. Tarawa

3. *Order of Spatial Arrangement* in an essay dealing with "Palm Tree and Oak Tree":
I. Foliage and branches
A. Palm
B. Oak
II. Trunk
A. Palm
B. Oak
III. Root system
A. Palm
B. Oak

4. *Climactic Order* in an essay dealing with "Life in a Democracy Versus Life in a Totalitarian State":
I. Job opportunities
A. Democracy
B. Totalitarian state
II. Political and civic activities
A. Democracy
B. Totalitarian state
III. Religious activities
A. Democracy
B. Totalitarian state

5. *Anticlimactic Order* in an essay dealing with "Junior College and University":
I. Curriculum
A. Junior college
B. University
II. Extracurricular activities
A. Junior college
B. University
III. Housing accommodations
A. Junior college
B. University

Of course, not all of these five plans of organization would be suited to a discussion of "The Insect and the Spider." Random order should be avoided if a more logical arrangement is possible. Chronological order does not seem applicable to the subject of the essay. Order of spatial arrangement would be awkward, for the specific differences the writer wishes to present do not lend themselves to a steady progression from one end of the two creatures to the other, but would instead require a great deal of backtracking. The writer, then, must employ either climactic or anticlimactic order, and he finally selects the latter. He decides that the number of legs is the most obvious and important difference between the two animals, and he therefore places it first in his outline. Then he decides that the difference in number of body divisions is more significant than the presence or absence of such body structures as wings and antennae. Eventually, he produces the following essay using anticlimactic order:

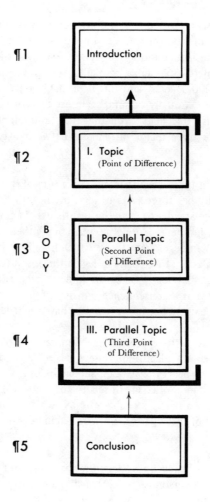

THE INSECT AND THE SPIDER

Sentence Summary:

A typical insect and a typical spider differ from one another in three main ways.

Outline:

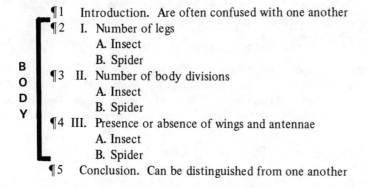

¶1   Introduction. Are often confused with one another
¶2   I. Number of legs
         A. Insect
         B. Spider
¶3   II. Number of body divisions
         A. Insect
         B. Spider
¶4   III. Presence or absence of wings and antennae
         A. Insect
         B. Spider
¶5   Conclusion. Can be distinguished from one another

Two classes of animals with jointed legs and a hard outer skeleton are widely distributed around the earth. These are the *insects* and the *spiders.* Insects constitute the largest group of animals in the world. Zoologists have so far named more than 900,000 species, and this may be only 10 per cent of the actual number in existence. Spiders are a smaller, though very important, group. Scientists have already identified over 30,000 species, and this is probably only 25 per cent of the eventual total. Since insects and spiders are extremely common, almost everyone has seen them. Yet many persons find it difficult to distinguish one class from the other and simply label them both incorrectly as "bugs." Actually, there are three major differences between a typical adult insect and a typical spider.

B O D Y

One difference between a typical adult insect and a typical spider is the number of legs that each possesses. The insect usually has three pairs of legs, often with one pair modified for some special function—for instance, the enlarged first pair the mantis uses in grasping its prey or the enlarged rear pair the grasshopper uses in jumping. A few insects, among them the female bagworm, are legless as adults; scientists consider them degenerate forms which have lost their legs. But no species of insects has *more* than six legs as an adult; three pairs of legs is the absolute maximum. Spiders, on the other hand, always have four pairs of legs. Since all spiders are predators, they are necessarily active creatures, and their legs have as a consequence remained functional. To repeat, most adult insects have six legs, though a few have none; but all spiders have eight legs.

There is also a difference with respect to the number of body divisions characteristic of each animal. When one examines a typical adult insect, he finds it composed of three distinct parts: a head; a thorax or chest, which bears the six legs; and an abdomen. If, however, one looks at a spider, he discovers that the head and thorax are fused to form a single part of the creature's body; so a spider is composed of only two parts: a cephalothorax, which bears the eight legs; and an abdomen. Thus, a specimen composed of three parts cannot be a spider, and one composed of two parts cannot be an insect.

The presence or absence of such body structures as wings and antennae is a final point of difference which can be helpful if a person is trying to distinguish between insects and spiders. A majority of insects have wings and antennae, but no spider has either of these structures. Of course, this distinction between the two classes of animals is not absolute since some species of insects also lack wings or antennae. But at least the *presence* of either of these features in a specimen indicates it is an insect rather than a spider.

If he keeps these characteristics in mind, anyone should be readily able to distinguish between an insect and a spider. It is true that some species possess traits which may at first be confusing. For instance, there are many kinds of insects which can spin silk, and there are some spiders which mimic the appearance of ants. Nevertheless, a person should have no difficulty determining the proper class for an individual specimen if he will only take time to count its legs, analyze the divisions of its body, and look to see whether it has wings or antennae.

You will find point-by-point contrast a good plan of organization for discussing subjects like the following: beef cattle and dairy cattle, coyote and timber wolf, fly rod and spincasting rod, grandmother's kitchen and the modern kitchen, a good teacher and a bad teacher, college football and professional football. Point-by-point contrast is an especially useful pattern if you wish to present a relatively large number of points of difference.

DO EXERCISE 39

C. SPECIAL TWO-POINT PATTERNS

You will find that some subjects can best be treated in a very flexible kind of *two-point Enumeration essay.* In this pattern, the essay body is devoted to different broad aspects of the subject.

For example, suppose you wish to discuss the extremely high salaries being paid to superstar professional athletes. You might decide first to examine the reasons why salaries have reached such high levels, and then to take up the effects of those salaries upon the financial health of professional sports. Here is a diagram of the body of such an essay:

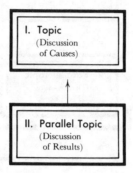

Besides this causes-results pattern, other common patterns are these: similarities-differences, advantages-disadvantages, and problem-solution. In addition, many other two-point combinations are possible—for example, changes-benefits, definition-example, comparison-example, difficulties-suggestions, shortcomings-virtues, and mistake-lesson.

Perhaps the most common of these two-point combinations is *similarities-differences.* One of the topics compares two things and explains how they are alike; the other topic contrasts them and explains how they are different from one another. This pattern would be appropriate if you should wish to discuss the revolver and the automatic, the German cockroach and the Oriental cockroach, or the coffee percolator and the drip coffee maker.

When using the similarities-differences pattern, you should always follow climactic order. If two things which you wish to discuss seem similar to most people but are actually quite different in certain important ways, you should treat the similarities first and then stress the significant differences. Such an arrangement would be appropriate for an essay body dealing with common measles and German measles. On the other hand, if two things seem quite different to most people but are actually alike in certain important ways, you should treat the differences first and then stress the significant similarities. Such an arrangement would be appropriate for an essay body dealing with fascism and communism.

Here is an essay employing the similarities-differences pattern. Note that it emphasizes the differences between moths and butterflies by treating that topic last:

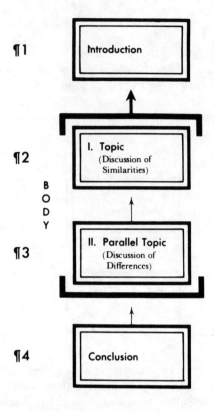

MOTHS AND BUTTERFLIES

Sentence Summary:

Although similar in many ways, moths and butterflies display certain marked differences.

Outline:

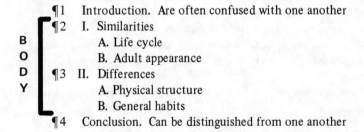

¶1   Introduction. Are often confused with one another
¶2   I. Similarities
      A. Life cycle
      B. Adult appearance
¶3   II. Differences
      A. Physical structure
      B. General habits
¶4   Conclusion. Can be distinguished from one another

Among the myriads of living creatures on this planet, some of the most beautiful are insects belonging to the order *Lepidoptera*. These are the moths and butterflies, of which more than 80,000 species are now known. Because of their striking appearance, moths and butterflies interest persons of all ages—children make butterfly collections, scientists study the migratory instincts of the Monarch butterfly, and poets write tributes to "beauty on wings." Yet the average person often confuses moths and butterflies, particularly when he encounters an unfamiliar specimen. It is therefore instructive to consider the similarities and differences between these two groups of insects.

The close similarity between moths and butterflies can be seen both in their life cycle and in the appearance of the adult insect. In each case, the egg hatches into a caterpillar, one of the most familiar and striking larvae in the insect world. After feeding energetically for a time, most often upon green vegetation, this creature goes through a dormant pupa stage and eventually emerges as an adult. The typical mature moth or butterfly has a small, rounded head bearing prominent jointed antennae; a pair of large compound eyes, and usually a pair of simple eyes as well; and a long, coiled "tongue" or sucking tube. The thorax bears three pairs of jointed legs and two pairs of large, membranous wings covered with tiny overlapping scales that give the wings a "dusty" appearance. The abdomen is composed of ten segments and terminates in the external reproductive organs.

B
O
D
Y

Despite the many similarities between moths and butterflies, it is possible to distinguish between these two groups of insects. First of all, there are certain significant differences in their physical structure. The most important of these involves the antennae. Moths almost always have either narrow, thread-like or broad, feather-like antennae *without* knobs at the end; butterflies, on the other hand, have club-like antennae which terminate in distinct knobs. Another physical difference is that moths frequently possess the frenulum, a group of bristles that helps to hold together the front and rear wing on each side of the insect, but butterflies invariably lack this structure. Fortunately, the few moths which have knobs on their antennae also have the frenulum, and thus can be readily distinguished from butterflies. One final physical difference is that the typical moth has a stouter body than the typical butterfly, as well as smaller wings in relation to body size. In addition to the physical differences between these insects, certain contrasting habits are also important. For example, a majority of moths are active by night, a majority of butterflies by day. Also, when resting, moths never hold their wings vertically over their backs; many butterflies do assume this position.

By remembering these characteristics of moths and butterflies, anyone should be able to tell them apart without difficulty. Superficially, the majestic Cecropia moth may seem to have more in common with the Swallowtail butterfly than with the tiny, drab clothes moth. But an examination of contrasting physical characteristics and habits will enable a person to establish the proper grouping. And in this manner he can increase his understanding of those scaled-wing insects, the *Lepidoptera*, whose many species include some of the most interesting and colorful creatures in existence.

DO EXERCISE 40

9

The Essay:
Equal-Pair and Unequal-Pair Patterns

A writer may wish to discuss his subject by presenting two topics which are *not* parallel. For example, his first topic might deal with the introduction of the Dutch elm disease to the United States, and his second topic might deal with the resulting destruction of the American elm. Or his first topic might summarize a recent decision of the Supreme Court, and his second topic might deal with the probable consequences of that decision.

If the two topics are of equal significance, the essay body will follow the *Equal-Pair Pattern*. On the other hand, if one of the topics is of more significance than the other, the essay body will follow the *Unequal-Pair Pattern*.

A. THE EQUAL-PAIR PATTERN

A writer may wish to present two contrasting topics, two alternative topics, two comparable topics, a circumstance and its result, a circumstance and its cause, an idea and a question suggested by that idea, or a question and its answer. In each instance, the two topics are of equal significance and are linked through an Equal Meaning Relationship. Therefore, the essay body follows the *Equal-Pair Pattern*.

In this variety of essay body, the Meaning Relationship which most frequently occurs is Contrast. We can diagram this arrangement as follows:

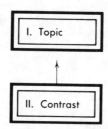

Suppose, for example, that you wish to discuss the differences between heatstroke and heat exhaustion. If you use this contrast pattern, your first topic will deal with heatstroke and your second topic with heat exhaustion (or *vice versa*). Such an arrangement is known as a *subject-by-subject contrast.*

Here is an example of an essay presenting a subject-by-subject contrast:

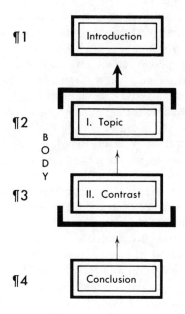

HEATSTROKE AND HEAT EXHAUSTION

Sentence Summary:

Although they are both caused by prolonged exposure to high temperature, heatstroke and heat exhaustion differ markedly.

Outline:

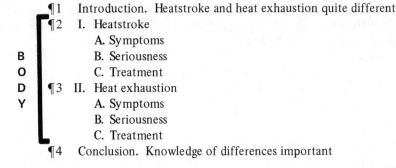

¶1   Introduction. Heatstroke and heat exhaustion quite different
¶2   I. Heatstroke
    A. Symptoms
    B. Seriousness
    C. Treatment
¶3   II. Heat exhaustion
    A. Symptoms
    B. Seriousness
    C. Treatment
¶4   Conclusion. Knowledge of differences important

During the summer months, many persons become ill after prolonged exposure to high temperatures, especially if the relative humidity is also high. Some are victims of *heatstroke,* also known as sunstroke; others suffer from *heat exhaustion,* also known as heat prostration. Since both conditions are caused by excessive heat, people often tend to confuse one with the other. Yet the two illnesses are actually quite different in their symptoms, relative seriousness, and recommended method of treatment.

B O D Y

Heatstroke results from a serious disturbance of the body's heat-regulating mechanism. Its onset is usually sudden. The victim's skin is flushed; to the touch it seems hot and dry. His pulse is rapid, his blood pressure often elevated. Although he may complain chiefly of dizziness, headache, and nausea, his most dangerous symptom is fever, which rises rapidly. Permanent brain damage results from a temperature over 108 degrees Fahrenheit, and it is therefore imperative that the victim's fever be reduced as quickly as possible to prevent coma, convulsions, even death. In heatstroke the mortality rate is high. First-aid treatment should begin at once. While the heatstroke patient lies with his head slightly elevated, the person giving first aid should bathe him with cold water or wrap him in a cold wet sheet. Ice packs and an electric fan are of some value. Massaging the victim's skin to promote circulation is highly desirable. In severe cases of heatstroke, an ice-water tub bath, accompanied by massage, is the preferred method of combatting fever. In any case, one should summon a physician promptly, for heatstroke victims usually require medical care for several days.

Heat exhaustion results from partial failure of the circulatory system. Its onset is usually gradual. The blood vessels of the skin become dilated as the body tries to radiate heat, and a great deal of blood collects there. Consequently, the volume of blood returning to the heart decreases, and the patient eventually becomes weak, or even collapses, because the brain is not receiving an adequate supply of blood. A person suffering from heat exhaustion has the appearance typical of fainting. His skin is pale; to the touch it is cold and damp with perspiration. His pulse is weak, his blood pressure often below normal. Despite his clammy skin, his body temperature is usually normal. Heat exhaustion is not ordinarily a serious condition; its mortality rate is very low. Therefore, first-aid treatment is comparatively simple. The victim should lie in a cool place with his head slightly lowered. The person rendering first aid should loosen or remove any tight clothing from the patient. Fanning him or applying cool compresses to his forehead and skin is often helpful. Usually it is desirable to give the victim salt tablets, or a drink of cool water with some salt added; however, the salt sometimes increases any tendency toward nausea that may be present. Although the patient may feel weak for some time, recovery is comparatively rapid. Except in cases of profound collapse, medical care is not required.

It is obvious, then, that heatstroke and heat exhaustion are dissimilar conditions. Each has its characteristic symptoms, and each requires its own method of treatment. If we keep these facts in mind during the hot summer months that lie just ahead, we shall be better able to distinguish between the two illnesses. And, if the need arises, we shall be able to render the proper form of first aid.

We have now studied three essay-body patterns involving some element of contrast: the *point-by-point contrast pattern,* the *similarities-differences pattern,* and the *subject-by-subject contrast pattern.* In order to understand these three patterns better, we shall now see how the same subject would be treated if arranged according to each pattern. Here are outlines for a discussion of moths and butterflies:

1. *Point-by-Point Contrast:*

    I.   Physical structure
       A. Moths
       B. Butterflies
   II.   General habits
       A. Moths
       B. Butterflies

2. *Similarities-Differences:*

   I. Similarities
      A. Life cycle
      B. Adult appearance
  II. Differences
      A. Physical structure
      B. General habits

3. *Subject-by-Subject Contrast:*

   I. Moths
      A. Physical structure
      B. General habits
  II. Butterflies
      A. Physical structure
      B. General habits

If a writer wishes to emphasize points of similarity as well as points of difference, he will probably use the similarities-differences pattern. On the other hand, if he is interested in discussing only points of difference, he may choose either of the other two patterns. A subject involving a relatively large number of points of difference (four or more) could probably best be treated through point-by-point contrast; otherwise, by the time the reader gets to the second subject, he might not remember all the points which were given about the first subject and hence would be unable to contrast them with the corresponding points which were given about the second subject. However, since the discussion of moths and butterflies involves only two points of difference, either point-by-point contrast or subject-by-subject contrast would be satisfactory.

Of course, as we have already seen, Contrast is not the only Meaning Relationship which occurs in an Equal-Pair essay body. The subject which a writer wishes to discuss may call for one of the other Equal Meaning Relationships to link the body topics. Here is an essay with its body topics linked through Cause. As the diagram indicates, the second topic presents the cause of the situation described in the first topic:

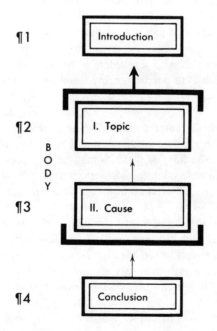

MAMIE'S PARROT FEVER

Sentence Summary:

My dog's altered behavior is due to her being jealous of my sister's parrot.

Outline:

B   ¶1   Introduction. Unreliability of ancient proverb concerning dogs
O   ¶2   I. Surprising change in behavior
D   ¶3   II. Violent jealousy toward parrot
Y   ¶4   Conclusion. Member of new class of dogs

According to an ancient saying, one cannot teach an old dog new tricks. I am not quite certain what that proverb means; but, if it implies that old dogs get so set in their ways that they cannot adopt new habit patterns, then I must dissent vigorously. For my dog Mamie, a venerable toy Manchester terrier twelve years old, has recently undergone a change as startling as Dr. Jekyll's celebrated transformation into Mr. Hyde.

During the past two months, Mamie has acquired a new disposition. Prior to that time, she was a lazy and placid little beast. So fat she could hardly waddle around the house, she nevertheless had a finicky appetite and often left her food untouched. She slept most of the day but could not reach her favorite snoozing place, the sofa, without help—someone always had to lift her up. And she greeted all comers with a friendly wag of the tail. Now, however, Mamie is both alert and aggressive. No longer overweight, she gobbles her food with wolf-like eagerness but still stays in fighting trim. She never seems to sleep but restlessly roams the house, day and night. She hops up on the sofa without difficulty, and I have even caught her atop the kitchen table. Worst of all, she snarls at strangers and even barks irritably at members of our family.

The reason for my dog's surprising metamorphosis is quite simple: she is violently jealous of Pete, the little half-moon parrot my sister recently acquired. Mamie is consumed with a smoldering resentment which periodically bursts into a flame of pure hatred. We call it "Mamie's parrot fever," and its symptoms are readily observable. When Pete eats sunflower seeds, Mamie also insists upon munching on a seed, apparently convinced that parrot food must be a special treat. When Pete is in his cage, Mamie sits nearby for hours at a time, directing an unwavering, baleful stare at him. When Pete flies around the house, Mamie stalks him with a murderous intensity that would do credit to the most bloodthirsty tomcat. And, when Pete perches on my shoulder and croaks softly in my ear, Mamie dances up and down in insane rage, yelping hysterically.

Although Mamie may eventually come to tolerate Pete's presence, that happy day is not yet in sight. In fact, Mamie has been so vocal in her displeasure that the first phrase Pete has learned to say, imitating my sister and me, is "Shut up, Mamie!" Sometimes I suspect that Mamie belongs to a class of dogs which has been hitherto unrecognized. Many persons can claim that they own bird dogs, but I am unique in owning what is obviously an anti-bird dog. Shut up, Mamie!

In the preceding essay, the body topics are linked through Cause. In similar fashion, a writer can use the other Equal Meaning Relationships to link the two topics of an Equal-Pair essay body. A subject involving alternatives would, of course, present topics linked through Alternative. The first topic might suggest a solution to a problem of unemployment among certain minority groups, and the second topic might suggest an alternate solution. A subject involving similarities would present two topics linked through Balanced Comparison. The first topic might discuss the trapdoor spider's habit of ambushing its prey, and the second topic might discuss the ant lion's similar behavior. A subject involving consequences or effects would present topics linked through Result. The first topic might deal with the development of the throw-away beverage can, and the second topic might discuss the consequences of its use.

The Equal Meaning Relationships we have just examined occur naturally as a result of the nature of the subject which the writer is discussing. Such is not the case with the Meaning Relationships of Question and Answer. If the topics of a two-point essay are linked through either of these Meaning Relationships, the writer has probably made a conscious decision to employ that pattern.

Fewer subjects lend themselves to development through Question or Answer than through the other Equal Meaning Relationships. Moreover, Question or Answer is usually appropriate only if the body topics are short. Still, either of these Meaning Relationships can sometimes produce an effective arrangement for a two-point essay body. If the Meaning Relationship is Question, the first topic might discuss the growing unionization of government employees, and the second topic might raise the question as to whether they should have the right to strike. If the Meaning Relationship is Answer, the first topic might ask why the Soviet Union continues to have great difficulty in producing enough food for its citizens, and the second topic might answer that question.

DO EXERCISE 41

B. THE UNEQUAL-PAIR PATTERN

Sometimes the subject a writer wishes to present does not lend itself to discussion in two parallel topics or two equal topics. Instead, it calls for two unequal topics—that is, topics linked through an Unequal Meaning Relationship. This is the *Unequal-Pair Pattern.*

In the treatment of some subjects, the second topic would be *subsidiary* to the first one. This would be true if the writer presented an idea plus a definition of a key word, an idea plus an amplification of some significant noun, an idea dealing with a general class followed by a discussion of a member of that class, a general idea plus a sample fact illustrating that idea, or an idea involving a hypothesis plus supporting data to support that hypothesis.

In the treatment of other subjects, the second topic would be *dominant.* This would be true if the writer presented an idea involving a sample fact plus a generalization based on that sample fact or an idea involving supporting data plus a hypothesis derived from that data.

If the subject of an essay leads the writer to follow the Unequal-Pair Pattern, the resulting composition is usually fairly short. We can illustrate this kind of essay body as follows:

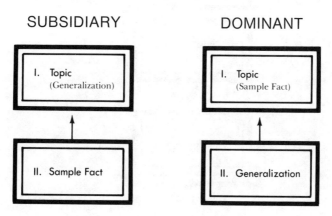

Let us suppose that a writer has a hypothesis or theory which he wishes to present, together with some evidence to support it. He can organize his essay body in this way:

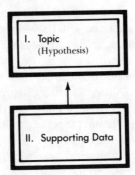

This is precisely the same sort of organization he would have used if he were presenting two independent clauses linked through Supporting Data:

As you can see, in each case the Meaning Relationship of Supporting Data links the two elements.

Here is an essay in which the topics are linked through Supporting Data. Note that the second topic is subsidiary to the first topic:

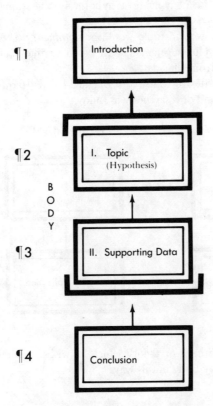

A CHILLING PROSPECT

Sentence Summary:

It now seems probable that the world is on the verge of another ice age.

Outline:

```
B    ¶1  Introduction.  Ice age of 20,000 years ago
O   ⌈¶2  I. Hypothesis of approaching ice age
D   ⌊¶3  II. Kinds of supporting evidence
Y    ¶4  Conclusion.  Resulting struggle for survival
```

Today, central Indiana is a pleasant region of wooded hillsides, fertile farms, and prosperous communities. But 20,000 years ago the situation was far different. The area lay buried under 1,500 feet of glacial ice. And, through long centuries of snowfall, the frozen wind howled across a scene of barren whiteness.

Until recently, scientists believed that ice ages like those of ancient times would not occur again and that our present weather patterns would continue more or less permanently, with only minor fluctuations. During the past few years, however, many climatologists have come to a disturbing conclusion. It now seems probable, they say, that the world is on the verge of another ice age.

Several kinds of evidence tend to support this hypothesis. Meteorologists report that the average annual temperature in the Northern Hemisphere has been dropping slowly but steadily for the past thirty years. Oceanographers state that the North Atlantic is undergoing significant cooling and that the Gulf Stream has migrated southward; indeed, in recent years Iceland's ports have been choked by winter ice for the first time in this century. Agriculturists say that the growing season in the English lowlands is two weeks shorter than it was in 1940, and our own upper Midwest has been experiencing midsummer frosts. Finally, geologists indicate that they have new evidence to show that there have been eight major periods of glaciation during the past million years, punctuated by "little ice ages" every 20,000 years. If they are correct and the 20,000-year cycle stays on schedule, another global deep freeze is due just about now.

If a new ice age does come, it will have a profound effect upon mankind. The changing weather will cause a drastic cut in our production of food, our dwindling sources of energy will be rapidly exhausted, and a majority of the areas now most heavily populated will be buried under hundreds of feet of glacial ice. In short, the human race will experience a harsh struggle for survival as it faces the chilling prospect of an ice age.

In the preceding essay, the body topics are linked through Supporting Data. The writer may find that his subject calls for one of the other subsidiary Unequal Meaning Relationships to link the topics of his essay body. An essay discussing the laser might present topics linked through Definition. The first topic might indicate the growing importance of the laser in scientific research, and the second topic might offer a definition of the term *laser*. An essay discussing some current social problem such as child abuse might present topics linked through Amplification. The first topic might include an anticipatory noun such as *problem* (usually at the end), and the second topic might amplify that noun by expanding it into a discussion of what the problem is. An essay dealing with those astronomical bodies known as asteroids might present topics linked through Sample Item. The first topic might discuss the general characteristics of asteroids, and the second topic might deal with one particular asteroid, Ceres. An essay dealing with diamond smuggling might present topics linked through Sample Fact. The first topic might indicate that diamond smugglers conceal their precious stones in many ingenious ways, and the second topic might give an example of an especially clever method of hiding them.

Of course, the writer may find that his subject calls for one of the two dominant Unequal Meaning Relationships to link the topics of his essay body. As you know, they are Generalization and Inference.

Study the following essay carefully. As you will discover, its body contains practically the same information as the body of the last essay you examined—namely, the hypothesis that another ice age is approaching, and data to support that hypothesis. However, the writer wishes to produce a different effect; so he gives the supporting data first and then presents his hypothesis. The resulting essay body contains two topics linked through the Meaning Relationship of Inference.

Note that this arrangement of topics makes it necessary for the essay to have a different kind of introduction. Since the writer wishes to delay discussing an ice age until he reaches the second body topic, he obviously cannot refer to it in the introduction:

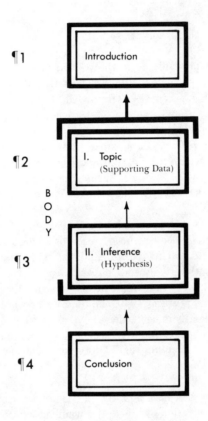

A CHILLING PROSPECT

Sentence Summary:

It now seems probable that the world is on the verge of another ice age.

Outline:

B   ¶1   Introduction. Greatest problem of human race
O   ¶2   I. Kinds of alarming evidence
D   ¶3   II. Hypothesis of approaching ice age
Y   ¶4   Conclusion. Coming struggle for survival

The human race always has a host of problems to occupy its attention. Today, for example, people worry about economic depression, corrupt government, injustice, discrimination, fires, floods, hurricanes, volcanic eruptions, earthquakes, pollution, hunger, pestilence, and even invaders from outer space. But mankind may soon be facing a more serious problem than any of these.

**B
O
D
Y**

Several kinds of rapidly accumulating evidence are very disquieting. Meteorologists report that the average annual temperature in the Northern Hemisphere has been dropping slowly but steadily for the past thirty years. Oceanographers state that the North Atlantic is undergoing significant cooling and that the Gulf Stream has migrated southward; indeed, in recent years Iceland's ports have been choked by winter ice for the first time in this century. Agriculturists say that the growing season in the English lowlands is two weeks shorter than it was in 1940, and our own upper Midwest has been experiencing midsummer frosts. Finally, geologists indicate they have new evidence to show that there have been eight major periods of glaciation during the past million years, punctuated by "little ice ages" every 20,000 years.

All of this evidence suggests strongly that the world is approaching another ice age. Indeed, if the 20,000-year cycle stays on schedule, a global deep freeze is due just about now. Until recently, scientists believed that ice ages like those of ancient times would not occur again and that our present weather patterns would continue more or less permanently, with only minor fluctuations. But now many climatologists are no longer confident that this is so. Weighing the evidence, they peer into the future and see the approaching ice and the long centuries of falling snow and howling wind.

If a new ice age does come, it will have a profound effect upon mankind. The changing weather will cause a drastic cut in our production of food, our dwindling sources of energy will be rapidly exhausted, and a majority of the areas now most heavily populated will be buried under hundreds of feet of glacial ice. In short, the human race will experience a harsh struggle for survival as it faces the chilling prospect of an ice age.

In the preceding essay, the body topics are linked through Inference. In similar fashion, a writer might find it desirable to use the other Unequal Meaning Relationship, Generalization, to link the two topics of an essay body. For example, a discussion of the use of television to bring important events to the viewing public might present topics linked through Generalization. The first topic might deal with the televising of the first moon walk, and the second topic might present, and discuss, the general idea that the TV camera is often present when modern history is being made.

DO EXERCISE 42

10

The Essay:
Chain and Leapfrog Patterns

Some subjects are too complex for satisfactory discussion in a two-point essay and need to be treated at greater length. Unlike the essay-body patterns which we have already studied, the final two patterns which we shall discuss always involve *three or more topics*. They are the *Chain Pattern* and the *Leapfrog Pattern*.

A. THE CHAIN PATTERN

The *Chain Pattern* consists of three or more topics linked in sequence through Equal Meaning Relationships. In other words, each topic (except, of course, the first one) is linked with the topic *immediately preceding it*.

Among the many possible combinations of Equal Meaning Relationships in the Chain Pattern, the following are the most common:

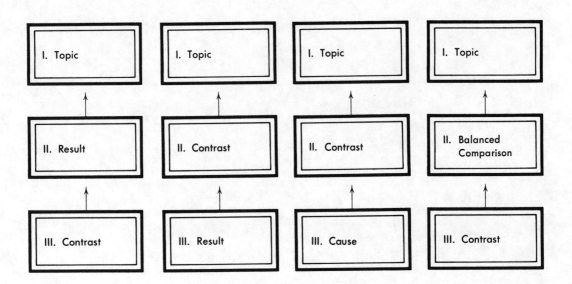

If it is suited to the development of your subject, you can use any of these combinations to form an effective Chain essay body.

For example, you might first cite the great number of automobiles in the Los Angeles area (Topic I), then discuss the air pollution which results from their use (Topic II), and finally contrast that condition with the clean air of the region fifty years ago (Topic III).

Or you might first describe nineteenth-century America as a nation of small towns and farms (Topic I), then present a contrasting picture of our present urban society (Topic II), and finally explain the consequences of that change (Topic III).

Here is an essay with its topics arranged in the Chain Pattern:

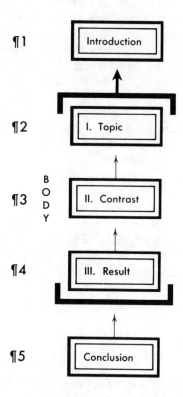

OIL ON TROUBLED WATERS

Sentence Summary:

Oil pollution is doing serious and increasing damage to our nation's coastline.

Outline:

B ¶1 Introduction. Heavy damage to America's coastline
O ¶2 I. Cases of oil pollution formerly rare
D ¶3 II. Cases of oil pollution now frequent
Y ¶4 III. Results of oil pollution extremely serious
   ¶5 Conclusion. Urgent need for adequate remedies

Along the 12,383 miles of United States coastline, oil is being accidentally leaked, spilled, or poured on waters that once were untroubled. The result is a black tide that causes billions of dollars' worth of damage every year.

B O D Y

Until recent years, oil pollution of our coasts was not a serious or frequent problem. There were, of course, occasional accidental leaks from oceangoing vessels, and the crews of some tankers followed the practice of flushing the storage compartments of their ships while at sea. Still, little harm was done, and oil pollution of our nation's shores was rare and relatively unimportant.

Within the past decade, however, oil pollution has become a critical problem. Our growing nation depends upon oil to satisfy about three-fourths of its energy requirements, and our consumption of it has risen nearly 20 per cent in the past five years, to its present level of 600,000,000 gallons per day. As more and more oil is produced, more and more of it gets spilled in our coastal waters. Many of the new jumbo tankers spring minor leaks, and a ship badly damaged in one of the two collisions occurring each week could spill up to 29,000,000 gallons. Likewise, any one of our thousands of offshore oil wells could "blow out" and pour 42,000 gallons or more a day into the sea. Indeed, within a single month, the beaches and waterways in four Florida areas were fouled by oil from storm-damaged tankers, a California bay was closed by oil pollution from a leaking offshore well, and there was an oil slick twelve miles long and a mile wide just off the Louisiana coast as the result of an accident on a drilling platform. The number of *significant* oil spills in American coastal waters is increasing by about 5 per cent each year, and a presidential task force has concluded that by 1980 our nation can expect at least one *disastrous* oil spill annually.

The damage resulting from oil pollution takes many forms. First, there is a vast destruction of wildlife—millions of sea gulls, grebes, and ducks; thousands of schools of fish; countless lobsters, crabs, shrimp, and squid; and even entire beds of oysters on the sea bottom. Second, there is the despoiling of beaches. In 1969, the oil from one leaking offshore well blackened 80 miles of beaches in the Santa Barbara Channel area, and it is estimated that the 284,000,000 gallons spilled annually into all of the world's oceans would be sufficient to coat a beach twenty feet wide with a half-inch layer for 8,633 miles. Finally, there may be long-term effects of oil pollution which will eventually render our planet unfit for human habitation—either by killing the ocean plankton which through photosynthesis produces much of the earth's oxygen, or by changing the thermal reflectivity of the ocean surface and thus altering the earth's average temperature.

There is, then, obviously a need for prompt action to solve the problem of oil pollution. In the first place, scientists must find an effective method of removing the oil already polluting the ocean waters. In the second place, state and federal agencies must tighten their regulations dealing with offshore drilling and the transporting of oil by tanker. Finally, legislative bodies must pass laws containing stiffer penalties for any person or corporation causing oil pollution. If these things are accomplished, perhaps we can eventually eliminate the black tide from our coastal waters. Then we will once again be able to proclaim that America stretches "from sea to shining sea."

B. THE LEAPFROG PATTERN

The *Leapfrog Pattern* consists of a non-sequential series of three or more topics. In other words, one of the topics has a Meaning Relationship with a *previous* topic rather than with the topic immediately preceding it. Thus, two of the topics in a Leapfrog Pattern are linked with the *same* earlier topic.

The kind of subject most often resulting in a Leapfrog arrangement is one about which the writer wishes to present both results *and* causes, or causes *and* results; such subjects would include political terrorism, inflation, the rising divorce rate, and the energy crisis.

Here is an essay with a Leapfrog-Pattern body. As the diagram indicates, the second topic is linked with the first topic through the Meaning Relationship of Result, and the third topic is also linked with the first topic through the Meaning Relationship of Cause:

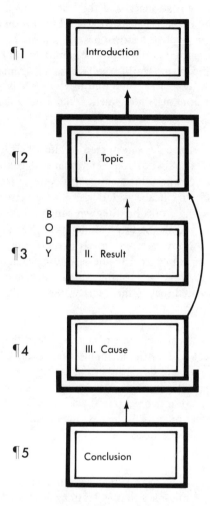

NOR ANY DROP TO DRINK

Sentence Summary:

When dead microorganisms fouled the water in my home town, people had to drink other beverages and modify their bathing habits.

Outline:

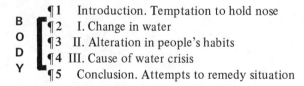

¶1   Introduction. Temptation to hold nose
¶2   I. Change in water
¶3   II. Alteration in people's habits
¶4   III. Cause of water crisis
¶5   Conclusion. Attempts to remedy situation

When you were small, you probably held your nose when you jumped—feet first—into a swimming pool. But have you ever been inclined to hold your nose while taking a bath or, for that matter, while drinking a glass of water? I was surely tempted to do so for several weeks last summer. And, if you had been living in my home town, you would have felt the same way.

About the middle of June, I began to notice a musty odor in the bathroom whenever I turned on the water at the sink. At first it was rather faint, and I therefore didn't pay much attention to it. However, day by day the odor got stronger, and the water also started to taste unpleasant. By the first of July, the odor was unbearable, particularly when I turned on the hot water, and the taste was nauseating. Everyone in our family had his own description of the water. I thought it smelled like rotten cabbage that had lain forgotten in the vegetable compartment of a refrigerator. My father, who was a soldier in the South Pacific during World War Two, said it reminded him of the odor of decayed vegetation and mud in a New Guinea swamp. And my younger brother, whose imagination works overtime, announced that our drinking water smelled like a soup made by boiling a pound of Limburger cheese, a pair of moldy old tennis shoes, and a couple of Egyptian mummies.

B **O** **D** **Y**   As a result of the foul water, people were forced to alter their habits. In the first place, nobody drank water. Since tea and coffee could not completely camouflage the taste and smell, many persons turned to milk. In fact, the editor of our local newspaper commented that a cow was the only filtering system that had proved effective in the water crisis. Some persons consumed large quantities of soft drinks, since the local bottling works had its own supply of pure water from deep wells. I suppose, too, that some citizens obeyed the Scriptural injunction, "Drink no longer water, but use a little wine for thy stomach's sake." At any rate, we all felt like Coleridge's Ancient Mariner—with water, water everywhere, "nor any drop to drink." In the second place, most people gave up hot baths and showers, which made them smell worse after bathing than they had beforehand. Some persons settled for cold showers and heavily scented soap. Others just washed as seldom as possible and used lots of body cologne.

According to the state public-health officers who investigated the case, the cause of our bad water was countless billions of dead bacteria, fungi, molds, and algae. Of course, those same microorganisms are always present, but they are usually there in far smaller numbers than they were last summer. For some reason which is still a mystery, last June they multiplied beyond all normal limits in the waters of the reservoir—a sort of microbial population explosion. When the water company treated the contaminated water, chlorination did kill them. However, the purification process did not remove their remains; and, as the myriads of little cells disintegrated, they gave our drinking water a foul smell and taste. It was safe to drink—but it was far from drinkable.

For nearly six weeks the water company tried everything possible to remedy the situation—extra chemicals, prolonged aeration, additional filtering. Nothing worked. Then in August there was a week of torrential rains, and suddenly the crisis was over. The heavy rains had flushed the impure water from the reservoir. They say that you never miss the water until the well runs dry. I can testify that you also miss it when it becomes unfit for human use. Certainly, no one in my home town will ever again take pure, sweet water for granted.

DO EXERCISE 43

11

The Essay: Expanded Patterns

In the basic essay-body patterns which we studied in Chapters 6 through 10, each main topic (or main point) was developed by one—and only one—paragraph. Now we shall examine *expanded essay-body patterns*. In these, at least one of the main topics is subdivided into two or more *subtopics* (or subpoints), each of which employs a paragraph for its development.

As its name suggests, an expanded pattern is always longer than the corresponding basic pattern. Obviously, if each main division of an essay body is a single paragraph, that essay must necessarily be shorter than a similar essay in which at least one main division of the body consists of two or more paragraphs.

Sometimes the use of two or more paragraphs to develop a main topic is due to the breadth of that topic. For instance, in a long essay dealing with organized crime, one main topic might be devoted to illegal gambling. Since this topic is quite broad, it might be subdivided into a number of subtopics dealing with the various kinds of illegal gambling, with each subtopic requiring a separate paragraph for its development.

At other times, the use of two or more paragraphs to develop a main topic is due to the writer's wish to present a detailed treatment of his subject. For instance, in a long essay dealing with the oil pollution of America's coastal waters, one main body topic might be concerned with developing the idea that the results of the oil pollution are extremely serious. In a short essay, this topic could be developed in a single paragraph (see page 138). But in a long essay, a separate paragraph might be devoted to each kind of result. Thus, there could be a paragraph on the destruction of wildlife, a second paragraph on the damage to beaches and other property, and a third paragraph on the additional long-term harmful effects.

If two or more paragraphs are used to develop the subtopics of a single main topic, they form a *paragraph cluster*. In this chapter we shall first become familiar with the varieties of paragraph clusters which can occur in expanded essay-body patterns. Next, we shall examine two ways of handling the topic and subtopic statements in a paragraph cluster. Finally, we shall see how a writer can progress from an accurate outline to a successful long essay with an expanded body pattern.

A. VARIETIES OF PARAGRAPH CLUSTERS

In Chapter 4 we learned that a cluster of independent clauses must belong to one of five classes: the Enumerative Cluster, the Equal-Pair Cluster, the Unequal-Pair Cluster, the Chain Cluster, or the Leapfrog Cluster. In similar fashion, a paragraph cluster must belong to one of the following classes: the *Enumerative Paragraph Cluster*, the *Equal-Pair Paragraph Cluster,* the *Unequal-Pair Paragraph Cluster,* the *Chain Paragraph Cluster,* or the *Leapfrog Paragraph Cluster.*

We can diagram the five varieties of paragraph clusters as follows, showing each as it would appear if functioning as the first topic of an expanded essay body:

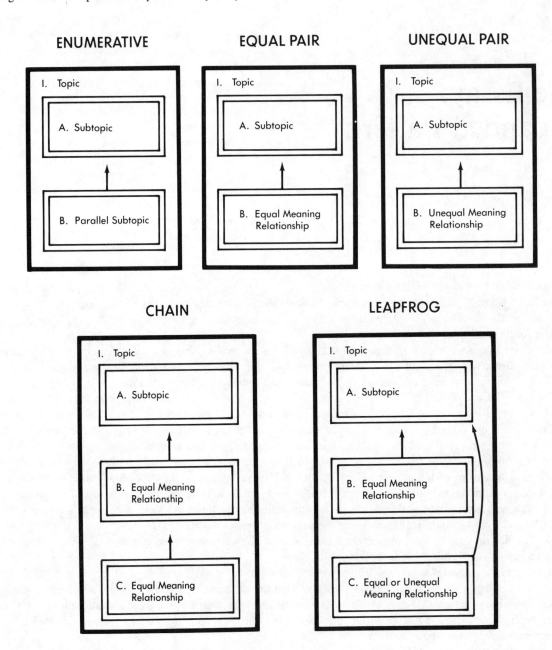

Note that the pattern within each cluster is essentially the same as that for the corresponding type of basic essay body.

We can best illustrate the relationship between the five basic essay-body patterns and the five varieties of paragraph clusters by showing the actual conversion of one to the other. In Chapter 9 we studied a short essay on "Mamie's Parrot Fever" which had a two-paragraph body treating a topic and its cause. It was accompanied by this outline:

B ¶1   Introduction. Unreliability of ancient proverb concerning dogs
O ┌¶2   I. Surprising change in behavior
D └¶3   II. Violent jealousy toward parrot
Y   ¶4   Conclusion. Member of new class of dogs

The two main topics which form the body of that short essay can be converted to two subtopics of a longer essay with an expanded body. Re-read the essay on page 130 and then examine the following:

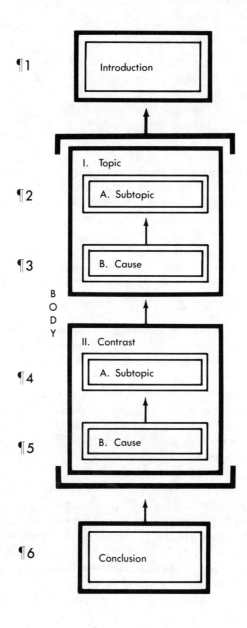

OLD DOGS AND NEW TRICKS

Sentence Summary:

My dog Mamie and my friend Lou's dog Miss Droopy have reacted differently to similar situations.

Outline:

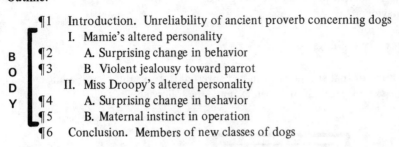

¶1   Introduction. Unreliability of ancient proverb concerning dogs

I. Mamie's altered personality

¶2   A. Surprising change in behavior

¶3   B. Violent jealousy toward parrot

II. Miss Droopy's altered personality

¶4   A. Surprising change in behavior

¶5   B. Maternal instinct in operation

¶6   Conclusion. Members of new classes of dogs

According to an ancient saying, one cannot teach an old dog new tricks. I am not quite certain what that proverb means; but, if it implies that old dogs get so set in their ways that they cannot adopt new habit patterns, then I must dissent vigorously. For I am acquainted with an elderly terrier and an aged basset which have recently undergone changes as startling as Dr. Jekyll's celebrated transformation into Mr. Hyde. Those changes represent very different reactions to similar situations.

First, consider the altered personality of my dog Mamie, a venerable Manchester terrier twelve years old. During the past two months, Mamie has acquired a new disposition. Prior to that time, she was a lazy and placid little beast. So fat she could hardly waddle around the house, she nevertheless had a finicky appetite and left her food untouched. She slept most of the day but could not reach her favorite snoozing place, the sofa, without help—someone always had to lift her up. And she greeted all comers with a friendly wag of the tail. Now, however, Mamie is both alert and aggressive. No longer overweight, she gobbles her food with wolf-like eagerness but still stays in fighting trim. She never seems to sleep but restlessly roams the house day and night. She hops up on the sofa without difficulty, and I have even caught her atop the kitchen table. Worst of all, she snarls at strangers and even barks irritably at members of our family.

The reason for my dog's surprising metamorphosis is quite simple: she is violently jealous of Pete, the little half-moon parrot my sister acquired recently. Mamie is consumed with a smoldering resentment which periodically bursts into a flame of pure hatred. We call it "Mamie's parrot fever," and its symptoms are readily observable. When Pete eats sunflower seeds, Mamie also insists upon munching on a seed, apparently convinced that parrot food must be a special treat. When Pete is in his cage, Mamie sits nearby for hours at a time, directing an unwavering, baleful stare at him. When Pete flies around the house, Mamie stalks him with a murderous intensity that would do credit to the most bloodthirsty tomcat. And, when Pete perches on my shoulder and croaks softly in my ear, Mamie dances up and down in insane rage, yelping hysterically.

Although Pete's arrival at our home has apparently stirred up Mamie's worst instincts, a similar situation has produced a very different kind of altered behavior on the part of Miss Droopy, an ancient basset hound belonging to my friend Lou. Nearly fourteen years old, Miss Droopy had reached the age where she had only one interest in life: sleeping in some warm, sunny spot. With her doddering gait and continual sad expression, she looked like a senile alcoholic enduring a perpetual hangover. Several months ago, however, this old basset hound contracted a severe and lingering case of maternal instinct. Now she tries to be a mother to everything that moves and is smaller than she is. She recently adopted a stray kitten and attempted to raise it. Before that, she found a sick baby squirrel somewhere and brought it back to her doghouse, where she fussed over it all day, and even attempted to nurse it—a gesture which, although appropriately symbolic, was completely futile. On several occasions, she has tried to stalk a young cottontail rabbit in Lou's back yard, and I am sure that she was motivated by mother love rather than hunger. Most startling of all, last week she went exploring in the woods and returned with a baby skunk, apparently with the intention of raising it to be a fine, upstanding dog. If every dog does, indeed, have its day, Miss Droopy must think that hers is Mother's Day.

The reason for this sudden upsurge of maternal instinct is rather surprising: Lou's younger brother acquired a pet baby duck at Easter. At first, Miss Droopy eyed the fluffy little intruder with melancholy disdain. Then, a tiny spark of sentiment began to glow amidst the cold ashes of her ancient heart. Heaving herself to her feet, she tottered over to the little duck and began to lick it. Before that day was over, the duckling was eating dog food from Miss Droopy's own dish, and that night they slept together, with the baby duck snuggled up beneath one of the dog's long ears. Their close relationship has continued. Although the duck is now half grown, Miss Droopy still keeps a fond, maternal eye on it as it marches around the yard, quacking and ruffling its feathers.

Sometimes I suspect that Mamie and Miss Droopy belong to two classes of dogs which have been hitherto unrecognized. With regard to Mamie, the evidence is clear. She has been so vocal in her dislike of Pete that the first word the little parrot has learned to say, imitating my sister and me, is, "Shut up, Mamie!" Therefore, although many persons can claim they own bird dogs, I am unique in possessing what is obviously an anti-bird dog. With regard to Miss Droopy, the situation is a bit more complicated, for the American Kennel Club has duly certified that Miss Droopy is a registered basset hound. Personally, I think somebody has made an error in classifying her. Since she is constantly trying to snuggle baby creatures of every species imaginable, it seems to me she is actually a bassinet hound. At any rate, both Miss Droopy and Mamie have demonstrated one thing: they may be old dogs, but they certainly have shown themselves capable of learning new "tricks."

If you compare "Old Dogs and New Tricks" with "Mamie's Parrot Fever" (pages 129-30), you will discover that the entire body of the short essay functions as the first main topic (with two subtopics) of the expanded essay body you have just finished studying. Except for a single difference, the two passages are identical. That one difference, however, is of great significance. When the two main topics of the short essay become subtopics in the longer essay, the main topic which results has no topic statement to express it explicitly. Therefore, the author of "Old Dogs and New Tricks" has inserted a new topic statement at the beginning of the first paragraph in the passage: "First, consider the altered personality of my dog Mamie, a venerable Manchester terrier twelve years old."

The addition of this topic statement greatly increases the clarity of the whole paragraph cluster, for the reader quickly grasps the main idea of the passage and is therefore better able to understand both the significance of the two subtopic statements and the purpose of the general development material in the two paragraphs.

Since the topic statements and subtopic statements are of key importance in any essay, the next section of this chapter will treat in some detail the two chief ways of handling these statements in a paragraph cluster. When you have studied it, re-examine the "Old Dogs and New Tricks" essay and ask yourself which method has been employed.

B. TOPIC STATEMENTS AND SUBTOPIC STATEMENTS

In Chapter 5, while studying paragraph structure, we learned that every paragraph contains a central idea which is usually expressed in a topic statement.

As applied to the paragraph, the term "topic statement" is appropriate when the paragraph in question is an isolated one, considered by itself. Moreover, it is equally appropriate when the paragraph in question functions within one of the five basic patterns of body development, in which each main topic of the essay body is developed by one (and only one) paragraph.

On the other hand, when a main division of an expanded essay body consists of two or more paragraphs, the central idea of each individual paragraph constitutes a *subtopic statement*. And the *topic statement* is the clause which expresses the central idea of the *entire group of subtopic paragraphs*.

Since each individual paragraph is devoted to the development of a subtopic statement, a question immediately arises concerning the best way of handling the topic statement: Where should it be located? There are two common ways of solving this problem. It is possible either to *absorb* the topic statement into the first subtopic paragraph or to *detach* the topic statement from the subtopics and present it as a separate paragraph. Thus, there may be an *absorbed topic statement* or a *detached topic statement*. We can diagram these constructions as follows:

ABSORBED TOPIC STATEMENT

(Topic Statement) _____

_____ . *(First Subtopic Statement)* _____

¶1 _____ . (Development of First Subtopic) _ _ _ _ _

_ _

_ _

_ _

(Second Subtopic Statement) _____

_____ . (Development of Second Subtopic) _ _ _ _

¶2 _

_ _

_ _

DETACHED TOPIC STATEMENT

(Topic Statement) _____

¶1 _____

_____

(First Subtopic Statement) _____

_____ . (Development of First Subtopic) _ _ _ _ _

¶2 _

_ _

_ _

(Second Subtopic Statement) _____

_____ . (Development of Second Subtopic) _ _ _ _

¶3 _

_ _

1. THE ABSORBED TOPIC STATEMENT

Of the two common varieties of topic statement which may occur in an expanded body pattern, the more common is the *absorbed topic statement.*

Let us suppose that a writer has produced the following paragraph:

> Every corporation may be placed in one of two classes on the basis of who owns its stock. In a close corporation, most or all of the stock is owned by a small number of persons, perhaps by members of a single family. On the other hand, in an open corporation, the stock is made available to the general public.

In this brief paragraph, the first independent clause functions as the topic statement, and the rest of the paragraph consists of development material. We can indicate its structure by printing the topic statement in boldface type and the development material in italics:

> **Every corporation may be placed in one of two classes on the basis of who owns its stock.** *In a close corporation, most or all of the stock is owned by a small number of persons, perhaps by members of a single family. On the other hand, in an open corporation, the stock is made available to the general public.*

Perhaps the writer decides that he should treat his material more fully. He may then produce the following paragraph. Note what happens to the development material of the original version:

> **Every corporation may be placed in one of two classes on the basis of who owns its stock.** *In a close corporation, most or all of the stock is owned by a small number of persons, perhaps by members of a single family.* For example, since most states require a corporation to have at least three stockholders, the stock of a drugstore organized as a close corporation might be distributed as follows: the druggist's wife, one share; some other member of the family, or the druggist's attorney, one share; the druggist himself, all the remaining shares. Obviously, for all practical purposes the druggist owns and controls his business. *On the other hand, in an open corporation, the stock is made available to the general public.* For example, the stock of such corporations as General Motors, United States Steel, American Airlines, General Electric, Sears Roebuck, International Business Machines, General Mills, or International Telephone and Telegraph is owned by thousands of persons. Moreover, the identities of the stockholders change constantly as shares are bought and sold, and the average small stockholder has no voice at all in company policy.

If this long paragraph seems awkward to the writer, he may decide to place each subtopic in a separate paragraph. But what, then, is to be done with the topic statement? Since it is relatively short, the best solution is to place it at the beginning of the first subtopic paragraph. The resulting paragraph, with its absorbed topic statement, would then read as follows:

> **Every corporation may be placed in one of two classes on the basis of who owns its stock.** *In a close corporation, most or all of the stock is owned by a small number of persons, perhaps by members of a single family.* For example, since most states require a corporation to have at least three stockholders, the stock of a drugstore organized as a close corporation might be distributed as follows: the druggist's wife, one share; some other member of the family, or the druggist's attorney, one share; the druggist himself, all the remaining shares. Obviously, for all practical purposes the druggist owns and controls his business.
>
> *On the other hand, in an open corporation, the stock is made available to the general public.* For example, the stock of such corporations as General Motors, United States Steel, American Airlines, General Electric, Sears Roebuck, International Business Machines, General Mills, or International Telephone and Telegraph is owned by thousands of persons. Moreover, the identities of the stock-

holders change constantly as shares are bought and sold, and the average small stockholder has no voice at all in company policy.

You will note that the preceding passage is easy to understand. The short paragraphs promote ready comprehension of the writer's message, and the structure of the passage also helps to make clear the relationships among the various ideas which are presented. Moreover, the topic statement blends smoothly into the initial paragraph and does not seem out of place. As a general rule, you will find the absorbed topic statement easy to use and effective in expressing your ideas.

2. THE DETACHED TOPIC STATEMENT

If the topic statement is long, or if there is development material which relates to it rather than to any of the subtopic statements, a writer may wish to employ a *detached topic statement.*

In this type of structure, the writer places the topic statement by itself in the initial paragraph of a passage and then devotes an additional paragraph to each of the subtopics. For example, suppose that the discussion of corporations which we have just examined contained an explanation of various kinds of stocks. It would then be very difficult to blend the topic statement into the first subtopic paragraph. Instead, the writer would probably employ a detached topic statement:

> **Every corporation may be placed in one of two classes on the basis of who owns its stock, those shares of ownership the company sells to raise capital which entitle the holder to dividends and to other rights of proprietorship.** A corporation may issue both common and preferred stock. Each has ownership rights, but the preferred normally has prior claim on dividends and, in the event of liquidation, on a share of the company assets.

> *In a close corporation, most or all of the stock is owned by a small number of persons, perhaps by members of a single family.* For example, since most states require a corporation to have at least three stockholders, the stock of a drugstore organized as a close corporation might be distributed as follows: the druggist's wife, one share; some other member of the family, or the druggist's attorney, one share; the druggist himself, all the remaining shares. Obviously, for all practical purposes the druggist owns and controls his business.

> *On the other hand, in an open corporation, the stock is made available to the general public.* For example, the stock of such corporations as General Motors, United States Steel, American Airlines, General Electric, Sears Roebuck, International Business Machines, General Mills, or International Telephone and Telegraph is owned by thousands of persons. Moreover, the identities of the stockholders change constantly as shares are bought and sold, and the average small stockholder has no voice at all in company policy.

As the preceding sample passage illustrates, the detached topic statement is often a very effective pattern. Nevertheless, when you write an essay which has an expanded body pattern, you should ordinarily prefer the absorbed topic statement and employ the detached variety only when it is not possible to blend the topic statement into the first subtopic paragraph.

C. PROGRESSING FROM ACCURATE OUTLINE TO SUCCESSFUL ESSAY

In Chapter 6 you learned the importance of constructing an accurate and well-organized formal outline before attempting actually to write your essay.

Now, note the ease with which you can proceed from outline to essay structure by using the following pattern:

SKELETON OUTLINE OF ESSAY BODY

  I. Topic One
    A. Subtopic A
    B. Subtopic B
 II. Topic Two
    A. Subtopic A
    B. Subtopic B

SKELETON ESSAY BODY

[I.] **(Topic Statement One)** _____

_____ . [A.] *(Subtopic Statement A)* _____

¶1 _____ . (Development of Subtopic A) _ _ _ _ _ _

_ _

_ _

[B.] *(Subtopic Statement B)* _____

_____ . (Development of Subtopic B) _ _ _ _ _ _

¶2 _

_ _

[II.] **(Topic Statement Two)** _____

_____ . [A.] *(Subtopic Statement A)* _____

¶3 _____ . (Development of Subtopic A) _ _ _ _ _ _

_ _

_ _

[B.] *(Subtopic Statement B)* _____

_____ . (Development of Subtopic B) _ _ _ _ _ _

¶4 _

_ _

As you can see, the preceding pattern is for an essay with absorbed topic statements. Since the expanded essay body containing absorbed topic statements is one of the most useful patterns which you can master, we shall end our study of expository prose by examining a complete essay organized in this fashion.

Here is an essay containing three examples of the absorbed topic statement. It happens to be an Enumerative essay, but this variety of expansion could be applied to any of the five essay-body patterns we have studied. In the diagram, note that the label "Absorbed Topic Statement," set off by a dotted line, is used to indicate an absorbed topic statement. In the body of the essay itself, topic statements appear in boldface type, subtopic statements in italics. In addition, marginal notations indicate the paragraph numbers, the topic and subtopic labels, and the material used to develop each subtopic. However, the customary heavy marginal brackets indicating the essay body are omitted. Study the essay carefully:

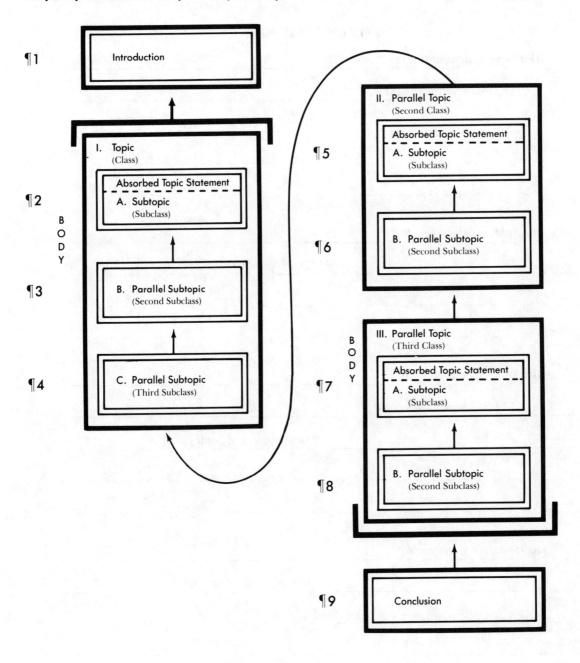

THE HAPPIEST PLACE ON EARTH

Sentence Summary:

The attractions at Disneyland are of three kinds: those appealing to the visitor's imagination and love of adventure, those appealing to his nostalgic fondness for the past, and those appealing to his curiosity about the future.

Outline:

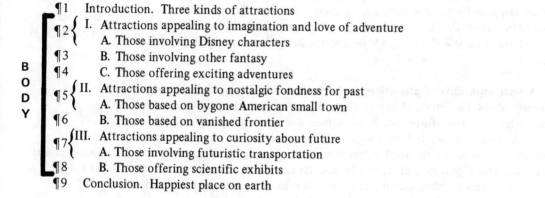

B
O
D
Y

¶1   Introduction. Three kinds of attractions
¶2   I. Attractions appealing to imagination and love of adventure
         A. Those involving Disney characters
¶3   B. Those involving other fantasy
¶4   C. Those offering exciting adventures
¶5   II. Attractions appealing to nostalgic fondness for past
         A. Those based on bygone American small town
¶6   B. Those based on vanished frontier
¶7   III. Attractions appealing to curiosity about future
         A. Those involving futuristic transportation
¶8   B. Those offering scientific exhibits
¶9   Conclusion. Happiest place on earth

¶1   In 1960 Premier Nikita Khrushchev of the Soviet Union threw a temper tantrum when he was refused permission to go to Disneyland. In 1975 Emperor Hirohito of Japan insisted on visiting the park during his tour of the United States. Since Disneyland opened in 1955, thousands of world-famous figures and millions of ordinary persons have passed through its gates. The exciting attractions which drew them there are of three kinds: those appealing to the visitor's imagination and love of adventure, those appealing to his nostalgic fondness for the past, and those appealing to his curiosity about the future.

I
A
¶2   **Perhaps the most enticing attractions are those which appeal to the visitor's imagination and love of adventure.** *Some of these feature well-known Disney characters.* Actors dressed as Mickey Mouse, Goofy, Donald Duck, the Three Little Pigs, and other cartoon characters stroll around Disneyland streets. The visitor can inspect Sleeping Beauty's castle, ride in a giant tea cup from the Mad Tea Party, witness Snow White's scary adventures, go aboard Captain Hook's pirate ship, ride on the flying elephant Dumbo, or watch Tinker Bell fly through the summer night sky.   Development of Subtopic A

B
¶3   *Other attractions draw upon fantasy not rooted in Disney cartoons.* The visitor can tour a haunted mansion in which chills and chuckles alternate as monsters scowl and playful spooks cavort. He can listen and watch as full-sized automated bears make jokes, sing, and play musical instruments in a jamboree of country music. Or he can sit quietly and be serenaded by tropical flowers and birds which sing with human voices.   Development of Subtopic B

C
¶4   The Walt Disney organization is well aware that every child craves excitement, and that every adult is a child at heart. *Therefore, another group of attractions appeals to the visitor's love of adventure.* He can cruise down a jungle river and see hippos, crocodiles, elephants, lions, gorillas, and even cannibals. He can watch Caribbean pirates sack a coastal town. Or he can plunge down the Matterhorn on a bobsled.   Development of Subtopic C

II
A

¶5

A second main class of attractions includes those which appeal to the visitor's nostalgic fondness for the past. *Many of these attempt to recreate life as earlier generations of small-town Americans knew it.* The visitor can stroll down Main Street as it was during the 1890's. He can ride in a horse-drawn street car, in a horseless carriage, or on an old-fashioned train. He can watch silent movies. Indeed, he can even meet President Lincoln and listen to him deliver a brief address.

Development of Subtopic A

B

¶6

Other attractions reproduce the thrilling sights and sounds of the vanished frontier. The visitor can board a stern-wheel steamboat for a trip past replicas of an Indian camp and a burning settler's log cabin. He can ride on a Mike Fink keel boat or in a Davy Crockett canoe. He can hop on a creaky little mine train for a tour of the Rainbow Caverns. Or he can try his luck in an Old West shooting gallery.

Development of Subtopic B

III
A

¶7

A final main class of attractions includes those which appeal to the visitor's curiosity about the future. *Many of them are concerned with futuristic forms of transportation.* The visitor can board a monorail train which glides noiselessly along an elevated concrete "beamway." He can travel underwater in a "nuclear" submarine, listening to recorded ocean sounds and looking out a porthole at animated fish and a graveyard of wrecked ships. He can ride a rocket jet which whirls at a dizzying speed. Most exciting of all, he can even take a cleverly simulated trip to the moon which will make him feel like an apprentice astronaut.

Development of Subtopic A

B

¶8

In addition, there are exhibits designed to make the visitor more aware of the other wonders of science. He can visit aeronautical, electronic, and industrial displays of things to come. Indeed, he can even take a journey into the heart of the atom. When one visits the Tomorrowland section of the park, he gains a better understanding of Walt Disney's comment that he enjoyed the past but lived for the future.

Development of Subtopic B

¶9

Although it occupies an area of less than 3,000 acres, Disneyland is a park which can kindle the imagination and make the pulse race with excitement. Moreover, it allows the visitor to enjoy both the past and the future. No wonder millions of people continue to enter the Magic Kingdom, which well deserves its reputation as "the Happiest Place on Earth."

A careful examination of "The Happiest Place on Earth" will illustrate the use of topic statements and subtopic statements, as well as the use of Transitional Elements to join topics and subtopics:

Paragraph 2. The first sentence is the absorbed topic statement for Topic I; it contains the Transitional Element *most enticing,* which points forward to Topics II and III. The second sentence is the subtopic statement for Subtopic A. The remainder of the paragraph is a development of Subtopic A.

Paragraph 3. The first sentence is the subtopic statement for Subtopic B; it contains the Transitional Element *other,* which points back to Subtopic A. The remainder of the paragraph is a development of Subtopic B.

Paragraph 4. The second sentence is the subtopic statement for Subtopic C; it contains the Transitional Element *another,* which points back to Subtopics A and B. The remainder of the paragraph is a development of Subtopic C.

Paragraph 5. The first sentence is the absorbed topic statement for Topic II; it contains the Transitional Element *second,* which points back to Topic I. The second sentence is the subtopic statement for Subtopic A. The remainder of the paragraph is a development of Subtopic A.

Paragraph 6. The first sentence is the subtopic statement for Subtopic B; it contains the Transitional Element *other,* which points back to Subtopic A. The remainder of the paragraph is a development of Subtopic B.

Paragraph 7. The first sentence is the absorbed topic statement for Topic III; it contains the Transitional Element *final,* which points back to Topics I and II. The second sentence is the subtopic statement for Subtopic A. The remainder of the paragraph is a development of Subtopic A.

Paragraph 8. The first sentence is the subtopic statement for Subtopic B; it contains the Transitional Element *in addition,* which points back to Subtopic A. The remainder of the paragraph is a development of Subtopic B.

With this discussion of expanded essay-body patterns, our examination of expository prose comes to an end. In the first chapter of this text you discovered that good prose is a logical sequence of related ideas, and everything you have studied since that time has been designed to increase your skill in organizing your ideas into logical, coherent patterns of thought.

First, you practiced connecting one independent clause with another independent clause through the use of Meaning Relationships and Linking Devices. Next, you became familiar with the five basic patterns of prose. Then, you took up materials of increasing complexity and learned to write clusters, paragraphs, and short essays incorporating the basic patterns of body development. Finally, you have become acquainted with expanded essay-body patterns. When you have mastered these expanded patterns, you should be able to plan and compose well-organized, clear, and effective long essays. Then you will have achieved the goal of this book: you will be able to write good expository prose.

DO EXERCISE 44

EXERCISES 157

APPENDIX: Punctuation and Mechanics 259

Exercise 1
MEANING RELATIONSHIPS

By writing "Yes" or "No" in the blank, indicate whether there is a Meaning Relationship linking each pair of independent clauses below.

1. _____ Meanwhile, American intelligence experts had achieved a major victory. They had "cracked" the Japanese code.

2. _____ Many vegetables reach the table minus valuable vitamins because of improper preparation. Baking powder is a leavening which produces the carbon dioxide necessary to make dough rise.

3. _____ A study of ancient civilizations reveals much about our present civilization. Furthermore, President Wilson repeatedly urged the formation of an international council of nations.

4. _____ When Mark Twain began writing a story, he usually had no idea how it would end. However, he composed the final episode of *A Connecticut Yankee* before working out the rest of the plot.

5. _____ Not all baby birds are helpless nestlings. For example, Australian bush turkeys are fully fledged when hatched and can therefore fly as soon as they emerge from the shell.

6. _____ The popular musical comedy *My Fair Lady* is based upon Shaw's play *Pygmalion*. Richard Armour and Phyllis McGinley, for instance, are outstanding writers of light verse.

7. _____ Sensory nerves carry impulses *to* the central nervous system from the various parts of the body; motor nerves carry impulses *from* the central nervous system to the muscles and glands.

8. _____ The great increase in scientific and technical research makes it difficult to find out whether any particular experiment has already been carried out. Nevertheless, a scientist will usually earn much more money in industry than he will in a university.

9. _____ The jazz pianist played "How High the Moon." Consequently, the automobile industry is rather slow to change its ideas of what a car should look like.

10. _____ Many scientists are becoming interested in exobiology. This is the study of life that may exist beyond the earth.

Exercise 2
REPETITION AND PRONOUN REFERENCE

In each pair of independent clauses below, identify the Linking Device involving Repetition or Pronoun Reference.

First, underline the *single* word in the second clause which is most closely linked with the italicized word or word-group in the first clause. *Select only one word.*

Second, indicate whether that word is a Linking Device involving Repetition or a Linking Device involving Pronoun Reference by writing in the appropriate column the single word that you have underlined.

Repetition	Pronoun Reference	
1. _____	_____	*Football* requires weight, power, and ruggedness. Basketball demands height, speed, and stamina.
2. _____	_____	Ben trudged out to the barnyard to feed the *livestock*. Hearing footsteps, the old sow grunted eagerly, heaved herself to her feet, and waddled over to the feed trough.
3. _____	_____	*Huck Finn* was startled to discover the smoking ashes of a campfire. He realized that someone else must be on the island.
4. _____	_____	At the end of World War II, the *United States* was the unquestioned mistress of the seas. The American fleet was the most powerful naval force the world had ever known.
5. _____	_____	The *fountain pen* was no good. The point was broken.
6. _____	_____	The *teacher* knew that Bobby was the culprit. When she looked at him, he hung his head and blushed furiously.
7. _____	_____	*Women* are showing increased interest in the legal profession. During the past decade, the number of women lawyers in the United States has more than doubled.
8. _____	_____	The ordinary *cumulus cloud* has a rounded top; the thunderhead has a flattened top resembling an anvil.
9. _____	_____	Perhaps the most common foot in English poetry is the *iambic*. It consists of an unstressed syllable followed by a stressed syllable.

Repetition **Pronoun Reference**

10. _____ _____ Betty likes to eat *persimmons* fresh from the tree. I much prefer persimmon pudding.

Exercise 3
PARALLELISM

Examine the following pairs of clauses and use the specified abbreviations to indicate whether the clauses show *Desirable Parallelism* (P), *Lack of Parallelism* (L), or *False Parallelism* (FP).

1. _____ I like the teacher, but I am not liked by him.

2. _____ The cook first cuts the chicken into serving pieces and browns them in six tablespoons of butter. She then covers the pan tightly and continues to cook them over a low flame for thirty minutes.

3. _____ The President's speech dealt primarily with foreign policy, but certain domestic issues were also touched on briefly by him.

4. _____ Sara Johnson is a senior in the College of Liberal Arts and Sciences, and she is Homecoming Queen.

5. _____ Did the last shipment arrive on time? Did it arrive in good condition?

6. _____ Check the compression of all the cylinders. Then inspect the spark plugs and distributor points.

7. _____ Heroin is a drug derived from the opium poppy, and it is a dangerous, habit-forming drug.

8. _____ The first step would be to enforce all traffic laws strictly. Requiring that all applicants for a driver's license pass a rigorous driving test would be the next step.

9. _____ The Norway rat has a tail shorter than its head and body; a tail longer than its head and body is characteristic of the black rat.

10. _____ Zachary Taylor was the twelfth President of the United States, and he was a Whig.

Name _____ Section _____

Date _____ Grade _____

Exercise 4

NOUNS SUMMARIZING PREVIOUS ASSERTIONS
AND MEANING LINKS

In each pair of independent clauses below, identify the Noun Summarizing a Previous Assertion or the Meaning Link.

First, underline the *single* word in the second clause which functions as a Noun Summarizing a Previous Assertion or as a Meaning Link. *Select only one word.*

Second, indicate whether that word is a Noun Summarizing a Previous Assertion or a Meaning Link by writing in the appropriate column the single word that you have underlined.

Noun Summarizing a Previous Assertion	Meaning Link	
1. _____	_____	Scientists estimate that throughout the universe the ratio of hydrogen to helium is 10 to 1, but in the atmosphere of the planet Jupiter the ratio is only 3 to 1.
2. _____	_____	My grandfather somehow became convinced that the grapefruit is a cross between an orange and a lemon. He clung stubbornly to that mistaken idea for the rest of his life.
3. _____	_____	When he was running for Governor, he repeatedly stated that he would give homeowners relief from high property taxes. He has not carried out that promise.
4. _____	_____	I had often warned my brother against missing class; he therefore had no excuse for failing the course.
5. _____	_____	The African lungfish, which has an airbladder "lung" as well as gills, comes to the surface at frequent intervals in order to breathe air. Behaving quite differently, the Australian lungfish rises to breathe air only occasionally.
6. _____	_____	Most college students choose electives closely related to their major fields. Employers, however, prefer to hire people with broad educational backgrounds.

Noun Summarizing a Previous Assertion	Meaning Link	
7. _____	_____	One nineteenth-century scholar insisted that Shakespeare was actually a woman. This theory has at present very few supporters.
8. _____	_____	Socrates' friends had bribed the jailers. Consequently, he could have escaped from prison without any difficulty.
9. _____	_____	I had a splitting headache; so I decided not to watch television.
10. _____	_____	American frontiersmen thought that bears hug their enemies to death; naturalists know that this belief has no basis in fact.

Exercise 5
MEANING LINKS POINTING BACKWARD

Rewrite the *second sentence* of each pair below, inserting a Meaning Link selected from the list in the margin. In every instance, use the Meaning Link which is most appropriate. Place the Meaning Link in such a position that it will fit smoothly into the sentence; your grade will be lowered if your sentence is awkward. Underline the Meaning Link in the rewritten sentence.

1. He failed to slow down for the curve. He lost control of his car, skidded into the wrong lane, and collided head-on with a trailer truck.

as a result
for example
however
nevertheless
yet

_____

_____

_____

2. Robert may have left high school in order to help support his widowed mother. He may have quit because of his dislike for school discipline.

after all
consequently
in fact
on the other
  hand
therefore

_____

_____

_____

3. A person who has just finished a big dinner doesn't want more food. A brook trout won't display any interest in a lure if it isn't hungry.

as a result
for instance
however
in fact
similarly

_____

_____

_____

4. My cousin Agatha always "speaks her mind" bluntly. She has very few friends.

again
consequently
for example
on the other
  hand
yet

_____

_____

_____

5. The meaning of a word can change drastically. The adjective *lurid,* which once meant "pale or wan," now means "shining with a fiery or harshly vivid glare."

also
for example
furthermore
however
on the
    contrary

_____

_____

_____

6. Present parking facilities in the central business district are hopelessly inadequate. The Chamber of Commerce has urged that the city administration build a large high-rise parking garage in the heart of the downtown shopping area.

for example
likewise
nevertheless
therefore
yet

_____

_____

_____

7. I rarely eat any breakfast. My brother always starts the day by consuming fruit juice, cereal, bacon, two eggs, toast, milk, and coffee—plus a stack of wheatcakes, if he is really hungry.

consequently
for instance
likewise
on the other
    hand
similarly

_____

_____

_____

8. Look up the spelling of all words about which you have any doubts. Check your punctuation carefully.

as a result
as a matter
    of fact
however
nevertheless
next

_____

_____

_____

9. Today, any ship can travel freely on the high seas. The spaceships of all nations will someday have an equal right to navigate the vacuum of outer space.

for example
in fact
nevertheless
similarly
yet

_____

_____

_____

Exercise 5 (continued)

Name _____

after all
for example
in addition
specifically
that is

10. Each volume in the series costs $8.75. There is a small charge to cover the cost of handling and mailing.

_____

_____

_____

Name _____   Section _____

Date _____   Grade _____

Exercise 6
RELATED ACTION AND PARALLEL IDEA

First, in the left-hand column indicate the Meaning Relationship linking each pair of independent clauses below. In every instance it will be the relationship of the *second* clause to the *first*. Your choices in this exercise are Related Action and Parallel Idea. If neither of these Meaning Relationships is present, write "Neither" in the left-hand column.

Second, examine each pair of independent clauses below to see whether a Meaning Link is present (this Meaning Link may consist of more than one word). Underline the Meaning Link, and then write it in the right-hand column. Be sure that this word or word-group is a *Meaning Link*—not some other type of Linking Device. If no Meaning Link is present, write "None" in the right-hand column. No pair of clauses contains more than one Meaning Link.

Meaning Relationship	Meaning Link	
1. _____	_____	My sister has very little knowledge of foreign affairs. Furthermore, she usually misinterprets what little information she has.
2. _____	_____	I need a new bicycle. My old one is completely worn out.
3. _____	_____	Lord Byron did not have a particularly profound knowledge of politics. Moreover, he did not have any desire to learn anything about political fundamentals.
4. _____	_____	Depress the gas pedal to the floor for an instant. Then release it, stopping when the pedal is halfway up.
5. _____	_____	Wading into the middle of the creek, the white-tail deer kicked several fish out of the water and onto the bank. Then it trotted ashore and ate the fish with obvious pleasure.
6. _____	_____	A quarterback must be a skillful field general; furthermore, he must be a good ball handler.

Meaning Relationship	Meaning Link	
7. _____	_____	Boil the snails from three to four hours in diluted white wine. Add vegetables suitable for soup and seasonings of choice—onions, celery, parsley, carrots, bay leaves, cloves, thyme, crushed cloves of garlic.
8. _____	_____	Mike Fink is the state high-school wrestling champion, and he holds a black belt in karate.
9. _____	_____	A great sheet of white flame belched from the base of the rocket. With an earth-shaking roar, the missile lifted slowly from its silo, seemed to hover for a moment, and streaked upward into the night sky.
10. _____	_____	The surgeon made a two-inch incision over the lower portion of the spine. Then he pushed the muscles aside until he had exposed a yellow-ish ligament.

Name _____ Section _____

Date _____ Grade _____

Exercise 7
RELATED ACTION AND PARALLEL IDEA

Illustrate each Meaning Relationship specified below by adding *one* (and only one) independent clause (which may contain Linking Devices) to the clause already given. Each pair of independent clauses thus produced may function as separate sentences or as parts of a single long sentence.

Be sure your examples are well-developed, meaningful, and sensible; and observe standard usage in grammar, punctuation, spelling, and capitalization. Your grade will be lowered if you fail to follow these instructions.

1.

| Statement (Action) | ← | Related Action |

The dog scrambled to his feet and began to growl angrily. _____

_____

_____

_____

2.

| Statement | ← | Parallel Idea |

In the first place, the coat was too expensive. _____

_____

_____

_____

Write a pair of independent clauses illustrating each specified Meaning Relationship and containing the specified Linking Devices. The two independent clauses may function as separate sentences or as parts of a single long sentence.

Be sure your examples are well-developed, meaningful, and sensible; and observe standard usage in grammar, punctuation, spelling, and capitalization. Do *not* imitate the over-all phrasing of the examples given in the text—show some originality.

3.

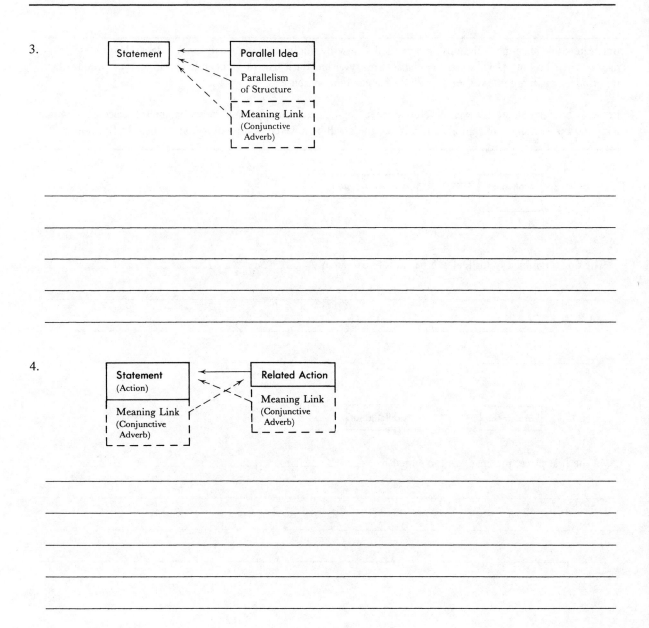

4.

Exercise 8
CONTRAST, ALTERNATIVE, AND BALANCED COMPARISON

First, in the left-hand column indicate the Meaning Relationship linking each pair of independent clauses below. In every instance it will be the relationship of the *second* clause to the *first*. Your choices in this exercise are Contrast, Alternative, and Balanced Comparison. If none of these Meaning Relationships is present, write "None" in the left-hand column.

Second, examine each pair of independent clauses below to see whether a Meaning Link is present (this Meaning Link may consist of more than one word). Underline the Meaning Link, and then write it in the right-hand column. Be sure that this word or word-group is a *Meaning Link*—not some other type of Linking Device. If no Meaning Link is present, write "None" in the right-hand column. No pair of clauses contains more than one Meaning Link.

Meaning Relationship	Meaning Link	
1. _____	_____	If your house has enough bedrooms but still seems crowded, you can add a family room at the back of the house near the kitchen. An alternate plan would be to convert your basement into a recreation room.
2. _____	_____	Most railroads are attempting to eliminate passenger service as rapidly as possible, since it is unprofitable. A few lines, however, are trying to attract more passengers and solve their financial problems through increased volume.
3. _____	_____	The city-manager system often brings about greater efficiency and economy in municipal government; similarly, a state-manager plan frequently offers the taxpayers better state government at a lower cost.
4. _____	_____	The directors may decide to omit the dividend entirely, or they may approve a stock dividend, which would not reduce cash reserves.
5. _____	_____	Today, any ship can travel freely on the high seas. Similarly, when interplanetary flight becomes commonplace, the spaceships of all nations will have an equal right to navigate the vacuum of outer space, governed only by international law.

Meaning Relationship	Meaning Link	
6. _____	_____	There are many worthwhile programs on TV, but you can waste a lot of time waiting for one to come along.
7. _____	_____	According to the state police, the station wagon had been going more than ninety miles per hour. The truck had been traveling much slower.
8. _____	_____	Thompson is one of the best relief pitchers in professional baseball. His batting average, however, is not impressive.
9. _____	_____	The male heron often woos his future mate by offering her bits of nesting material, usually sticks or twigs. The male penguin is similarly inclined to court the female by giving her gifts of nesting material, usually small pebbles from the sea bottom.
10. _____	_____	If I put up a convincing hard-luck story, my English teacher may excuse me from the examination. Again, she may laugh at my efforts to fool her.

Exercise 9
CONTRAST, ALTERNATIVE, AND BALANCED COMPARISON

Illustrate each Meaning Relationship specified below by adding *one* (and only one) independent clause (which may contain Linking Devices) to the clause already given. Each pair of independent clauses thus produced may function as separate sentences or as parts of a single long sentence.

Be sure your examples are well-developed, meaningful, and sensible; and observe standard usage in grammar, punctuation, spelling, and capitalization. Your grade will be lowered if you fail to follow these instructions.

1.

| Statement | ← | Alternative |

I may get a full-time job next summer. _____

_____

_____

_____

2.

| Statement | ← | Balanced Comparison |

The squirrel, which is normally a timid creature, may attack a person savagely if it is cornered. _____

_____

_____

_____

Write a pair of independent clauses illustrating each specified Meaning Relationship and containing the specified Linking Device. The two independent clauses may function as separate sentences or as parts of a single long sentence.

Be sure your examples are well-developed, meaningful, and sensible; and observe standard usage in grammar, punctuation, spelling, and capitalization. Do *not* imitate the over-all phrasing of the examples given in the text—show some originality.

3.

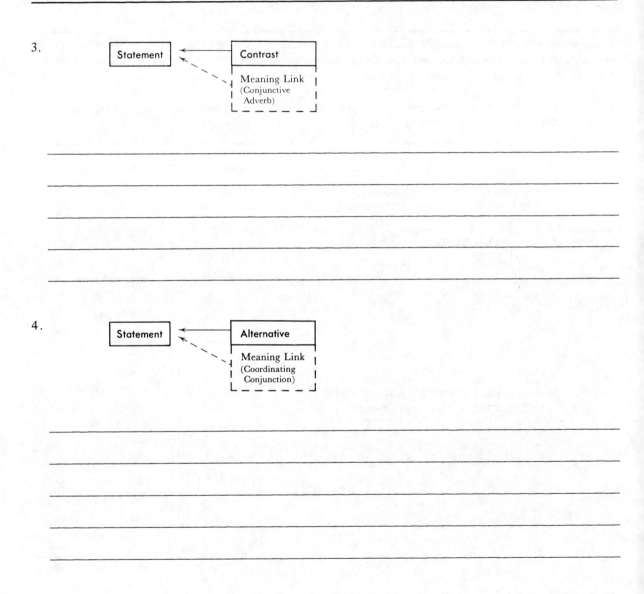

4.

Exercise 10
RESULT, CAUSE, QUESTION, AND ANSWER

First, in the left-hand column indicate the Meaning Relationship linking each pair of independent clauses below. In every instance it will be the relationship of the *second* clause to the *first*. Your choices in this exercise are Result, Cause, Question, and Answer. If none of these Meaning Relationships is present, write "None" in the left-hand column.

Second, examine each pair of independent clauses below to see whether a Noun Summarizing a Previous Assertion or a Meaning Link is present (this Meaning Link may consist of more than one word). Underline the Noun Summarizing a Previous Assertion or the Meaning Link, and then write it in the right-hand column. If the Meaning Relationship between two clauses is Question, the Meaning Link may indicate a secondary Meaning Relationship. If no Noun Summarizing a Previous Assertion or Meaning Link is present, write "None" in the right-hand column. No pair of clauses contains more than one of these Linking Devices.

Meaning Relationship	Noun Summarizing a Previous Assertion, or Meaning Link	
1. _____	_____	The students had failed to read the history assignment. Therefore, they were very unhappy when the teacher gave a "pop quiz."
2. _____	_____	We found our once-beautiful Christmas tree in ruins. Our half-grown cat had used it as a jungle gym.
3. _____	_____	I had spent most of my money; so I lived on peanut-butter sandwiches until the end of the month.
4. _____	_____	The price of meat is higher now than it has ever been. Who can afford even to look at a T-bone steak these days?
5. _____	_____	Frank Zebrowski is a small man, measuring barely five feet in height and weighing 115 pounds; his brother Adam is a giant, standing nearly eight feet tall and tipping the scales at over 300 pounds.

Meaning Relationship	Noun Summarizing a Previous Assertion, or Meaning Link	
6. _____	_____	Mars has white polar "ice caps." But are they composed of real ice, thin hoarfrost, or crystals of solidified carbon dioxide?
7. _____	_____	My mother's tulips did not come up this spring. Ground squirrels had eaten all of the bulbs.
8. _____	_____	Bob never studies until the night before an examination. Consequently, after he completes a course, he retains very little of the material covered.
9. _____	_____	A spark from a welder's torch ignited the gasoline fumes. The result was an explosion which injured eight men, destroyed two buildings, and shattered windows for miles around.
10. _____	_____	Why do baboons dwell on the ground rather than in trees? It seems probable that a change in climate destroyed the forests in which their ancestors lived, forcing them to adapt themselves to a terrestrial existence.

Exercise 11
RESULT, CAUSE, QUESTION, AND ANSWER

Illustrate each Meaning Relationship specified below by adding *one* (and only one) independent clause (which may contain Linking Devices) to the clause already given. Each pair of independent clauses thus produced may function as separate sentences or as parts of a single long sentence.

Be sure your examples are well-developed, meaningful, and sensible; and observe standard usage in grammar, punctuation, spelling, and capitalization. Your grade will be lowered if you fail to follow these instructions.

1.

| Statement | ← | Cause |

The road across the mountain is closed to traffic. _____

_____

_____

_____

2.

| Question | ← | Answer |

What do I like most about this school? _____

_____

_____

_____

Write a pair of independent clauses illustrating each specified Meaning Relationship and containing the specified Linking Device. The two independent clauses may function as separate sentences or as parts of a single long sentence.

Be sure your examples are well-developed, meaningful, and sensible; and observe standard usage in grammar, punctuation, spelling, and capitalization. Do *not* imitate the over-all phrasing of the examples given in the text—show some originality.

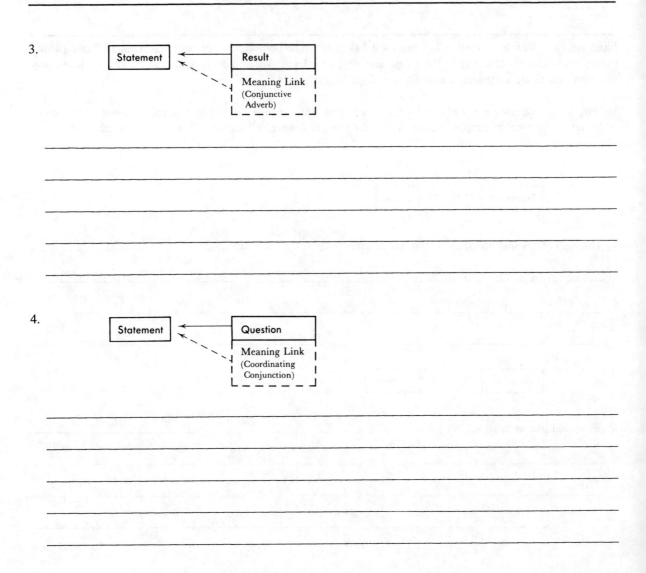

3.

4.

Exercise 12
DEFINITION AND AMPLIFICATION

First, in the left-hand column indicate the Meaning Relationship linking each pair of independent clauses below. In every instance it will be the relationship of the *second* clause to the *first*. Your choices in this exercise are Informal Definition, Formal Definition, and Amplification. For the words "Informal Definition" and "Formal Definition," use the abbreviations "Informal Def." and "Formal Def." If none of these Meaning Relationships is present, write "None" in the left-hand column.

Second, examine each pair of independent clauses below to see whether a Meaning Link is present (this Meaning Link may consist of more than one word). Underline the Meaning Link, and then write it in the right-hand column. Be sure that this word or word-group is a *Meaning Link*—not some other type of Linking Device. If no Meaning Link is present, write "None" in the right-hand column. No pair of clauses contains more than one Meaning Link.

Meaning Relationship	Meaning Link	
1. _____	_____	The experience has taught me a very obvious lesson. People who live in glass houses shouldn't throw parties.
2. _____	_____	In Guatemala I was first introduced to the cow tree. It is an evergreen which oozes a whitish, milklike juice when its trunk or branches are cut.
3. _____	_____	In small Ozark communities, the shivaree still occurs frequently. It is, of course, a mock serenade of a newly married couple, usually on their wedding night.
4. _____	_____	According to the judge, the pawnbroker was guilty of usury. In other words, he had loaned money at an unlawfully high rate of interest.
5. _____	_____	While I was calling on Janice, her little brother took the opportunity to play two jokes on me. Specifically, he hid my coat and let the air out of the tires of my car.
6. _____	_____	The bank robber made a most embarrassing error. He jumped into the wrong car while trying to make his getaway.

Meaning Relationship	Meaning Link

7. _____ _____ It has been suggested that the Biblical manna may have been a form of honeydew. Briefly, this is a sugary liquid given off by the leaves of certain plants during hot weather.

8. _____ _____ When I opened the bread box, I got quite a surprise. A mouse hopped out and scurried across the kitchen floor.

9. _____ _____ In Dickens' *Pickwick Papers,* the Fat Boy is a victim of narcolepsy. That is, he displays an uncontrollable tendency to fall asleep under all sorts of conditions.

10. _____ _____ Apollo 12's scientific instruments revealed an astonishing fact about the moon. It rings like a bell when struck.

Name _____ Section _____

Date _____ Grade _____

Exercise 13
DEFINITION AND AMPLIFICATION

Illustrate each Meaning Relationship specified below by adding *one* (and only one) independent clause (which may contain Linking Devices) to the clause already given. Each pair of independent clauses thus produced may function as separate sentences or as parts of a single long sentence.

Be sure your examples are well-developed, meaningful, and sensible; and observe standard usage in grammar, punctuation, spelling, and capitalization. Your grade will be lowered if you fail to follow these instructions.

1.

| Statement (Containing Anticipatory Noun) | ← | Amplification |

General Starr made a very unfortunate mistake. _____

_____

_____

_____

2.

| Statement | ← | Definition (Formal) |

The shipwrecked sailor finally reached an atoll. _____

_____

_____

_____

Write a pair of independent clauses illustrating each specified Meaning Relationship and containing the specified Linking Device. The two independent clauses may function as separate sentences or as parts of a single long sentence.

Be sure your examples are well-developed, meaningful, and sensible; and observe standard usage in grammar, punctuation, spelling, and capitalization. Do *not* imitate the over-all phrasing of the examples given in the text—show some originality.

3.

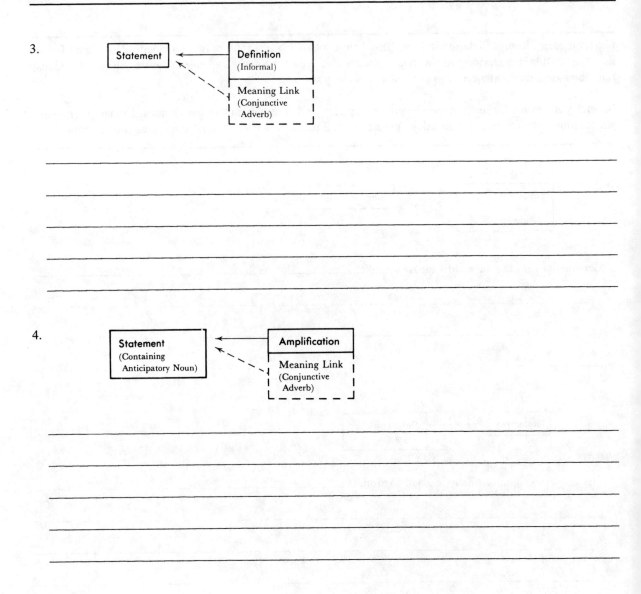

4.

Exercise 14
SAMPLE ITEM, SAMPLE FACT, AND SUPPORTING DATA

First, in the left-hand column indicate the Meaning Relationship linking each pair of independent clauses below. In every instance it will be the relationship of the *second* clause to the *first*. Your choices in this exercise are Sample Item, Sample Fact, and Supporting Data. If none of these Meaning Relationships is present, write "None" in the left-hand column.

Second, examine each pair of independent clauses below to see whether a Meaning Link is present (this Meaning Link may consist of more than one word). Underline the Meaning Link, and then write it in the right-hand column. Be sure that this word or word-group is a *Meaning Link*—not some other type of Linking Device. If no Meaning Link is present, write "None" in the right-hand column. No pair of clauses contains more than one Meaning Link.

Meaning Relationship	Meaning Link	
1. _____	_____	My cousin practices thrift to the point of eccentricity. For instance, he always saves his cigarette butts, tears them up, and smokes the tobacco in his pipe.
2. _____	_____	My neighbors have some peculiar hobbies. One of them makes costume jewelry out of gold-plated cockroaches.
3. _____	_____	This car has probably been in a wreck. The frame is twisted.
4. _____	_____	Some birds avoid all parental responsibilities by laying their eggs in the nests of other species. Typical of these feathered parasites is the common cowbird.
5. _____	_____	I must be coming down with a cold. I've been sniffling and sneezing all morning.
6. _____	_____	A picaresque novel is a loosely constructed work of fiction which relates the adventures of a likeable rogue. One well-known example from eighteenth-century English literature is Tobias Smollett's *Roderick Random*.

Meaning Relationship	Meaning Link

7. _____ _____ My father dearly loves old Humphrey Bogart movies. He has a regular passion for "The Maltese Falcon," staying up to watch it every time it appears on the television late-late show.

8. _____ _____ This car seems to have a twisted frame. Could it have been in a wreck?

9. _____ _____ California ice-cream companies offer their customers some unusual flavors. Last year, for example, a Los Angeles firm sold pizza-flavored ice cream.

10. _____ _____ The Greek gods and goddesses often displayed human emotions. Aphrodite, for instance, revenged herself upon Hippolytus because he neglected to worship her.

Exercise 15
SAMPLE ITEM, SAMPLE FACT, AND SUPPORTING DATA

Illustrate each Meaning Relationship specified below by adding *one* (and only one) independent clause (which may contain Linking Devices) to the clause already given. Each pair of independent clauses thus produced may function as separate sentences or as parts of a single long sentence.

Be sure your examples are well-developed, meaningful, and sensible; and observe standard usage in grammar, punctuation, spelling, and capitalization. Your grade will be lowered if you fail to follow these instructions.

1.

| Statement (Containing Name of Class) | ← | Sample Item |

Several of the animals which man uses for food are ruminants. _____

_____

_____

_____

2.

| Statement (Generalization) | ← | Sample Fact |

Many high-school graduates receive scholarships from colleges and universities. _____

_____

_____

_____

Write a pair of independent clauses illustrating each specified Meaning Relationship and containing the specified Linking Device. The two independent clauses may function as separate sentences or as parts of a single long sentence.

Be sure your examples are well-developed, meaningful, and sensible; and observe standard usage in grammar, punctuation, spelling, and capitalization. Do *not* imitate the over-all phrasing of the examples given in the text—show some originality.

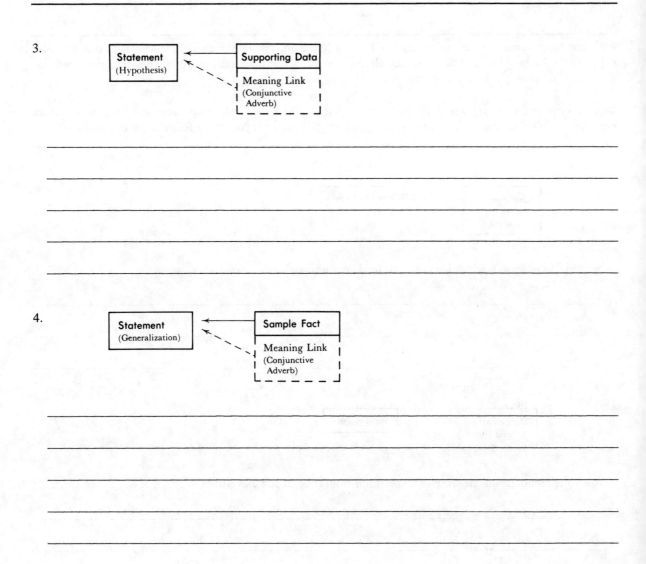

3.

Statement
(Hypothesis)

Supporting Data

Meaning Link
(Conjunctive
Adverb)

_____

_____

_____

_____

_____

4.

Statement
(Generalization)

Sample Fact

Meaning Link
(Conjunctive
Adverb)

_____

_____

_____

_____

_____

Exercise 16
GENERALIZATION AND INFERENCE

First, in the left-hand column indicate the Meaning Relationship linking each pair of independent clauses below. In every instance it will be the relationship of the *second* clause to the *first*. Your choices in this exercise are Generalization and Inference. If neither of these Meaning Relationships is present, write "Neither" in the left-hand column.

Second, examine each pair of independent clauses below to see whether a Noun Summarizing a Previous Assertion or a Meaning Link is present (this Meaning Link may consist of more than one word). Underline the Noun Summarizing a Previous Assertion or the Meaning Link, and then write it in the right-hand column. If no Noun Summarizing a Previous Assertion or Meaning Link is present, write "None" in the right-hand column. No pair of clauses contains more than one of these Linking Devices.

Meaning Relationship	Noun Summarizing a Previous Assertion, or Meaning Link	
1. _____	_____	He did not take any money or extra clothing with him. He obviously had not planned to leave town.
2. _____	_____	When Winston Churchill was a schoolboy, his teachers considered him a stupid lad who would never amount to anything. Teachers sometimes misjudge their students' potentialities.
3. _____	_____	My mother's tulips did not come up this spring. Ground squirrels must have eaten all of the bulbs.
4. _____	_____	This car has a twisted frame. It has probably been in a wreck.
5. _____	_____	Last summer my brother worked as a bellhop at a resort hotel in Colorado. During vacations many students take temporary jobs which provide opportunities for recreation as well as a chance to earn some money.
6. _____	_____	Alice and Bob must have broken their engagement. She's not wearing his ring any more.

Meaning Relationship	**Noun Summarizing a Previous Assertion, or Meaning Link**	

7. _____ _____ The Renault gets up to forty miles per gallon. Small foreign cars use very little gas.

8. _____ _____ A forty-watt bulb gives off as much light as do 200 tons of the sun's mass. Ounce for ounce of mass, many common light sources here on earth shine more brightly than does the sun.

9. _____ _____ A human body "shines"—that is, gives off energy—at a rate 10,000 times greater than a piece of the sun of equal size. Obviously, the sun's great brilliance must be due entirely to its enormous volume.

10. _____ _____ The TV police drama showed three assaults, two murders, and one attempted rape. Many TV programs present violent episodes to entertain the viewing public.

Name _____ Section _____

Date _____ Grade _____

Exercise 17
GENERALIZATION AND INFERENCE

Illustrate each Meaning Relationship specified below by adding *one* (and only one) independent clause (which may contain Linking Devices) to the clause already given. Each pair of independent clauses thus produced may function as separate sentences or as parts of a single long sentence.

Be sure your examples are well-developed, meaningful, and sensible; and observe standard usage in grammar, punctuation, spelling, and capitalization. Your grade will be lowered if you fail to follow these instructions.

1.

| Statement (Sample Fact) | ← | Generalization |

My next-door neighbor raises boa constrictors. _____

_____

_____

_____

| Statement (Supporting Data) | ← | Inference (Hypothesis) |

She has a very sore throat, generalized muscle ache, and a fever of 103. _____

_____

_____

_____

Write a pair of independent clauses illustrating each specified Meaning Relationship and containing the specified Linking Device. The two independent clauses may function as separate sentences or as parts of a single long sentence.

Be sure your examples are well-developed, meaningful, and sensible; and observe standard usage in grammar, punctuation, spelling, and capitalization. Do *not* imitate the over-all phrasing of the examples given in the text—show some originality.

3.

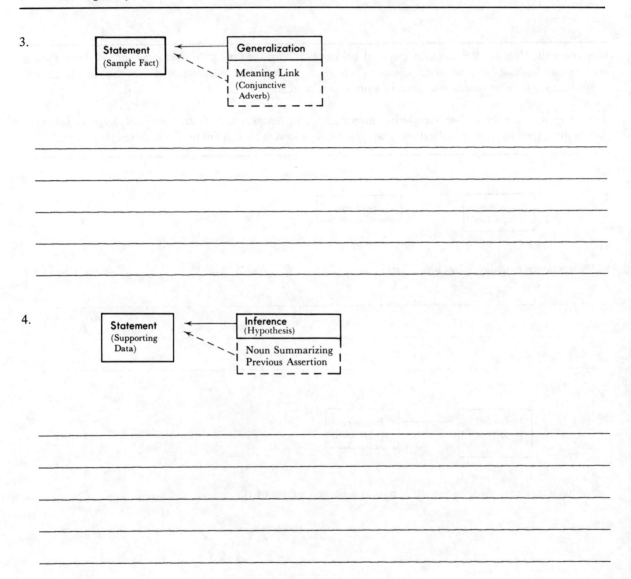

4.

Exercise 18
COORDINATION VERSUS SUBORDINATION

Each of the following sentences can be improved through some form of subordination.

If you feel that one of the independent clauses in a sentence presents a minor idea, convert that clause to a construction of lesser grammatical rank by turning it into an appositive, an adjective clause, an adverb clause, or a phrase.

If you feel that the two independent clauses in a sentence present ideas which are actually equal parts of one major idea, convert the two clauses to a single clause with a compound predicate.

Write the revised sentence in the space provided. Observe standard usage in grammar, punctuation, spelling, and capitalization. Your grade will be lowered if you fail to follow these instructions.

1. President James A. Garfield could turn perfect handsprings; he was forty-nine years old.

_____

_____

_____

_____

2. The cook broiled the steak, and he fried the potatoes.

_____

_____

_____

_____

3. The little sparrow hawk is common in Indiana; it often attacks birds ten times its size.

_____

_____

_____

_____

4. He held his breath; he took careful aim and fired.

_____

_____

_____

_____

5. Walt Disney's "Snow White and the Seven Dwarfs" appeared in 1938; it was the first feature-length movie cartoon.

_____

_____

_____

_____

Exercise 19
REVIEW

First, in the left-hand column indicate the Meaning Relationship linking each pair of independent clauses below. In every instance it will be the relationship of the *second* clause to the *first*.

Second, examine each pair of independent clauses below to see whether a Noun Summarizing a Previous Assertion or a Meaning Link is present (this Meaning Link may consist of more than one word). Underline the Noun Summarizing a Previous Assertion or the Meaning Link, and then write it in the right-hand column. If no Noun Summarizing a Previous Assertion or Meaning Link is present, write "None" in the right-hand column. No pair of clauses contains more than one of these Linking Devices.

Meaning Relationship	Noun Summarizing a Previous Assertion, or Meaning Link	
1. _____	_____	Every spring, my father turns up dozens of arrowheads while plowing his fields. Probably our farm was once an Indian hunting ground.
2. _____	_____	Elmer Zilch must have written the unsigned letter threatening to blow up the Capitol. According to the FBI, his fingerprints are on it.
3. _____	_____	His abdominal pain may indicate acute appendicitis, or it may be a symptom of typhoid fever.
4. _____	_____	Old Dr. Watson puffed thoughtfully on his pipe for several minutes. Then he swiveled his chair around and stared quizzically at his visitor's indignant face.
5. _____	_____	Spanish senoritas used to squeeze orange juice into their eyes to make them lustrous. Through the ages, women have always been willing to undergo discomfort in the pursuit of beauty.
6. _____	_____	George Washington's false teeth did not fit properly. Therefore, as he complained to his dentist, they forced "the lips out just under the nose," spoiling the General's appearance.

Meaning Relationship	Noun Summarizing a Previous Assertion, or Meaning Link	
7. _____	_____	The Senator was guilty of nepotism. That is, he had placed his relatives on the payroll as "special assistants," even though they were not performing any real services.
8. _____	_____	The Restoration comedy of manners ridiculed the social follies and private vices of its time. One of the most famous of these plays is William Congreve's *The Way of the World.*
9. _____	_____	A liquid-fuel rocket is a very complex mechanism. Furthermore, it is a very expensive one.
10. _____	_____	A distinguished scientist has said that the earth has a mass of nearly 6,000,000,000,000,000,-000,000,000 kilograms but a weight of zero kilograms. Does this mean that the earth, which is in orbit around the sun, is in a state of weightlessness like that of an astronaut who is in orbit around the earth or the moon?

Exercise 19 (continued)

Name _____

Illustrate each Meaning Relationship specified below by adding *one* (and only one) independent clause (which may contain Linking Devices) to the clause already given. Each pair of independent clauses thus produced may function as separate sentences or as parts of a single long sentence.

Be sure your examples are well-developed, meaningful, and sensible; and observe standard usage in grammar, punctuation, spelling, and capitalization. Your grade will be lowered if you fail to follow these instructions.

11.

| Statement
(Containing
Anticipatory Noun) | ← | Amplification |

My automobile accident had one serious consequence. _____

_____

_____

_____

12.

| Statement
(Generalization) | ← | Sample Fact |

Animal characters appear in a number of cartoon strips. _____

_____

_____

_____

Write a pair of independent clauses illustrating the specified Meaning Relationship and containing the specified Linking Device. The two independent clauses may function as separate sentences or as parts of a single long sentence.

Be sure that your example is well-developed, meaningful, and sensible; and observe standard usage in grammar, punctuation, spelling, and capitalization. Do *not* imitate the over-all phrasing of the examples given in the text—show some originality.

13.

EXAMINATION: CHAPTERS 1 AND 2

At the beginning of the examination, your instructor will tell you what labels to insert in the various boxes. Your instructor may also wish to furnish the first clause for some or all of the units.

Write a pair of independent clauses illustrating each specified Meaning Relationship and containing whatever Linking Devices may be specified. You may, of course, use any appropriate Linking Devices in addition to those specified by your instructor. The two independent clauses which you compose may function as separate sentences or as parts of a single long sentence.

Be sure your examples are well-developed, meaningful, and sensible; and observe standard usage in grammar, punctuation, spelling, and capitalization. *Do not repeat any examples which appear in the text or which you have used in the exercises.* Your grade will be lowered if you fail to follow these instructions.

1.

```
┌──────────────┐        ┌──────────────┐
│              │ ◄──────│              │
│              │        │              │
└──────────────┘        └──────────────┘
```

_____

_____

_____

_____

_____

2.

```
┌──────────────┐        ┌──────────────┐
│              │ ◄──────│              │
│              │        │              │
└──────────────┘        └──────────────┘
```

_____

_____

_____

3.

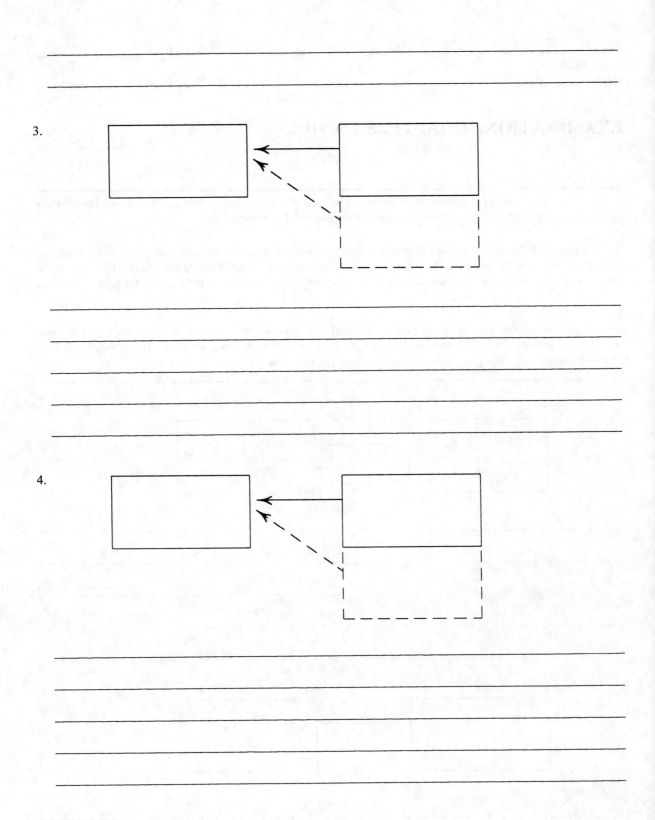

4.

Exercise 20
THE FIVE PATTERNS OF PROSE

First, in the left-hand column indicate the Meaning Relationships occurring in each group of clauses. List them in the order of their occurrence. In the blank opposite *A* write "Statement," "Statement (Action)," or "Question," whichever is appropriate. In the blanks opposite *B* and *C*, write the names of the Meaning Relationships employed. (For example, if the pattern is *Statement ← Contrast ← Result,* write "Statement" in the blank opposite *A,* write "Contrast" in the blank opposite *B,* and write "Result" in the blank opposite *C*; or, if the pattern is *Question ← Answer,* write "Question" in the blank opposite *A,* write "Answer" in the blank opposite *B,* and leave the blank opposite *C* empty.)

Second, in the right-hand column indicate the pattern represented by each group of clauses below. Do so by writing the appropriate abbreviation in the proper blank: *Enumeration* (E), *Equal Pair* (EP), *Unequal Pair* (UP), *Chain* (C), or *Leapfrog* (L).

	Meaning Relationships	**Pattern**	
1.	A. _____	_____	The bull alligator clamped its jaws around Will's chest and pulled him under water. In a panic, the boy kicked to the surface, still caught in the beast's powerful jaws. The alligator dragged him down again.
	B. _____		
	C. _____		
2.	A. _____	_____	My father has always wanted me to become an engineer. I have decided, however, that I would rather be a physician, and I therefore plan to register for twelve hours of pre-medical courses next semester.
	B. _____		
	C. _____		
3.	A. _____	_____	The Centerville grade school was badly damaged by fire last night. Consequently, it will be necessary to hold classes in the basement of Grace Church until the school building can be repaired. According to Fire Chief Melvin Anderson, the blaze was caused by faulty wiring in the school cafeteria.
	B. _____		
	C. _____		
4.	A. _____	_____	The city park certainly isn't very green this spring. Pedestrians taking "shortcuts" have trampled the tender new grass into the ground.
	B. _____		
	C. _____		

	Pattern
Meaning Relationships	

5. A. _____   _____ The unconscious man's breathing was weak and irregular.
    B. _____   His skin was a bright cherry-red.
    C. _____

6. A. _____   _____ My brother made straight A's in high school, but he has
    B. _____   difficulty maintaining a C average in college.
    C. _____

7. A. _____   _____ When his ship reached port, the sailor was shocked to
    B. _____   learn that his darling Clementine had married another
    C. _____   man. What disturbed him most about this turn of
                                           events? He had just had her name tattooed across his
                                           chest in inch-high letters.

8. A. _____   _____ Some scientists have come to a surprising conclusion
    B. _____   concerning the dinosaurs. They believe that these ancient
    C. _____   reptiles were warm-blooded.

9. A. _____   _____ Racing across the infield, the shortstop scooped up the
    B. _____   hard-hit grounder. Then he whirled and threw the ball to
    C. _____   the first baseman.

10. A. _____   _____ During his study of animal behavior, Professor Pryor
    B. _____   has attached tiny radio transmitters to many different
    C. _____   kinds of wild creatures. For example, he has glued them
                                           to vampire bats, surgically implanted them in salmon,
                                           and strapped them around the necks of tigers.

Exercise 21
THE FIVE PATTERNS OF PROSE

Complete the patterns below by adding independent clauses containing the specified Meaning Relationships to the clauses already given. The clauses which you add may, of course, contain Linking Devices. You must decide whether the clauses in each pattern would function best as separate sentences or as parts of a single long sentence.

Be sure your clauses are well-developed, meaningful, and sensible; and observe standard usage in grammar, punctuation, spelling, and capitalization. Your grade will be lowered if you fail to follow these instructions.

1.

| Statement | ← | Result |

While my sister was entertaining her bridge club, a mouse scurried across the living-room carpet. _____

_____

_____

_____

_____

_____

2.

| Statement (Containing Anticipatory Noun) | ← | Amplification |

After much thought, Mary reached a decision. _____

_____

_____

_____

_____

_____

3.

Statement ← Result ← Cause

The basketball team has lost its last twelve games. _____

_____

_____

_____

_____

4.

Statement ← Question ← Answer

There is a widespread rumor that many members of the faculty have threatened to resign. _____

_____

_____

_____

_____

Exercise 22
VARIETIES OF CLUSTERS

First, examine each of the following passages carefully to determine whether or not it contains a cluster. Underline the cluster if one is present. Be sure that the underlined clauses function as a unit in relation to some other independent clause.

Second, determine the Meaning Relationship or Meaning Relationships which link the clauses in the cluster. Write each Meaning Relationship in the appropriate blank in the left-hand column. If the cluster contains two independent clauses, write their Meaning Relationship in the blank opposite *A*. If the cluster contains three independent clauses, write the Meaning Relationship between the first two clauses of the cluster in the blank opposite *A*, and then write the Meaning Relationship between the second and third clauses of the cluster (or between the first and third clauses if the pattern is Leapfrog) in the blank opposite *B*. If no cluster is present, write "None" in the blank opposite *A*.

Third, determine whether the cluster is an *Enumerative Cluster* (E), an *Equal-Pair Cluster* (E-P), an *Unequal Pair Cluster* (U-P), a *Chain Cluster* (C), or a *Leapfrog Cluster* (L). Write the appropriate abbreviation in the right-hand column. If no cluster is present, write "None" in the right-hand column.

Meaning Relationship(s) within Cluster	**Variety of Cluster**	
1. A. _____ B. _____	_____	Homonyms are pairs of words which have the same pronunciation but which differ in meaning. One example is *meet* and *meat*; another is *bear* and *bare*.
2. A. _____ B. _____	_____	Priscilla is rather reserved and does not make friends easily. As a result, many persons consider her conceited and arrogant. My sister, for instance, calls her a "stuck-up snob."
3. A. _____ B. _____	_____	Eric Goodman, the concert violinist, has two broken fingers on his left hand. Therefore, he has been forced to cancel his appearance as guest soloist with the Metropolitan Symphony Orchestra. According to newspaper stories, his injury was caused by his wife's accidentally slamming a car door on his hand.
4. A. _____ B. _____	_____	After we had unloaded the boat and pitched our tent, we made an annoying discovery. Most of the food for our camping trip was in cans, but neither of us had remembered to bring a can opener.

Meaning Relationship(s) within Cluster	**Variety of Cluster**

5. A. _____

   B. _____

_____ Foolishly trying to drive while drowsy, I fell asleep at the wheel. As a result, my car was demolished when it left the road and struck a tree, and I received a broken collarbone and a cut cheek.

6. A. _____

   B. _____

_____ Today I noticed a red leaf on a maple tree, and yesterday I spotted a flock of geese flying south. Autumn must be here once again.

7. A. _____

   B. _____

_____ My brother, who is a sophomore at the state university, has a difficult problem to solve. He needs to work in order to pay his expenses, but working interferes seriously with his studying and may even cause him to fail some of his courses.

8. A. _____

   B. _____

_____ Why did the once-abundant moose vanish from the Adirondack Mountains? According to Forest Service officials, the huge beasts contracted a disease of the nervous system which was highly contagious. As a result, they died in large numbers and were soon extinct. The disease was caused by a parasitic roundworm infesting the whitetail deer which flocked to the region after its forests had been lumbered.

9. A. _____

   B. _____

_____ The consumer wants lower prices. The manufacturer wants bigger profits. Is there any way to reconcile these conflicting desires?

10. A. _____

    B. _____

_____ While flying to Los Angeles last summer, I was involved in a mishap which was quite minor but could have been rather serious. The jetliner lurched violently just as the stewardess was serving my lunch. Consequently, she spilled coffee all over me. However, I was only drenched, not scalded.

Name _____ Section _____

Date _____ Grade _____

Exercise 23
VARIETIES OF CLUSTERS, AND CLUSTERS WITHIN CLUSTERS

Add independent clauses containing the specified Meaning Relationships to the clauses already given. The clauses which you add may, of course, contain Linking Devices.

You must decide whether each independent clause would function best as a separate sentence or as part of a longer sentence. Notice that there is no period or other punctuation mark after any of the independent clauses already given. Your punctuation should help to show the relationships among the ideas expressed by the various clauses. Your grade will be lowered if you use punctuation, obscures the relationships among the clauses.

In addition, make sure your clauses are well-developed, meaningful, and sensible; and observe standard usage in grammar, spelling, and capitalization. Your grade will also be lowered if you fail to follow these instructions.

1.

Statement (Containing Anticipatory Noun)	←	Amplification
		Statement (Amplification) ← Parallel Idea (Second Amplification)

He made two surprising discoveries _____

_____

_____

_____

_____

2.

Statement	←	Contrast
Statement (Hypothesis) ← Supporting Data		

The bank robber was probably a novice _____

_____

_____

_____

_____

3.

```
┌─────────────────────────────────┐      ┌────────┐
│         Statement               │ ◄─── │ Result │
│ ┌───────────┐    ┌──────────┐  │      └────────┘
│ │ Statement │ ◄──│ Contrast │  │
│ └───────────┘    └──────────┘  │
└─────────────────────────────────┘
```

Aunt Helen wanted to go to the seashore _____

_____

_____

_____

4.

```
┌───────────┐      ┌──────────────────────────────────────────────────┐
│ Statement │ ◄─── │                     Contrast                     │
└───────────┘      │ ┌──────────────┐   ┌──────────────────────────┐  │
                   │ │  Statement   │   │       Amplification      │  │
                   │ │ (Containing  │◄──│ ┌───────────┐ ┌────────┐ │  │
                   │ │ Anticipatory │   │ │ Statement │◄│Contrast│ │  │
                   │ │   Noun)      │   │ └───────────┘ └────────┘ │  │
                   │ └──────────────┘   └──────────────────────────┘  │
                   └──────────────────────────────────────────────────┘
```

My wife and I hold similar views concerning most political issues _____

_____

_____

_____

Exercise 24
GROUPING AND PUNCTUATION OF CLAUSES
IN PATTERNS CONTAINING CLUSTERS

Each of the following passages contains a cluster. If the grouping and the internal punctuation of the passage are acceptable, write "A" in the blank. If they are unacceptable, write "U" in the blank.

1. _____ The killer whale probably deserves its reputation as "the wolf of the sea"; it is a fierce predator. And it hunts in a pack with highly organized tactics.

2. _____ A study of malpractice suits against physicians has uncovered two surprising facts; there are more suits against doctors who do not perform surgery than against those who do. Moreover, among surgeons, there are more suits against those who do only minor surgery than against those who do major surgery.

3. _____ Since ancient times, perfume makers have used true musk to make their products more distinctive and long-lasting; this is a substance obtained from a small gland near the navel of the male musk deer. However, American perfume makers usually substitute a less expensive synthetic musk made from coal tar.

4. _____ My brother's wife is furious with him; consequently, I was acutely uncomfortable the last time I visited their home; apparently she had dropped numerous hints that she wanted a fur coat for Christmas; but he bought her a new vacuum cleaner instead.

5. _____ Cockroaches can adapt themselves to almost any environment. Furthermore, they quickly develop an immunity to new insecticides; therefore, the pesky cockroach will probably survive mankind's efforts to destroy him.

6. _____ First, disconnect the ignition wire from the spark plug. This will prevent the power mower from starting accidentally and possibly injuring you; second, tip the mower on its side, with the carburetor upward.

7. _____ For many centuries the Chinese have regarded the ginseng root as an elixir of youth; moreover, modern Oriental armies use it for added stamina. For instance, Japanese soldiers during World War Two and Viet Cong officers in recent years received regular issues of the highly regarded herb in order to combat fatigue.

8. _____ For the average American household, tax increases are outstripping all other rising costs in the family budget. For example, federal tax increases are growing twice as fast as increases in the cost of food and housing; consequently, millions of taxpayers are searching for ways— legal or illegal—to escape the burden.

9. _____ Physicians have studied fever for thousands of years. But they have not yet discovered its cause, and they are not sure whether it is generally harmful or beneficial to the patient.

10. _____ The New York City Fire Department is starting to use water to which a small amount of polyethylene-oxide has been added. The resulting "slippery water" flows through a fire hose 70 per cent faster than ordinary water. Moreover, after leaving the nozzle, it travels twice as far.

Name _____ Section _____

Date _____ Grade _____

Exercise 25
GROUPING AND PUNCTUATION OF CLAUSES
IN PATTERNS CONTAINING CLUSTERS

Each of the following passages contains a cluster. Note that there are no punctuation marks either within or at the end of any of the independent clauses. Note also that none of the clauses, except for the first, begins with a capital letter.

Copy each passage in the space provided, adding any punctuation marks and capital letters which you feel are needed. Be sure that the punctuation marks and capital letters which you add are in accordance with standard usage. Also, be sure that they help to show the relationships among the ideas expressed by the clauses.

1. My new cassette tape deck must need adjustment or repair the sound seems to flutter when I play a tape moreover the noise level is quite high

_____

_____

_____

_____

_____

2. The inhabitants of one Parsi community in India can no longer dispose of their dead in the traditional way by putting the corpses on top of a Tower of Silence where vultures congregate several of the scavenging birds were killed by cyanide in the body of a suicide victim and as a result the other vultures are avoiding the tower

_____

_____

_____

_____

_____

_____

_____

3. During the Victorian era artists fashioned jewelry from human hair   today they are making it from even stranger substances   for example one artist is creating brooches and other ornaments from dried elk manure

_____

_____

_____

_____

_____

4. A recent study of mass transportation has uncovered an interesting paradox   the trolley car has almost disappeared from the American scene   but many urban planners believe it will soon be in widespread use again   for it is not only pollution-free but also efficient and relatively inexpensive to operate

_____

_____

_____

_____

_____

_____

_____

Exercise 26
BASIC PATTERNS OF PARAGRAPH DEVELOPMENT

Indicate which basic pattern of paragraph development occurs in each of the paragraphs below. Do so by writing the appropriate abbreviation in the proper blank: *Enumerative Paragraph* (E), *Equal-Pair Paragraph* (E-P), *Unequal-Pair Paragraph* (U-P), *Chain Paragraph* (C), or *Leapfrog Paragraph* (L). Some of the paragraphs contain clusters.

1. _____ A shoplifter successfully stole a matching bathroom set of toilet, bathtub, and sink from a floor display in a large department store. The thief was apparently brazen, clever, and resourceful; and the store employees were obviously negligent, stupid, or asleep.

2. _____ The coyote is undoubtedly too smart and adaptable to be in any danger of extinction. Once almost exclusively a Western animal, it has increased its range by 400 per cent since North America was colonized and is now found as far east as Maine. Moreover, it has successfully established itself in many—perhaps most—of the nation's urban areas.

3. _____ My arms loaded with packages, I walked across the parking lot to my car. I placed the packages and my purse on the hood while I unlocked the car. Suddenly a young boy appeared out of nowhere, grabbed my purse, and ran off with it. "Stop! Stop, thief!" I yelled in panic.

4. _____ Wherever Jo Ellen goes in the house or yard, her pet baby chick scurries after her, peeping plaintively. The reason for the chick's odd behavior is clear. It thinks Jo Ellen is its mother.

5. _____ A wild rabbit ate my mother's tulips last spring and is now wrecking our vegetable garden. Therefore, I want to set out some traps, and my father wants to put out poison. But my mother and sister will not let us do these things because they think rabbits are "cute."

Create a paragraph by adding *at least* two additional independent clauses to the clause already given. The paragraph may contain a cluster. The clauses which you add may, of course, contain Linking Devices, and you must decide whether they would function more effectively as separate sentences or as parts of a longer sentence.

Be sure your clauses are well-developed, meaningful, and sensible; and observe standard usage in grammar, punctuation, spelling, and capitalization. Your grade will be lowered if you fail to follow these instructions.

After you have composed your paragraph, decide which of the five basic patterns of paragraph development it follows, and write the name of that pattern in the blank.

Today's teenagers are facing some very difficult problems. _____

_____

_____

_____

_____

_____

_____

_____

_____

_____

_____

Pattern of Paragraph Development: _____

Exercise 27
THE PARAGRAPH
The Topic Statement

Study each of the paragraphs below. First, determine its central idea. Then, by writing "Yes" or "No" in the proper blank, indicate whether that central idea is expressed in a specific topic statement. Underline the topic statement if there is one.

1. _____ Money spent on space-travel schemes is money spent very foolishly. The dollars that have been required to place astronauts on the surface of the moon could have been used to solve problems affecting millions of human beings here on the surface of the earth. Surely, preserving the life of one child is much more important than determining how and when the moon was formed.

2. _____ A brown pelican flapped awkwardly overhead. Suddenly it folded its wings and dropped like a stone into the ocean, producing a noisy splash. After a moment it reappeared on the surface of the water, struggled clumsily into the air, and continued its flight with its pouch distended by the fish it had just caught.

3. _____ All morning the air had been oppressive and still, but now a fresh breeze was blowing steadily from the west. Thick banks of clouds hid the sun, growing blacker and more ominous every second. Lightning flickered on the horizon, with an occasional fiery streak zigzagging high across the heavens. The low, shuddering roll of distant thunder was almost continuous. Suddenly the wind blew harder, in gusts which set the tree limbs to tossing and turned up the pale underside of the leaves. The thunder rumbled louder and closer, and a few preliminary raindrops splattered on the sidewalk. Apparently, a severe thunderstorm was fast approaching.

4. _____ Small, compact automobiles have both advantages and disadvantages. Their purchase price is comparatively low, they get good gas mileage, and they are easy to park. On the other hand, they provide rather limited space for passengers and luggage, they have less power than most big cars, and they cannot deliver as smooth a ride.

5. _____ There was a heavy frost last night, the water in the bird bath is frozen, and the weatherman says it may snow. Obviously, winter is at hand. So tomorrow I'll carry the lawn furniture to the basement, put up the storm windows, and take the car to the filling station to have the snow tires mounted.

Consider each italicized clause below to be the topic statement for a paragraph, and compose at least three additional clauses or clusters which will serve as suitable development material for that topic statement. The resulting paragraph should follow one of the five basic patterns of paragraph development, and the clauses or clusters which you compose should appropriately develop the topic statement so that the full implications of the central idea of the paragraph are clear to the reader.

Observe standard usage in grammar, punctuation, spelling, and capitalization.

1. *Our urban areas are ugly, polluted, and congested.* _____

_____

_____

_____

_____

_____

_____

_____

2. *As a society, America has changed significantly in many ways during recent years.* _____

_____

_____

_____

_____

_____

_____

_____

Exercise 28
THE "LAWS" OF THE PARAGRAPH

Carefully examine each of the following paragraphs to see whether it violates the principle of Unity, Coherence, Completeness, Emphasis, or Variety. Write the name of the principle violated in the proper blank. If no violation is present, write "None" in the blank.

1. _____   Pigeons spread several diseases which can be fatal to human beings.

2. _____   Many children considered "slow learners" by their teachers are in reality suffering from impaired hearing, a difficulty which can usually be remedied. Many forms of deafness respond to medical or surgical treatment. Every child's hearing should be checked periodically by a doctor. Missing much of what is said in class, he may seem dull, inattentive, even stupid. Experts claim that over 2,000,000 school children have subnormal hearing. Most of the children whose impaired hearing cannot be cured medically or surgically can be helped by a good hearing aid. Those whose deafness cannot be remedied should receive special training in lip reading.

3. _____   Ants construct several different kinds of nests. Many species dig tunnels and galleries in the earth, usually piling up a characteristic anthill above ground. Some species, including the well-known "carpenter ants," inhabit hollow tree limbs or invade the timbers of dwellings, chewing out extensive galleries. Other ants fashion nests from chewed wood cemented with saliva. And a few tropical species use leaves held together with a sticky silk which the workers secrete.

4. _____   First of all, I object to the plan because it would involve a great deal of unnecessary expense, the total cost having been estimated at $475,000.

5. _____   Many historical figures did not make the statements attributed to them. For example, Nathan Hale, the American spy hanged by the British in 1776, never uttered those often quoted words, "I only regret that I have but one life to lose for my country."

6. _____   Corky, my pet boxer, must be an unusually smart dog. He quickly learned to sit up, lie down, roll over, and bring in the evening paper. Moreover, he has recently mastered some difficult tricks. For example, he can walk across the room on his hind legs while our parakeet perches on his head. Of course, feeding a big dog like Corky is something of a problem. He can devour half a pound of hamburger in a single gulp, and my father says he will bankrupt the family. Nevertheless, it is wonderful to have an intelligent pet that is eager to please us by learning tricks.

7. _____ After inspecting the house, we decided not to buy it. The bathroom was decorated in the most hideous colors imaginable. The furnace needed replacing. There was a foot of water in the basement. Because of a leaky roof, plaster had fallen in one upstairs bedroom. There were only three closets in the entire house. Finally, the front yard was filled with dandelions. Their yellow blooms were sprinkled liberally throughout the grass, and along the side fence they were so thick that they resembled a flower bed. Moreover, many of the plants had ripened flower heads, and every breeze filled the air with winged seeds that would spread the weed further.

8. _____ When a faculty member wears academic costume, the edging of his hood reveals his subject. For example, light blue indicates education, orange indicates engineering, purple indicates law, green indicates medicine, pink indicates music, and dark blue indicates philosophy.

9. _____ My uncle was snoozing peacefully. The telephone began to ring. He awakened with a start. He jumped out of bed. He tripped over his dog. The startled animal bit him.

10. _____ Contrary to what many people think, the speed of light is not constant. In a perfect vacuum, light travels approximately 186,282 miles per second, but it goes more slowly through any other transparent medium. For example, it goes approximately 140,000 miles per second through water, 128,000 miles per second through quartz, and 77,000 miles per second through diamond.

Exercise 29
REVIEW

Examine each of the following paragraphs to see whether it contains a clause or cluster which functions as a topic statement. If so, underline the topic statement.

1. The babysitter spent the evening talking on the telephone instead of keeping an eye on my little brother. Consequently, there is a large root-beer stain on the davenport, the television picture tube is broken, the dining-room wallpaper is decorated with murals executed in peanut butter, and the hall carpeting is a soggy mess as the result of the bathtub's having overflowed.

2. Overhead, a bat wheeled and dipped in the evening dusk as it pursued insects. Bill watched it in silence for several minutes. Then, picking a green grape from Grandmother's arbor, he hurled it straight upward. Instantly the bat veered from its course and followed the grape as it fell back to earth. Bill and I gasped as the bat dived to within inches of the ground and then banked sharply upward. Hastily we began to pick more grapes.

3. When I went camping last summer, the mosquitoes and deer flies were both numerous and bloodthirsty. Therefore, I covered myself with insect repellent. Unfortunately, however, it proved to be completely ineffective, and I was soon covered with hundreds of welts from the bites I received.

4. The blue whale is probably the largest animal that has ever existed on this planet. It may reach a weight of 1,470 tons. In contrast, the heaviest dinosaur known to science did not exceed 111 tons.

5. Mineral wool is fire-resistant and water-resistant. Vermin do not damage it, and it is non-decaying. Finally, it is easy to install in blanket or pellet form. Therefore, mineral wool is widely used as an insulating material.

6. Astronomers have been unable to explain a curious fact concerning the satellites of Jupiter. The four outermost moons revolve around the planet from east to west; but the eight inner moons revolve in the opposite direction, from west to east.

7. Flowering plants employ many ingenious methods of attracting insects to pollinate their blossoms. The moss rose signals passing bees with its bright hues. The honeysuckle appeals to night-flying moths with its strong perfume. The pelican flower of South America draws flies with its pungent, rotten-meat smell. One tropical orchid even closely mimics the shape of a female moth and in this way lures the eager male.

8. Most bats feed either on insects or on some other form of animal life. Many species live primarily on the moths and beetles which they capture in flight. Other species prey on rodents, frogs, fish, and other bats. And, of course, the vampire has a liquid diet, the blood of its victims.

9. There was a bad fire at the Platt-Sheridan Hotel last night. Consequently, several hundred guests had to flee their rooms in pajamas or nightgowns. According to Fire Chief O'Leary, the blaze was started by an arsonist. Oil-soaked rags, together with a wad of excelsior and a piece of candle, were discovered in a ventilator shaft.

10.   My mother bought some herbicide last spring, but my father wouldn't let her use it. She wanted to kill the dandelions in our lawn, but he wanted to make salads from the young leaves and dandelion wine from the flowers.

Name _____ Section _____

Date _____ Grade _____

EXAMINATION: CHAPTERS 3, 4, AND 5

At the beginning of the examination, your instructor will tell you what labels to insert in the various boxes. Your instructor may also wish to furnish the first clause for some or all of the units.

In accordance with the diagrams, write clause-groups and paragraphs containing the specified Meaning Relationships. The clause-groups and paragraphs may, of course, contain Linking Devices. You must decide whether the independent clauses you compose would function best as separate sentences or as parts of longer sentences.

Be sure your clauses are well-developed, meaningful, and sensible; and observe standard usage in grammar, punctuation, spelling, and capitalization. *Do not repeat any examples which appear in the text or which you have used in the exercises.* Your grade will be lowered if you fail to follow these instructions.

Clause-Groups (no indentation)

1.

_____

_____

_____

_____

_____

_____

_____

2.

_____

_____

_____

_____

_____

_____

_____

Paragraphs (use indentation)

3.

_____

_____

_____

_____

_____

_____

_____

_____

Name _____

4.

_____
_____
_____
_____
_____
_____
_____
_____

Exercise 30
THE PARTS OF AN ESSAY

Each italicized sentence below is the topic statement for a paragraph. Write the specified number of additional clauses or clusters to complete the paragraph. When you have completed this exercise, you will have composed a brief essay.

Make sure that each paragraph follows one of the five basic patterns of paragraph development; and observe standard usage in grammar, punctuation, spelling, and capitalization. Your grade will be lowered if you fail to follow these instructions.

1. INTRODUCTION (Supply ONE additional clause or cluster):

   Our nation is faced with a real crisis. _____

   _____

   _____

   _____

2. TOPIC ONE (Supply THREE additional clauses or clusters):

   Each citizen must do everything possible to solve the problem. _____

   _____

   _____

   _____

   _____

   _____

   _____

   _____

   _____

3. TOPIC TWO (Supply THREE additional clauses or clusters):

To supplement the efforts of individual citizens, the government must take prompt corrective action. _____

_____

_____

_____

_____

_____

_____

_____

_____

4. CONCLUSION (Supply ONE additional clause or cluster):

Our nation can successfully meet the challenge which faces it. _____

_____

_____

_____

_____

Exercise 31
OUTLINING

Carefully examine the outlines given below. Then decide which of the following statements best describes each outline:

1. Parallel items are not indented equally.
2. Parallel items do not bear parallel labels.
3. Parallel items are not expressed in parallel phrasing.
4. The body contains too many main divisions.
5. The divisions of the outline overlap.
6. Items are listed under incorrect headings.
7. There is an illogical single subdivision of a division.
8. The outline contains irrelevant items.
9. The outline is incomplete.
10. The outline is correct.

Write the number of the appropriate statement in the proper blank. Only one statement applies to each outline.

1. _____   OUR POLLUTED ENVIRONMENT

    Introduction. Our environment rapidly being destroyed
    I. Air pollution by emissions from automobiles and airplanes
    II. Air pollution by smoke from factories and power plants
    III. Air pollution by smoke from home heating units
    IV. Air pollution by smoke and fumes from incinerators
    V. Water pollution by sewage from cities and towns
    VI. Water pollution by chemical wastes from industrial operations
    VII. Water pollution by heat and radioactivity from nuclear power plants
    VIII. Water pollution by pesticides, herbicides, and fertilizers from farms
    Conclusion. Massive clean-up campaign needed

2. _____   MY TWO BEST FRIENDS

    Introduction. Fascinated by their dissimilar personalities
    I. Mary Sue
        A. Excellent student
        B. Serious-minded
        C. She has very few dates
    II. Karen
        A. Makes poor grades
        B. Happy-go-lucky outlook
        C. Very popular with boys
    Conclusion. Fond of both girls

3. _____   THE BENEFITS OF AUTOMATION

Introduction. Definition of term
I.   Benefits to individual worker
    A. Places premium upon intelligence and education
    B. Provides additional time for leisure activities
II. Benefits to business world
    A. Decreases production time per unit
    B. Decreases production costs per unit
    C. Ensures greater uniformity of product
    D. Frees the worker from dull, routine tasks
Conclusion. Future of automation

4. _____   RHEUMATIC FEVER
               AND RHEUMATOID ARTHRITIS

Introduction. Should not confuse two diseases
I.   Rheumatic fever
    A. Cause
    B. Symptoms
    C. Seriousness
    D. Treatment
II. Rheumatoid arthritis
    A. Cause
    B. Symptoms
    C. Treatment
Conclusion. Should remember differences

5. _____   AUTOMOBILES FOR THE YOUNG AND
               THE NOT-SO-YOUNG AT HEART

Introduction. Reasons for survey
I.   Automobiles owned by persons over 35
    A. Low-priced
    B. Medium-priced
    C. High-priced
    D. Foreign-made
II. Automobiles owned by persons under 35
    A. Low-priced
    B. Medium-priced
    C. High-priced
    D. Foreign-made
Conclusion. Significance of findings

Name _____

Assume that you are planning to write an essay about "A Tragic Forest Fire." You have just jotted down your ideas on that subject as they occurred to you, and the result is the following list of items.

Study the list carefully. Next, convert it into a topic outline of the *body* of your essay. Use all of the items in the list. Finally, compose suitable entries for the *introduction* and the *conclusion* of your essay. Write your outline in the space provided.

ORIGINAL LIST

1. The total property damage has been estimated at $20,000,000.
2. Thirteen campers killed, more than fifty injured
3. Nearly 2,000 square miles of woodland laid waste
4. Eight fire-fighters killed, twenty-three seriously injured
5. Several thousand deer killed
6. Destruction of 250 lakeside cottages and summer homes
7. Game birds almost completely wiped out
8. Many power lines destroyed
9. Countless rabbits killed
10. Destruction of the woodland means that the area is now of no value as a timber-producing region, as a vacation spot, as a game refuge, or as forest cover to prevent erosion and flash flooding in the Crystal Lake watershed area.

ESSAY OUTLINE

Exercise 32
VARIETIES OF INTRODUCTIONS

Carefully examine the introductory paragraphs given below. Then decide which of the following statements best describes each paragraph:

1. The introduction presents a *general explanation* of the subject.
2. The introduction presents one or more *examples*.
3. The introduction presents a *definition*.
4. The introduction presents one or more *causes* of a situation.
5. The introduction presents one or more *results* of a situation.
6. The introduction presents both *causes* and *results* of a situation.
7. The introduction presents one or more *comparisons*.
8. The introduction presents one or more *contrasts*.
9. The introduction presents both *comparison* and *contrast*.
10. The introduction presents one or more *rhetorical questions*.
11. The introduction presents *narrative materials*.

Write the number of the appropriate statement in the proper blank. Write only one number in each blank.

1. _____ One of the characteristics of a truly great scientist is serendipity. Webster defines this strange word as the "gift of finding valuable or agreeable things not sought for." In simpler language, it is the habit of having lucky accidents.

2. _____ A balmy spring breeze wafted in the open window, bringing with it the scent of apple blossoms and the joyous notes of a robin's song. Boy, I told myself, it's great to be alive on a day like this! For the fifth time, I paused to scrutinize my reflection in the mirror: Really cool, man! At this point, the door opened, and my brother entered. For a long moment he gazed at me in silence, while I waited for him to pay tribute to my appearance. Then, at last, he spoke. "Say, Bob," he said, "do you realize that you're starting to get bald in back?"

3. _____ My friend Sue, ordinarily a blithe spirit if there ever was one, is steeped in gloom these days. She made a C– on her last chemistry test, instead of the A she had been expecting. She had a quarrel with her boyfriend. She accidentally knocked her typewriter off her study desk, smashing it beyond repair. And, last but apparently not least, she recently gained another three pounds, despite her heroic efforts to reduce.

4. _____ As much as I hate to admit it, my Aunt Gertrude bears a marked resemblance to an oversized squirrel. She is a small woman with fluffy, sandy red hair; bright, beady little eyes; large protruding front teeth; and a high-pitched, chattering voice. Moreover, she is a restless person, and her sudden nervous movements are like those of a half-frightened animal.

5. _____   Shocked librarians have found some surprising objects used as bookmarks in the books returned to them by library patrons. For instance, a librarian in Illinois discovered a well-fried egg, and a librarian in New Jersey encountered a crisp strip of bacon. Moreover, librarians elsewhere have extracted money, love letters, airline tickets, potato chips, nail files, safety matches, playing cards, bobby pins, pocket combs, pawn tickets, rubber snakes, soda crackers, tooth brushes, pearl necklaces, and chocolate bars from the library books in their care.

Create an introductory paragraph by adding one or more clauses or clusters to the topic statement given below. Make the introduction one of the seven common varieties discussed in Chapter 6.

Observe standard usage in grammar, punctuation, spelling, and capitalization. Your grade will be lowered if you fail to follow these instructions.

After you have composed the introductory paragraph, decide which of the statements listed on page 231 best describes the paragraph. Write the appropriate number in the blank.

According to the Surgeon General of the United States, cigarette smoking is dangerous to one's health. _____

_____

_____

_____

_____

_____

_____

_____

_____

Statement Number _____

Exercise 33
VARIETIES OF CONCLUSIONS

Carefully examine the concluding paragraphs given below. Then decide which of the following statements best describes each paragraph:

1. The conclusion presents a *summary*.
2. The conclusion presents a *final generalization*.
3. The conclusion presents a *final inference*.
4. The conclusion presents a *striking example*.
5. The conclusion presents an *analogy*.
6. The conclusion presents a *parting question*.
7. The conclusion presents a *call to action*.
8. The conclusion presents a *forecast*.
9. The conclusion presents a *denouement*.
10. The conclusion presents *narrative materials*.

Write the number of the appropriate statement in the proper blank. Write only one number in each blank.

1. _____ The so-called "military mind" is, then, a baffling phenomenon. As a final instance, consider this incident from the hectic days of World War II. When 1,400 soldiers assigned to an army student-training program arrived at one Southern university, school officials discovered that 1,398 of them were named Brown. According to campus legend, military officials explained that they were merely "simplifying clerical procedures." The reply of the harried, confused, and baffled academicians has, unfortunately, been lost to posterity.

2. _____ As the above examples demonstrate, the rapidly whirling blades of a power mower can maim or even kill the person operating it. Consequently, anyone using this machine should always exercise the greatest caution. The power mower is potentially a lethal weapon, and a moment's carelessness is sometimes enough to produce real tragedy.

3. _____ Such evidence suggests that many diseases are probably spread by the water we drink. For our present system of purifying water through filtration, aeration, and chlorination is effective only against disease-producing bacteria. It is completely incapable of safeguarding us against harmful viruses. Therefore, there is clearly an urgent need for further research into improved methods of water purification.

4. _____ In a very real sense, then, the poet and his work are like a mother and child. A poem is the result of its author's passion and labor; yet, once conceived and brought into existence, the poem must make its own way in the world. Like a fond parent, the poet may wish great success for his offspring, but he cannot control its destiny. For, like a child who has grown up and left home, a published poem has its own individual "career."

5. _____ Several months later, while repairing the sink in that motel room, a plumber happened to find the ring in the gooseneck trap of the drain pipe. Thus, my sister did eventually recover her engagement ring. The incident, however, made a lasting impression upon her. When she wishes to wash her hands, she no longer casually slips the ring from her finger and places it on the edge of the wash basin. Instead, before going into the bathroom, she removes the ring carefully and places it in a special small box that she carries in her purse. She is determined never again to risk losing, through carelessness, her precious "diamond from Tom."

Create a concluding paragraph by adding one or more clauses or clusters to the topic statement given below. Make the conclusion one of the ten common varieties discussed in Chapter 6.

Observe standard usage in grammar, punctuation, spelling, and capitalization. Your grade will be lowered if you fail to follow these instructions.

After you have composed the concluding paragraph, decide which of the statements listed on page 233 best describes the paragraph. Write the appropriate number in the blank.

Law-enforcement officials cannot successfully combat organized crime without the help of the general public.

_____

_____

_____

_____

_____

_____

_____

_____

_____

_____

Statement Number _____

Exercise 34
TRANSITIONAL ELEMENTS

First, in the passage below taken from a longer prose composition, underline all of the Transitional Elements belonging to the following classes: *Parallelism* (P), *Nouns Summarizing Previous Assertions* (NSPA), *Meaning Links* (ML), *Transitional Adverb Phrases* (TAP), *Transitional Adverb Clauses* (TAC), *Transitional Paragraphs* (TP). Remember that a Transitional Element is a specific verbal bond between paragraphs or even larger units of prose; do *not* underline a Deliberate Linking Device which functions only *inside* the paragraph in which it is located. If a short Transitional Element (for example, a Meaning Link) occurs within a longer Transitional Element (for example, a parallel element), underline the short Transitional Element *twice*.

Second, indicate the class to which each underlined Transitional Element belongs by writing the appropriate abbreviation in the proper blank in the left-hand margin. If you encounter Parallelism, be sure to underline each of the parallel elements and write the appropriate abbreviation for each. If a Transitional Element extends to more than one line of the passage, write the abbreviation in the blank opposite the line where it *begins*. If two Transitional Elements occur in the same line, write the abbreviations for both in the *same* blank.

1. _____
2. _____
3. _____
4. _____
5. _____
6. _____
7. _____
8. _____
9. _____
10. _____
11. _____
12. _____
13. _____
14. _____
15. _____
16. _____
17. _____
18. _____
19. _____
20. _____
21. _____
22. _____
23. _____
24. _____
25. _____
26. _____
27. _____
28. _____

     Moreover, despite numerous attempts of the food industry to increase efficiency, the production of natural meat protein is still a slow and costly process. Meat prices therefore remain high, and millions of families must omit this important but expensive food from their diet. A punster might sum up the situation by stating that neither the producer nor the consumer is able to "make ends meat."

     As a result, hundreds of low-cost, low-calorie "meatless meat" or "meat analog" products are now on the market. Some resemble bacon bits or strips. Others imitate hamburger patties, meat loaf, ground beef for chili or "Sloppy Joe" sandwiches, and meat chunks for stews or casseroles. A few varieties even simulate slices of ham or pieces of steak.

     The food industry is, in addition, currently spending millions of dollars annually in an attempt to develop further kinds of synthetic meat. Among the companies actively engaged in such research are Swift, General Mills, Ralston Purina, Worthington Foods, and Archer-Daniels-Midland. As one corporation president commented recently, "Before our industry is finished, we'll duplicate every natural-meat product under the sun."

     Thus far, we have been considering the current increased interest in meat analogs; now let us examine briefly the ways in which these new foods are produced. For it is one thing to tell the public that there is valuable protein in soy beans, cottonseed meal, seaweed, or other vegetable substances; and it is quite another thing to convert those raw materials into an appetizing food which successfully duplicates the taste and appearance of meat.

     One technique that has proved to be very valuable is the *fiberspinning process*, which was borrowed from the textile industry. For example, in making artificial bacon bits, General Mills extracts the protein from soybeans and then spins it into very fine fibers which, under the magnifying lens, look like frizzled hairs. Next, the General Mills workers bond the fibers with fats and add substances which give flavor, aroma, and color to the food. The result is a very close imitation of natural bacon.

     Another technique that is proving to be quite useful is the *extrusion process*, which was adapted from the plastics industry. For instance, Swift and Company reduces soybeans to a kind of gritty flour, adds flavoring and coloring, and then forces the mixture through a die to

29. _____ form small cubes or rolls. These closely resemble small chunks of ham, beef, or chicken and are
30. _____ suitable for use in casseroles or stews.
31. _____   But how successful are the various kinds of imitation meat? According to experts in the
32. _____ food industry, they are not all equally faithful reproductions. Most agree that the meat analogs
33. _____ used in stews, chili, and "Sloppy Joe" sandwiches are the ones which come closest to the real
34. _____ thing. On the other hand, some of the more ambitious imitations are not very convincing; for
35. _____ example, none of the synthetic "steaks" now available is either very realistic or very appealing.
36. _____   Moreover, even though most meat analogs are generally acceptable in flavor and appearance,
37. _____ people tend to dislike the *idea* of eating artificial meat. So, even though the *product* itself may
38. _____ be satisfactory, the *concept* underlying it is not. The public is inclined to have a built-in preju-
39. _____ dice against synthetic food. Since the producer is required by federal regulations to label his
40. _____ product in such a way that the consumer will clearly understand the true nature of the food,
41. _____ there is no possibility of allowing the public to enjoy meatless meat in blissful ignorance. Con-
42. _____ sequently, the food industry will have to undertake a large-scale program of customer educa-
43. _____ tion in order to combat the prejudice against artificial foods which is rather widespread at
44. _____ present.
45. _____   If this psychological problem can be solved, meatless meat may eventually become the chief
46. _____ source of protein for the average family. Indeed, the day may come when only the very rich
47. _____ will dine on real meat. As one researcher has recently proclaimed, "By the year 2000, half of
48. _____ the 'meat' in the typical supermarket will actually be non-meat protein."

Name _____ Section _____

Date _____ Grade _____

Exercise 35
THE NARRATIVE ESSAY

First, either select one of the essay subjects listed, or use a subject provided by your instructor.

Second, construct a topic outline for an essay dealing with that subject. Be sure that it conforms to the principles of effective outlining. The essay body should consist of a series of paragraphs linked through Related Action.

Third, write an essay based upon the outline you have constructed. The essay should constitute a complete, clear, and effective discussion of the subject you have selected.

Fourth, compose a suitable title for your essay.

Special Instructions:

1. Be sure to write either on one of the subjects listed or on a subject provided by your instructor.
2. Be sure to follow the prescribed pattern of body development.
3. Be sure that each paragraph is fully developed. It should conform to the principles of Unity, Coherence, Completeness, and Emphasis; and it should avoid monotony of sentence type, sentence length, and sentence organization.
4. Write your essay upon paper measuring 8½ by 11 inches.
5. Type your essay, or use blue or black ink.
6. Write on only one side of each page.
7. Leave a margin of at least 1½ inches at the top, bottom, and sides of each page.
8. Follow standard usage in grammar. This includes the avoidance of sentence fragments.
9. Follow standard usage in punctuation.
10. Follow standard usage in spelling.
11. Follow standard usage in capitalization.
12. Follow standard usage in diction (word choice).
13. When you have finished writing your essay, check it carefully for errors. Make any necessary revisions before submitting it to the instructor.

ESSAY SUBJECTS

1. A Tragic (or Hilarious) Experience
2. Training My Hunting Dog
3. Buying a Used Car
4. A Hunting Accident
5. Getting Mugged
6. An Encounter with a High-Pressure Salesperson
7. Woes of an Amateur Home Decorator (or Home Repairman)
8. A Bad Auto Accident
9. The Worst Mistake I Ever Made

10. My Most Embarrassing Experience
11. Hunting for a Job
12. My Most Exciting Experience
13. The Fire Department to the Rescue
14. Woes of an Inexperienced Babysitter
15. A Hunting or Fishing Incident

ESSAY OUTLINE

Exercise 36
THE PROCESS-EXPLANATION ESSAY

First, either select one of the essay subjects listed, or use a subject provided by your instructor.

Second, construct a topic outline for an essay dealing with that subject. Be sure that it conforms to the principles of effective outlining. The essay body should consist of a series of paragraphs linked through Related Action.

Third, write an essay based upon the outline you have constructed. The essay should constitute a complete, clear, and effective explanation of the process.

Fourth, compose a suitable title for your essay.

Special Instructions:

1. Be sure to write either on one of the subjects listed or on a subject provided by your instructor.
2. Be sure to follow the prescribed pattern of body development.
3. Be sure that each paragraph is fully developed. It should conform to the principles of Unity, Coherence, Completeness, and Emphasis; and it should avoid monotony of sentence type, sentence length, and sentence organization.
4. Write your essay upon paper measuring 8½ by 11 inches.
5. Type your essay, or use blue or black ink.
6. Write on only one side of each page.
7. Leave a margin of at least 1½ inches at the top, bottom, and sides of each page.
8. Follow standard usage in grammar. This includes the avoidance of sentence fragments.
9. Follow standard usage in punctuation.
10. Follow standard usage in spelling.
11. Follow standard usage in capitalization.
12. Follow standard usage in diction (word choice).
13. When you have finished writing your essay, check it carefully for errors. Make any necessary revisions before submitting it to the instructor.

ESSAY SUBJECTS

1. How to Select a Puppy (or Other Pet)
2. How to Prepare a Bed for Rosebushes
3. How to Render First Aid for Some Specific Injury
4. How to Install a Three-Way Electrical Switch
5. How to Build a Fire in an Indoor Fireplace
6. How to Refinish a Piece of Furniture
7. How to Develop a Certain Type of Photographic Film
8. How to Clean a Hunting Rifle
9. How to Service a Power Mower for Winter Storage

10. How to Quick-Freeze Strawberries (or Some Other Fruit or Vegetable)
11. How to Bathe a Dog
12. How to Prepare and Cook Some Specific Food
13. How to Park a Car Parallel to the Curb
14. How to Give a Manicure
15. How to Re-pot a House Plant

ESSAY OUTLINE

Exercise 37
THE DESCRIPTIVE ESSAY

First, either select one of the essay subjects listed, or use a subject provided by your instructor.

Second, construct a topic outline for an essay dealing with that subject. Be sure that it conforms to the principles of effective outlining. The essay body should consist of a series of paragraphs linked through Parallel Idea.

Third, write an essay based upon the outline you have constructed. The essay should constitute a complete, clear, and effective description of the subject you have selected.

Fourth, compose a suitable title for your essay.

Special Instructions:

1. Be sure to write either on one of the subjects listed or on a subject provided by your instructor.
2. Be sure to follow the prescribed pattern of body development.
3. Be sure that each paragraph is fully developed. It should conform to the principles of Unity, Coherence, Completeness, and Emphasis; and it should avoid monotony of sentence type, sentence length, and sentence organization.
4. Write your essay upon paper measuring 8½ by 11 inches.
5. Type your essay, or use blue or black ink.
6. Write on only one side of each page.
7. Leave a margin of at least 1½ inches at the top, bottom, and sides of each page.
8. Follow standard usage in grammar. This includes the avoidance of sentence fragments.
9. Follow standard usage in punctuation.
10. Follow standard usage in spelling.
11. Follow standard usage in capitalization.
12. Follow standard usage in diction (word choice).
13. When you have finished writing your essay, check it carefully for errors. Make any necessary revisions before submitting it to the instructor.

ESSAY SUBJECTS

1. A Typical Home Stereo System
2. A Home Aquarium (or Terrarium)
3. The Human Eye
4. A Pressure Cooker
5. An Aqualung (or Other Diving Equipment)
6. A Coffee Percolator
7. A Simple Telescope
8. A Living Cell
9. A Fire Extinguisher

10. A Flashlight Battery
11. A Golf Ball
12. A Vacuum Bottle
13. A Perfume Atomizer
14. A Shotgun Shell
15. The Organization of a Typical Business Corporation (or Military Unit)

ESSAY OUTLINE

Exercise 38
THE LISTING-OF-POINTS ESSAY

First, either select one of the essay subjects listed, or use a subject provided by your instructor.

Second, construct a topic outline for an essay dealing with that subject. Be sure that it conforms to the principles of effective outlining. The essay body should consist of a series of paragraphs linked through Parallel Idea. You must decide whether *random order, chronological order, order of spatial arrangement, climactic order,* or *anticlimactic order* is best suited to the development of your subject.

Third, write an essay based upon the outline you have constructed. The essay should constitute a complete, clear, and effective discussion of the subject you have selected.

Fourth, compose a suitable title for your essay.

Special Instructions:

1. Be sure to write either on one of the subjects listed or on a subject provided by your instructor.
2. Be sure to follow the prescribed pattern of body development.
3. Be sure that each paragraph is fully developed. It should conform to the principles of Unity, Coherence, Completeness, and Emphasis; and it should avoid monotony of sentence type, sentence length, and sentence organization.
4. Write your essay upon paper measuring 8½ by 11 inches.
5. Type your essay, or use blue or black ink.
6. Write on only one side of each page.
7. Leave a margin of at least 1½ inches at the top, bottom, and sides of each page.
8. Follow standard usage in grammar. This includes the avoidance of sentence fragments.
9. Follow standard usage in punctuation.
10. Follow standard usage in spelling.
11. Follow standard usage in capitalization.
12. Follow standard usage in diction (word choice).
13. When you have finished writing your essay, check it carefully for errors. Make any necessary revisions before submitting it to the instructor.

ESSAY SUBJECTS

1. Why I Am Planning a Career in _____
2. Why I Like (or Dislike) Living in the City
3. What's Wrong with Automobile Insurance (or Health Insurance, or Social Security)
4. Some Things Anyone Can Do to Improve the Environment
5. The Sources of Air Pollution in This Town
6. Why Young Adults Often Have Difficulty Communicating with Older Adults
7. The Causes of a Certain School (or National, or Social) Problem

8. Things to Remember When Buying a Used Car (or Some Other Thing)
9. How the Problem of "Hard-Core" Unemployment Might Be Solved
10. Rules of Some Sport Which Should Be Changed or Eliminated
11. Some Major Contributions to Our Society by Black Citizens
12. My Pet Peeves
13. Sounds I Like (or Dislike) to Hear at Night
14. Some American Women I Admire Greatly
15. Ambitions Other Persons Have Had for Me

ESSAY OUTLINE

Note: Indicate whether you have employed (1) *random order,* (2) *chronological order,* (3) *order of spatial arrangement,* (4) *climactic order,* or (5) *anticlimactic order* in your outline. Do so by writing the appropriate number in this blank: _____.

Exercise 39
THE POINT-BY-POINT CONTRAST ESSAY

First, either select one of the essay subjects listed, or use a subject provided by your instructor.

Second, construct a topic outline for an essay dealing with that subject. Be sure that it conforms to the principles of effective outlining. The essay body should consist of a series of paragraphs which are linked through Parallel Idea and are devoted to *point-by-point contrast*. You must decide whether *random order, chronological order, order of spatial arrangement, climactic order,* or *anticlimactic order* is best suited to the development of your subject.

Third, write an essay based upon the outline you have constructed. The essay should constitute a complete, clear, and effective discussion of the subject you have selected.

Fourth, compose a suitable title for your essay.

Special Instructions:

1. Be sure to write either on one of the subjects listed or on a subject provided by your instructor.
2. Be sure to follow the prescribed pattern of body development.
3. Be sure that each paragraph is fully developed. It should conform to the principles of Unity, Coherence, Completeness, and Emphasis; and it should avoid monotony of sentence type, sentence length, and sentence organization.
4. Write your essay upon paper measuring 8½ by 11 inches.
5. Type your essay, or use blue or black ink.
6. Write on only one side of each page.
7. Leave a margin of at least 1½ inches at the top, bottom, and sides of each page.
8. Follow standard usage in grammar. This includes the avoidance of sentence fragments.
9. Follow standard usage in punctuation.
10. Follow standard usage in spelling.
11. Follow standard usage in capitalization.
12. Follow standard usage in diction (word choice).
13. When you have finished writing your essay, check it carefully for errors. Make any necessary revisions before submitting it to the instructor.

ESSAY SUBJECTS

1. The Economy Car Versus the Luxury Automobile
2. The Suburban Shopping Center and the Downtown Business District
3. Two Different "Rock" Groups
4. The Spy in Fact and Fiction
5. Police Investigations in Real Life and in TV Drama
6. Two Kinds of Dogs (or Some Other Animal)

7. Two Popular Comic Strips
8. Good and Bad Drivers (or Teachers)
9. Grandmother's Kitchen and the Modern Kitchen
10. The Career Woman—Now and Fifty Years Ago
11. The Republican Party and the Democratic Party
12. Life in the City Versus Life in the Suburbs
13. Social Protest Movements—Today and Ten Years Ago
14. The Fashionable Department Store Versus the Discount Store
15. Women's (or Men's) Clothing Styles—Five Years Ago and Today

---

ESSAY OUTLINE

Note: Indicate whether you have employed (1) *random order,* (2) *chronological order,* (3) *order of spatial arrangement,* (4) *climactic order,* or (5) *anticlimactic order* in your outline. Do so by writing the appropriate number in this blank: _____.

Exercise 40
SPECIAL TWO-POINT ENUMERATION ESSAYS

First, either select one of the essay subjects listed, or use a subject provided by your instructor.

Second, construct a topic outline for an essay dealing with that subject. Be sure that it conforms to the principles of effective outlining. The essay body should consist of two paragraphs linked through Parallel Idea.

Third, write an essay based upon the outline you have constructed. The essay should constitute a complete, clear, and effective discussion of the subject you have selected.

Fourth, compose a suitable title for your essay.

Special Instructions:

1. Be sure to write either on one of the subjects listed or on a subject provided by your instructor.
2. Be sure to follow the prescribed pattern of body development.
3. Be sure that each paragraph is fully developed. It should conform to the principles of Unity, Coherence, Completeness, and Emphasis; and it should avoid monotony of sentence type, sentence length, and sentence organization.
4. Write your essay upon paper measuring 8½ by 11 inches.
5. Type your essay, or use blue or black ink.
6. Write on only one side of each page.
7. Leave a margin of at least 1½ inches at the top, bottom, and sides of each page.
8. Follow standard usage in grammar. This includes the avoidance of sentence fragments.
9. Follow standard usage in punctuation.
10. Follow standard usage in spelling.
11. Follow standard usage in capitalization.
12. Follow standard usage in diction (word choice).
13. When you have finished writing your essay, check it carefully for errors. Make any necessary revisions before submitting it to the instructor.

ESSAY SUBJECTS

1. Tornado and Hurricane
2. Commercial Television and Public Television
3. Foreign Movies and Hollywood Movies
4. Some Particular Amateur Sport and the Corresponding Professional Sport
5. The Advantages and Disadvantages of Wage and Price Controls
6. The Virtues and Shortcomings of the Social Security System (or the Welfare System)
7. A Serious Problem and Its Solution
8. The Causes and Consequences of Inflation

9. A Bad Mistake I Made, and the Lesson I Learned From It
10. The U.S. Postal Service and the United Parcel Service
11. The Advantages and Disadvantages of No-Fault Divorce
12. The Virtues and Shortcomings of a Certain New Law
13. The Causes and Consequences of the Energy Crisis
14. The Grasshopper and the Cricket
15. The Advantages and Disadvantages of Strict Gun Control

ESSAY OUTLINE

Exercise 41
THE EQUAL-PAIR ESSAY

First, either select one of the essay subjects listed, or use a subject provided by your instructor.

Second, construct a topic outline for an essay dealing with that subject. Be sure that it conforms to the principles of effective outlining. The essay body should consist of two paragraphs linked through Contrast, Alternative, Balanced Comparison, Result, or Cause.

Third, write an essay based upon the outline you have constructed. The essay should constitute a complete, clear, and effective discussion of the subject you have selected.

Fourth, compose a suitable title for your essay.

Special Instructions:

1. Be sure to write either on one of the subjects listed or on a subject provided by your instructor.
2. Be sure to follow the prescribed pattern of body development.
3. Be sure that each paragraph is fully developed. It should conform to the principles of Unity, Coherence, Completeness, and Emphasis; and it should avoid monotony of sentence type, sentence length, and sentence organization.
4. Write your essay upon paper measuring 8½ by 11 inches.
5. Type your essay, or use blue or black ink.
6. Write on only one side of each page.
7. Leave a margin of at least 1½ inches at the top, bottom, and sides of each page.
8. Follow standard usage in grammar. This includes the avoidance of sentence fragments.
9. Follow standard usage in punctuation.
10. Follow standard usage in spelling.
11. Follow standard usage in capitalization.
12. Follow standard usage in diction (word choice).
13. When you have finished writing your essay, check it carefully for errors. Make any necessary revisions before submitting it to the instructor.

ESSAY SUBJECTS

1. What This School Needs Most
2. The Consequences of the Population Explosion
3. Possible Solutions to a Serious Local Problem
4. Automation
5. Man's Increasing Life Span
6. The True Signs of Spring
7. Changing Customs
8. How Medical Care Might Be Improved

9. The Teenager's Outlook Versus That of His Parents
10. The Central City Area Versus the Suburbs
11. The Need for Self-Discipline
12. Careless Drivers
13. Why Everyone Needs a Hobby
14. What May Happen to Our Space Program
15. The Greatest Mistake Our National Government Has Made in the Past Five Years

ESSAY OUTLINE

Exercise 42
THE UNEQUAL-PAIR ESSAY

First, either select one of the essay subjects listed, or use a subject provided by your instructor.

Second, construct a topic outline for an essay dealing with that subject. Be sure that it conforms to the principles of effective outlining. The essay body should consist of two paragraphs linked through Sample Fact, Supporting Data, Generalization, or Inference.

Third, write an essay based upon the outline you have constructed. The essay should constitute a complete, clear, and effective discussion of the subject you have selected.

Fourth, compose a suitable title for your essay.

Special Instructions:

1. Be sure to write either on one of the subjects listed or on a subject provided by your instructor.
2. Be sure to follow the prescribed pattern of body development.
3. Be sure that each paragraph is fully developed. It should conform to the principles of Unity, Coherence, Completeness, and Emphasis; and it should avoid monotony of sentence type, sentence length, and sentence organization.
4. Write your essay upon paper measuring 8½ by 11 inches.
5. Type your essay, or use blue or black ink.
6. Write on only one side of each page.
7. Leave a margin of at least 1½ inches at the top, bottom, and sides of each page.
8. Follow standard usage in grammar. This includes the avoidance of sentence fragments.
9. Follow standard usage in punctuation.
10. Follow standard usage in spelling.
11. Follow standard usage in capitalization.
12. Follow standard usage in diction (word choice).
13. When you have finished writing your essay, check it carefully for errors. Make any necessary revisions before submitting it to the instructor.

ESSAY SUBJECTS

1. The Possibility of World Famine
2. How the War Against Crime Is Going
3. How Sports Cars Are Changing
4. The Costly Damage Done by Rats
5. Man's Courage (or Cruelty)
6. Current Business Conditions
7. The Sinister Operations of the Loan Shark
8. The American City in the Year 2000 A.D.
9. Unusual Jobs Held by Students

10. Popular Music as a Form of Propaganda
11. Social Changes Brought About by Violence
12. The Danger of Improper Reducing Diets
13. Equality of Opportunity for All Americans
14. "Pollution" of the Air Waves by Radio and Television Commercials
15. The Chances of Detecting Intelligent Life Elsewhere in the Universe.

ESSAY OUTLINE

Exercise 43
CHAIN AND LEAPFROG ESSAYS

First, either select one of the essay subjects listed, or use a subject provided by your instructor.

Second, construct a topic outline for an essay dealing with that subject. Be sure that it conforms to the principles of effective outlining. The essay body should consist of three or more paragraphs. If you compose a Chain Essay, the body paragraphs will form a sequential series linked through Equal Meaning Relationships. If you compose a Leapfrog Essay, use a Topic-Result-Cause pattern like that discussed on pages 139–40.

Third, write an essay based upon the outline you have constructed. The essay should constitute a complete, clear, and effective discussion of the subject you have selected.

Fourth, compose a suitable title for your essay.

Special Instructions:

1. Be sure to write either on one of the subjects listed or on a subject provided by your instructor.
2. Be sure to follow the prescribed pattern of body development.
3. Be sure that each paragraph is fully developed. It should conform to the principles of Unity, Coherence, Completeness, and Emphasis; and it should avoid monotony of sentence type, sentence length, and sentence organization.
4. Write your essay upon paper measuring 8½ by 11 inches.
5. Type your essay, or use blue or black ink.
6. Write on only one side of each page.
7. Leave a margin of at least 1½ inches at the top, bottom, and sides of each page.
8. Follow standard usage in grammar. This includes the avoidance of sentence fragments.
9. Follow standard usage in punctuation.
10. Follow standard usage in spelling.
11. Follow standard usage in capitalization.
12. Follow standard usage in diction (word choice).
13. When you have finished writing your essay, check it carefully for errors. Make any necessary revisions before submitting it to the instructor.

ESSAY SUBJECTS

1. The Problem of Drug Addiction
2. The Missile Race
3. The Problem of Overpopulation
4. The Campaign for Women's Rights
5. The Development of "Instant" Foods
6. Life in the Central City (or in the Suburbs or in a Small Town)

7. Sea-Floor Spreading and Continental Drift
8. Turning Over a New Leaf
9. The Development of Disposable Clothing
10. Recent Developments in Electronics (or Medicine or Science)
11. The Current Interest in Astrology
12. Recent Trends in Leisure-Time Activities
13. The Decline of Good Manners
14. My Personal Unbalanced Budget
15. The Split Between Russia and China

ESSAY OUTLINE

Note: Indicate whether you have composed a Chain Essay or a Leapfrog Essay. Do so by writing "Chain" or "Leapfrog" in this blank: _____ .

Exercise 44
EXPANDED ESSAY PATTERNS

First, either select one of the essay subjects listed, or use a subject provided by your instructor.

Second, construct a topic outline for an essay dealing with that subject. Be sure that it conforms to the principles of effective outlining. Every main division (or topic) of the essay body should be composed of two or more paragraphs. Use *absorbed* topic statements rather than *detached* topic statements.

Third, write an essay based upon the outline you have constructed. The essay should be from 500 to 900 words in length; and it should constitute a complete, clear, and effective discussion of the subject you have selected.

Fourth, compose a suitable title for your essay.

Special Instructions:

1. Be sure to write either on one of the subjects listed or on a subject provided by your instructor.
2. Be sure to follow the prescribed pattern of body development.
3. Be sure that each paragraph is fully developed. It should conform to the principles of Unity, Coherence, Completeness, and Emphasis; and it should avoid monotony of sentence type, sentence length, and sentence organization.
4. Write your essay upon paper measuring 8½ by 11 inches.
5. Type your essay, or use blue or black ink.
6. Write on only one side of each page.
7. Leave a margin of at least 1½ inches at the top, bottom, and sides of each page.
8. Follow standard usage in grammar. This includes the avoidance of sentence fragments.
9. Follow standard usage in punctuation.
10. Follow standard usage in spelling.
11. Follow standard usage in capitalization.
12. Follow standard usage in diction (word choice).
13. When you have finished writing your essay, check it carefully for errors. Make any necessary revisions before submitting it to the instructor.

ESSAY SUBJECTS

1. Corruption in Government
2. The Changing Moral Values of Our Society
3. Modern Man and His Polluted World
4. Where Is Science Taking Us?
5. The Future of the Labor Movement
6. The Future of the Free-Enterprise Economic System
7. Our National Defense Strategy
8. Should the United States Use Food as an Economic Weapon?

9. The Quest for Peace
10. Why the Crime Rate Continues to Increase
11. After the American Woman Is Liberated, Then What?
12. Vandalism and Its Significance
13. The Future of American Political Parties
14. The American Family
15. Recent Developments in _____

ESSAY OUTLINE

EXAMINATION: CHAPTERS 6 THROUGH 11

At the beginning of the examination, your instructor will provide you with a subject for an impromptu essay.

First, construct a topic outline for an essay dealing with that subject. Be sure that it conforms to the principles of effective outlining.

Second, write an essay based upon the outline you have constructed. Your essay should constitute a complete, clear, and effective discussion of the subject.

Third, compose a suitable title for your essay.

Special Instructions:

1. Be sure to write on the assigned subject.
2. Be sure to follow one of the patterns of body development which you have studied.
3. Write your outline in the space provided on page 258.
4. Be sure that each paragraph is fully developed. It should conform to the principles of Unity, Coherence, Completeness, and Emphasis; and it should avoid monotony of sentence type, sentence length, and sentence organization.
5. Write your essay upon paper measuring 8½ by 11 inches.
6. Use blue or black ink.
7. Write on only one side of each page.
8. Leave a margin of at least 1½ inches at the top, bottom, and sides of each page.
9. Follow standard usage in grammar (including the avoidance of sentence fragments), punctuation, spelling, capitalization, and diction (word choice).
10. When you have finished writing your essay, check it carefully for errors. Make any necessary revisions before submitting it to the instructor.

ESSAY OUTLINE

APPENDIX: PUNCTUATION AND MECHANICS

A. THE COMMA

1. Commas are used to separate the units of certain types of compounds.

Compounds consisting of single-word units, compounds consisting of predicates, compounds consisting of phrases, and compounds consisting of dependent clauses follow identical punctuation patterns.

Punctuation patterns:

_____and _____

_____ , _____

_____ , _____ , and _____

_____ and _____ and _____

_____ , _____ , _____

Examples:
My father sealed the package and typed the letter.
She is a beautiful, charming girl.
The secretary needed pencils, erasers, and paper.
The child ran and jumped and played.
I felt numb, empty, lost.
I wondered when to go, what to say, and when to leave.
We knew that the faculty would adopt the resolution and that the dean would approve it.

2. Commas are used to separate the independent units of certain compound and compound-complex sentences.

a. If there is no internal comma punctuation near a break between independent units, a sentence containing independent units connected by a single coordinating conjunction normally follows one of two punctuation patterns.

Punctuation patterns:

$$_____ , \begin{Bmatrix} \text{and} \\ \text{but} \\ \text{or} \\ \text{for} \\ \text{nor} \end{Bmatrix} _____ .$$

$$_____ , _____ , \begin{Bmatrix} \text{and} \\ \text{or} \end{Bmatrix} _____ .$$

Examples:
I wanted a car for Christmas, but I didn't expect to get one.
Beth is studying, Sue is reading, and Veronica is watching TV.

b. If there is no internal comma punctuation near the break between independent units, a sentence containing independent units connected by a pair of conjunctions normally has a comma separating the units.

Punctuation patterns:
Not only _____, but (also) _____.
Either _____, or _____.

Examples:
Not only did he date my girl, but he also borrowed my clothes.
Either stop complaining, or leave the room.

3. Commas are used to set off non-restrictive modifiers.

a. Adjectival modifiers

(1) Non-restrictive adjectives are set off by commas.

Examples:
Remorseful, he apologized to the hostess.
My cousin, furious, locked the child in the bedroom.

(2) Non-restrictive participles and participial phrases are set off by commas.

Examples:
Laughing, the director returned to the stage.
The team, having lost, left the field slowly.
Having broken my watch, I had no idea what time it was.
The driver, apparently growing impatient, pulled out of line.

(3) Non-restrictive adjective clauses are set off by commas.

Examples:
His father, who owns an oil well, hates to pay taxes.
I attended the conference basketball tournament, which was held in Atlanta.

b. Adverbial modifiers

(1) Non-restrictive adverbs are set off by commas.

Example:
He climbed the stairs, slowly and painfully.

(2) Non-restrictive adverbial phrases are set off by commas.

Example:
The motion was carried, despite his opposition.

(3) Non-restrictive adverb clauses are set off by commas.

Examples:
He must have recognized you, since he turned and ran.
We read the assignment, though we didn't understand it.

4. Commas are usually employed to set off non-restrictive appositives.

Examples:
Mary Henderson, the valedictorian, applied for a scholarship.
We met the English teacher, Miss Jones.

5. A comma usually follows an introductory expression used with an appositive.

Examples:
My roommate failed one course—namely, chemistry.
I dislike many television programs—for example, Western movies and panel shows.

6. Commas are used to set off certain independent sentence elements.

a. Mild exclamatory expressions are often set off by commas.

Examples:
Well, it seems very unlikely.
Oh, he isn't as unfriendly as he looks.

b. Vocatives are set off by commas.

Examples:
Barbara, there is a letter for you on the table.
I hope, Jim, that you will change your mind.

7. Commas are used to set off most sentence modifiers.

a. Commas are used to set off most single-word sentence modifiers.

Examples:
Honestly, I do not know what he said.
No, I don't believe that he will come.

b. Commas are used to set off phrases functioning as sentence modifiers.

Examples:
To tell the truth, he has already written the letter.
As a general rule, it is unwise to pet a strange dog.

c. Commas are used to set off clauses functioning as sentence modifiers.

Example:
Mary, you know, was the person who invited him.

d. Commas are used to set off certain conjunctive adverbs.

Examples:
The result, however, was not what I expected.
Consequently, Anna now refuses to speak to me.

e. Commas are used to set off nominative absolute constructions.

Example:
The bell having rung, the teacher ended his lecture.

8. Commas are used to set off certain elements when they occur in specified positions in the sentence.

a. A long prepositional phrase preceding the subject is set off by comma punctuation.

Example:
In spite of overwhelming opposition, he continued the fight.

b. An infinitive or an infinitive phrase functioning as an adverb is set off by comma punctuation when it precedes the element it modifies.

Examples:
To succeed, you must work hard.
An athlete, to keep in condition, must exercise daily.

c. An adverb clause preceding or falling within the independent clause to which it belongs is set off by comma punctuation.

Examples:
If he returns the book, I would like to borrow it.
The treasurer, as soon as he had collected the dues, left the meeting hurriedly.

9. **Commas are used to set off a short direct quotation functioning as the object of a verb of saying, commanding, exclaiming, asking, etc.**

Examples:
He said, "That is a serious mistake."
"Give me a second chance," she begged.

10. **Commas are used to set off parts of dates and addresses.**

Examples:
The celebration was held on February 3, 1959.
My parents live at 501 North Main Street, Barbourville, Kentucky.

11. **Commas are used to prevent misreading.**

Example:
Confusing: Below the football players were practicing.
Clarified: Below, the football players were practicing.

12. **Commas are used to set off a degree or title following the name of a person or institution.**

Examples:
The speaker at the banquet was George Samuelson, M.D.
Charles McDonnell, Jr., served as master of ceremonies.
He bought stock in Electronic Products, Incorporated.

13. **Commas are used to set off echo questions.**

Examples:
You brought the car, didn't you?
He is your cousin, isn't he?

14. **Commas are normally used to set off the second of two contrasted items.**

Examples:
I ordered tea, not coffee.
Hard work, not luck, brought him success.

B. PARENTHESES

1. **Parentheses may be used to enclose non-restrictive appositives which are loosely connected with the rest of the sentence.**

    Examples:
    Substantive modifiers (adjectives) have an important function.
    A few cities (Rector, Mendenhall, and Ashford) have adopted city-manager government.

2. **Parentheses may be used to enclose interpolated elements.**

    Example:
    Patsy (you met her last week) has gone to Tahiti.

C. THE DASH

1. **A dash is used to mark sudden shifting or interruption of thought in a sentence.**

    Examples:
    He said—I won't tell you what he said.
    I wonder what they—

2. **Dashes may be used to set off certain types of appositives.**

    a. A dash is used to set off an introductory appositive preceding a summarizing word or word-group.

    Example:
    To be rich and famous—that was all he wanted.

    b. A dash may be used to set off a non-restrictive appositive which comes at the end of the sentence and serves as the climax of the idea.

    Examples:
    We beat only one team—the Tigers.
    The committee finally selected three nominees—Don, Charles, and Keith.

    c. Dashes may be used to set off a non-restrictive appositive which is loosely connected with the rest of the sentence.

    Example:
    My brother—an expert swimmer—saved the woman's life.

    d. Dashes may be used to set off a non-restrictive appositive which contains internal comma punctuation.

    Examples:
    The three girls—Ann, Jean, and Karen—planned to visit the museum.
    We enjoy two spectator sports—namely, baseball and soccer.

3. **Dashes may be used to enclose interpolated elements.**

    Example:
    My brother—he's seven feet tall—received several scholarship offers.

4. A dash may be used to separate two parts of a sentence when the second explains or illustrates the first. The dash is less formal and more dramatic than the colon, which is also used to punctuate such constructions (see F3).

Example:
She isn't in love—she's merely insane.

D. BRACKETS

Brackets are used to enclose explanatory notes or additions inserted in quoted material.

Example:
Byron said: "He [Colonel Stanhope] leaves nothing untouched from the general government to the schools for children."

E. THE SEMICOLON

1. Semicolons are used to separate the independent units of certain compound and compound-complex sentences.

   a. If there is no conjunction connecting the independent units, a semicolon is used to separate the units.

   Punctuation patterns:

   _____ ; _____ .

   _____ ; _____ ; _____ .

   Examples:
   Senator Brown wanted to raise price supports; Senator Cook wanted to eliminate them entirely.
   The dog barked ferociously as I entered the yard; then it began to wag its tail.
   The lightning flashed; the thunder boomed; the rain poured down.

   b. If there is internal comma punctuation near a break between independent units, a semicolon is used to separate the units even though they are connected by a conjunction.

   Example:
   I interviewed Mr. Simpkins, the principal; and Charles interviewed Mr. Smith, the superintendent.

2. Semicolons are used instead of commas to separate the units of compounds containing internal comma punctuation.

   Example:
   We invited Jones, the banker; Smith, the merchant; and Johnson, the editor.

F. THE COLON

1. A colon is used before a direct quotation which is formally introduced. Usually such a quotation will be relatively long.

   Example:
   George Washington said: "A slender acquaintance with the world must convince every man that actions, not words, are the true criterion of the attachment of friends and that the most liberal professions of goodwill are very far from being the surest marks of it."

2. A colon may be used before non-restrictive appositives occurring at the end of a sentence.

Example:
The class selected three candidates: Sally, Linda, and Jo Ellen.

3. A colon may be used to separate two parts of a sentence when the second explains or illustrates the first.

Example:
Judy was obviously very angry: her face was pale, her jaw was thrust forward, and her blue eyes flashed ominously.

G. THE PERIOD

1. A period is used to close a declarative sentence.

Example:
My friend is particularly fond of pecans.

2. A period is used to close an imperative sentence, unless the sentence is also exclamatory.

Example:
Raise the mainsail.

3. A period is used after an abbreviation.

Examples:
Mr., Mrs., Dr., a.m., N.Y.

H. THE QUESTION MARK

1. A question mark is used to close an interrogative sentence.

Example:
Who wants to play tennis?

2. A question mark is used after an interrogative element which stands alone as a non-sentence.

Examples:
When? Day after tomorrow?

I. THE EXCLAMATION POINT

1. An exclamation point is used to close an exclamatory sentence.

Example:
I dropped my glasses!

2. An exclamation point is used after an exclamatory element.

Example:
Ouch! you stepped on my toe.

J. QUOTATION MARKS

1. **Quotation marks are used to enclose titles of relatively short literary compositions, such as essays, articles, short stories, and lyrics.**

   Titles of subordinate parts of long works are also enclosed in quotation marks.

   Examples:
   We read Shelley's "Ozymandias."
   The first chapter is "The Tennyson Legend."

2. **Quotation marks are used to enclose direct quotations.**

   Note the use of quotation marks and other marks of punctuation in the following examples:

   a. Direct quotations of sentences containing no punctuation

   Examples:

   Original sentence
   Your method of working is entirely wrong.

   Direct quotations
   He said, "Your method of working is entirely wrong."
   "Your method of working is entirely wrong," he said.
   "Your method of working," he said, "is entirely wrong."

   Punctuation patterns:

   He said, " _____ ."

   " _____," he said.

   " _____," he said, " _____ ."

   b. Direct quotations of sentences containing comma punctuation

   Examples:
   Original sentence
   I waited at the office, but the doctor did not come.

   Direct quotations
   He said, "I waited at the office, but the doctor did not come."
   "I waited at the office, but the doctor did not come," he said.
   "I waited at the office," he said, "but the doctor did not come."

   Punctuation patterns:

   He said, " _____ , but _____ ."

   " _____ , but _____," he said.

   " _____," he said, "but _____ ."

   c. Direct quotations of sentences containing semicolon punctuation

   Examples:

   Original sentence
   Our opponents have weight; we have skill and speed.

Direct quotations

He said, "Our opponents have weight; we have skill and speed."
"Our opponents have weight; we have skill and speed," he said.
"Our opponents have weight," he said; "we have skill and speed."

Punctuation patterns:

He said, " _____ ; _____ ."

" _____ ; _____ ," he said.

" _____ ," he said; " _____ ."

d. Direct quotations of more than one sentence

Examples:

Original sentences

She must be here. Her car is in the driveway.

Direct quotations

He said, "She must be here. Her car is in the driveway."
"She must be here. Her car is in the driveway," he said.
"She must be here," he said. "Her car is in the driveway."

Punctuation patterns:

He said, " _____ . _____ ."

" _____ . _____ ," he said.

" _____ ," he said. " _____ ."

3. **The position of various marks of punctuation in relation to the final set of a pair of quotation marks may be determined by the following rules:**

a. Commas and periods are placed *inside* the quotation marks.

Examples:
"I misplaced my notes," she explained.
The man replied, "I have not completed the work."

b. Colons and semicolons are placed *outside* the quotation marks.

Example:
I selected Poe's "The Raven"; she preferred Coleridge's "Kubla Khan."

c. Question marks and exclamation points are placed *inside* the quotation marks when they refer to the quotation itself.

Examples:
She asked, "When did you arrive?"
"What a surprise!" the girl exclaimed.

d. Question marks and exclamation points are placed *outside* the quotation marks when they refer to the entire sentence in which the quotation occurs.

Example:
Who said, "A little learning is a dangerous thing"?

4. **Single quotation marks are used to enclose a quotation within a quotation.**

Example:
Mary replied, "I'm sure the teacher said, 'We *may* have an exam.' "

K. THE APOSTROPHE

1. **The apostrophe is used in forming possessives of nouns and indefinite pronouns.**

Examples:
writer	writer's
Morris	Morris's
women	women's
girls	girls'
someone	someone's

2. **The apostrophe is used to indicate omitted letters in contractions.**

Examples:
don't, doesn't, I'm, you're

3. **The apostrophe is used in forming the plural of letters, figures, and words used as words.**

Examples:
There are two *m*'s in *committee.*
There are too many *and*'s in this paragraph.

L. THE HYPHEN

1. **The hyphen is used to divide compound words.**

Consult a good dictionary to determine whether a word is hyphenated.

2. **The hyphen is used to divide a word which is carried over from one line to another.**

A word may be divided only between syllables. Consult a good dictionary to determine the proper syllabication of a word.

M. ITALICS

Underlining is used in handwritten and typewritten material to indicate italics.

1. **Italics are used for titles of works of art, newspapers, magazines, and relatively long literary compositions, such as books, plays, and long poems.**

Examples:
He always reads the *Saturday Review.*
Did you see *Green Pastures*?

2. **Italics are used for names of ships, trains, and airplanes.**

> Example:
> She arrived on the *Mayflower*.

3. **Italics are used for letters used as letters and words used as words.**

> Example:
> The word *across* is spelled with one *c*.

4. **Italics are used for foreign words occurring in English sentences.**

> Example:
> They believed in the doctrine of *laissez faire*.

5. **Italics are used for emphasized words.**

> Example:
> I am certain that he *did* go.

N. CAPITAL LETTERS

1. **A capital letter is used at the beginning of a sentence.**

> Example:
> The car struck the wall.

2. **A capital letter is used at the beginning of a quoted sentence.**

> Example:
> The boy replied, "You should turn at the next corner."

3. **A capital letter is normally used at the beginning of every line of poetry.**

> Example:
> That time of year thou mayst in me behold
> When yellow leaves, or none, or few, do hang
> Upon those boughs which shake against the cold,
> Bare ruin'd choirs where late the sweet birds sang.

4. **Proper nouns and adjectives derived from proper nouns begin with capital letters. If a proper noun consists of several words, the important words are capitalized.**

> Examples:
> Franklin Pierce, Barbara Frietchie, Guy Fawkes, Alabama, the Constitution of the United States, a Keatsian poem, a British company

5. **The important words in titles are capitalized.**

> Example:
> Cooper wrote *The Last of the Mohicans*.

6. **The pronoun *I* is always capitalized.**

7. **Words which refer to Deity are always capitalized.**

> Examples:
> God, Jehovah, the Almighty, Christ, the Saviour

SYMBOLS FOR THEME CORRECTI

A   THE COMMA

A1   Compounds
A2   Compound and compound-complex
       sentences
A3   Non-restrictive modifiers
A4   Non-restrictive appositives
A5   Introductory expressions with appositives
A6   Independent sentence elements
A7   Sentence modifiers
A8   Elements not in normal sentence position
A9   Direct quotations
A10 Dates and addresses
A11 To prevent misreading
A12 Degrees and titles
A13 Echo questions
A14 Contrasted items

B   PARENTHESES

B1   Appositives
B2   Interpolated elements

C   THE DASH

C1   Shifting or interruption of thought
C2   Appositives
C3   Interpolated elements
C4   Explanatory elements

D   BRACKETS

Explanatory notes or additions

E   THE SEMICOLON

E1   Compound and compound-complex
       sentences
E2   Compounds with internal comma
       punctuation

F   THE COLON

F1   Direct quotations
F2   Appositives
F3   Explanatory elements

G   THE PERIOD

G1   Declarative sentences
G2   Imperative sentences
G3   Abbreviations

H   THE QUESTION MA

H1   Interrogative sentences
H2   Interrogative non-sentences

I   THE EXCLAMATION P

I1   Exclamatory sentences
I2   Exclamatory elements

J   QUOTATION MARK

J1   Titles
J2   Direct quotations
J3   Position of other marks of punctu
J4   Single quotation marks

THE APOSTROPHE

Possessives
Contractions
Plurals of letters, figures, and words

THE HYPHEN

Compound words
Divided words

ITALICS

Titles
Names of ships, trains, and airplanes
Letters and words used as such
Foreign words
Emphasized words

CAPITAL LETTERS

Beginning of sentence
Beginning of quoted sentence
Beginning of line of poetry
Proper nouns and adjectives
Important words in titles
Pronoun *I*
Words referring to Deity

OTHER SYMBOLS FOR CORRECTING THEMES

adj   Adjective
adv   Adverb
agr   Subject-verb agreement
awk   Awkward phrasing or construction
cap   Capital letter (See N in Appendix)
case   Wrong case
coh   Coherence
cs   Comma splice (See A2, E1, and G1 in Appendix)
cst   Construction; faulty sentence structure
dng   Dangling modifier
frag   Fragmentary sentence
id   Faulty idiom
inc comp   Incomplete comparison
inf   Too informal
ital   Italics (See M in Appendix)
lc   Lower case; do not capitalize
mean   Meaning not clear
mm   Misplaced modifier
no abb   Do not abbreviate
no ¶   No new paragraph
om   Omission of word or words
¶   New paragraph
‖ cst   Parallel construction
ref   Faulty pronoun reference
rep   Undesirable repetition
seq tn   Sequence of tenses
shift   Shift in tense, person, or number
sp   Spelling
sub   Subordinate this idea
tn   Wrong tense
tr   Trite
vb fm   Verb form
voice   Wrong voice of verb
wd ord   Word order
wdy   Wordy
ww   Wrong word

2   3945